Advance Praise for 99%

'If you are concerned about your future but would never dream of reading a book about the economy... you should read this one!'

Hugh Pym
BBC Health Editor
Former BBC Chief Economics Correspondent

'Policy-makers face stiff challenges. 99% will help them to navigate the minefield.'

Andrew Harrop
General Secretary of the Fabian Society

'In the age of Trump, Putin, and Brexit, it is difficult to be an optimist. But 99% opens a route forward – it deserves to be read by all those in a position of influence.'

Sten Scheibye
Former Chairman of Novo Nordisk

'Structural changes in society risk creating a generation poorer than its parents. 99% clearly sets out both the problem and its solution.'

Fiona Devine
Head of Alliance Manchester Business School and Professor of Sociology at The University of Manchester

'Without concerted action, many countries face the prospect of a lost generation. This book will start a movement to prevent that from happening.'

Nicholas Anderson
Chief Executive Officer, Spirax-Sarco Engineering plc

'Mark's book provides the story which is likely to drive material regime change in markets. All investors who purport to serve their clients should read it.'

Henry Maxey
Chief Investment Officer, Ruffer LLP

99%

Mass Impoverishment and How We Can End It

MARK E. THOMAS

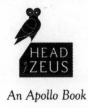

An Apollo Book

First published in the UK in 2019 by Apollo,
an imprint of Head of Zeus Ltd

9 7 5 3 1 2 4 6 8

A catalogue record for this book is available from
the British Library.

ISBN (FTPO) 9781789544503
ISBN (E) 9781789544527

Typeset by e-type

Graphs designed by Jeff Edwards

Printed and bound by CPI Group (UK) Ltd,
Croydon, CR0 4YY

Head of Zeus Ltd
First Floor East
5–8 Hardwick St
London EC1R 4RG

WWW.HEADOFZEUS.COM

99%

WHEN DARWIN proposed his Theory of Evolution based on natural selection, it took time to win over the scientific community. Although the general concept of evolution was quickly accepted, the specific mechanism Darwin proposed, natural selection, was not fully accepted by scientists until the 1940s.

The General Theory of Relativity was published in 1915 but not widely accepted until the 1960s.

And it took 359 years after Galileo's recantation for the Catholic Church to accept that the Earth moves around the Sun.

Clearly, accepting big ideas takes time.

But in the case of this book, we don't *have* much time. Our society is on a path towards self-destruction. And at the current rate, by 2050 it will no longer be recognizable.

So, I have an urgent request. Once you have read this book, please pass it on to a friend. Discuss the ideas with your family, with your colleagues, with your friends and acquaintances. And please *act* on the suggestions in Part Three.

Change will happen if we all play our part – please make sure you play yours.

MET, November 2018
99-percent.org

Table of Contents

Chapter 7: Eight Scenarios

Part 2: Why We Don't Act   131

Chapter 8: Going Post-Fact   136

Chapter 9: Myths and Metaphors   165

'It is never too late to give up our prejudices. No way of thinking or doing, however ancient, can be trusted without proof.'

Henry David Thoreau

How this book came about

My reason for writing this book is one that I hope will resonate with you. I want to help build a world fit for my children's generation – and their children – to live in.

In recent years, much as I'd like to believe the opposite, I've come to see that the world that we are building may well *not* be fit for future generations. If I can help to change this, I will – and that's why I want to share the information I've gathered with you so that, together, we can put the world back on track.

Let me explain. When my children were born, I took it for granted that economic progress would ensure that they would have more opportunities and probably become better off than I am. It seemed to me and, I suspect, to many other people at the time, that it was almost a law of nature that each generation would have greater opportunities than the last.

Certainly this was true for my predecessors. None of my grandparents went to university. My father's father worked for Ford Motor Company, while his wife stayed at home. They had a comfortable middle-class life. My mother's father was a bookkeeper and his wife was a nurse. They were slightly less comfortable, but not poor.

My parents came of age after the Second World War at a time when, if you were bright and worked hard, you could go to university. They both did – in fact, they met at university – my mother studying history, and my father engineering. As graduates, they had a greater choice of more interesting jobs: my mother as a journalist and as a teacher; and my father in research and development, technical journalism and, ultimately, press relations.

As a result, my parents were better off than my grandparents, just as I am better off than my parents.

Yet today, we are looking at the first generation in living memory who can expect to be poorer than their parents, even as the economy continues to grow.[1]

This is unprecedented.

No generation in modern history has been poorer than its parents.

And they could be quite a lot poorer.

It took me a long time to come to this shocking realization. Let me tell you how I came to it. It's a long story but the really crucial events leading me to write this book happened rapidly in the past few years.

I ran the strategy-consulting practice in a major international consulting firm, working with clients both in the private sector and in government to resolve strategic challenges, and to predict and manage developing trends in the world of business, and more broadly in global affairs. Exploring the future was part of my job.

One of my colleagues ran the defence and security practice. This was a large and successful part of the firm, which dealt with some huge and important public-sector projects. But it didn't have access to the top-level contacts we enjoyed in my own area. One day, my colleague asked me whether we might be able to work together to build a network of contacts at the most senior level in the defence and security services, and apply the analytical techniques of business strategy to urgent problems of national security.

It wasn't long before our first test came. In 2011, the Arab Spring erupted. Most Western countries were caught on the hop by a wave of revolutions that swept through the Arab countries. Yes, there were individual specialists within Western governments who had felt that something was brewing, but *institutionally*, collectively, the West was unprepared. Diplomatic services, armed forces and security services all had to scramble to react, to understand the global ramifications and to develop policy responses – and fast.

The Arab Spring raised some fundamental issues: What would be the impact on the West? Which country was next? How should we react now? I decided to focus on the question of predictability. Should we have been able to predict the Arab Spring?

At one level, the answer is an obvious 'No.' The Arab Spring began with the suicide of a hitherto unknown street vendor and erupted into revolts and revolutions in eighteen Middle Eastern nations, of which four led to chaotic regime change. No one, however sophisticated their analysis, could have predicted the sequence of events that unfolded in 2011.

But as the team conducted its analysis, we uncovered some very clear – and very worrying – problems shared by the countries which were hit by the Arab Spring. Of the four problems common to these countries – economic hardship, lack of a democratic safety-valve, ethnic or sectarian divisions and oppressive laws and policing – the one which grabbed my attention was *economic hardship*.

And the real shock came when we carried out the same analysis for other countries. I had been aware that rising inequality was an issue in the West, but it was not until our analysis was complete that I realized the extent of the problem.

We found that the continuation of current trends in economic inequality posed an *existential threat* to civilization in several major Western countries. Included in that list were the US and the UK. Our conclusion was terrifying.

If we carry on as we are going, the civilization we enjoy today will not last until 2050.

The early signs are already here. In 2017, we read that the economy was booming[2] and stock markets were at an all-time high[3], yet at the same time we heard that wages were not keeping pace with inflation[4] and food-banks had more 'customers' than ever before.[5]

If the economy is doing so well, *how can most people not be doing well?* If the pie is growing, why aren't we all getting bigger slices? If we are so well-off, why is our children's generation set to be the first in living memory to be worse-off than its predecessors? If you've read this far, you'll see the logical disconnect here straight away. And if you're like me, you'll want to know what you can do to change this state of affairs.

The emergence of mass impoverishment

Over the following chapters I'm going to use the phrase 'mass impoverishment' fairly frequently. This is a phrase I've coined to describe the state of affairs that could become the new normal if we don't initiate a course-correction fairly soon. Briefly put, it's the process by which, even as the pie continues to grow, most people find themselves forced to accept ever smaller slices.

If mass impoverishment continues at current rates, most Americans will be living in or near poverty before 2050. In fact, the world in 2050 will be unrecognizable to the average person living in the West today. If you have children, their world in 2050 will not be the one you share with them now. We'll explore this further in Chapter One.

But that dystopian future in 2050 isn't inevitable. If we take a step back and question some of our assumptions about the basics of making, taking and sharing wealth, we see that there are alternative options to explore. A sceptic might say that most countries do a worse job for their populations than the US and the UK, and this is true, but there are quite a few which consistently do better – in terms of poverty rates, wage growth, social mobility and overall life satisfaction. We can learn from these countries.

We can also learn from our own history – it wasn't so long ago that we were experiencing a 'Golden Age of Capitalism' – the period after the Second World War in which most developed countries, including the US and the UK, experienced an economic miracle. It is still quite possible for us to create a similar period of prosperity. Where children can again expect to become wealthier than their parents. Where they contribute more to society and take a firm hand in determining the world's future.

If you are already thinking that a lot of what this book tells you is hard to believe, then I sympathize. A few years ago, I would have said the same. It flies in the face of what you will hear from many politicians or read in your newspapers.

But the facts are out there – and they tell a clear story. The official statistics paint a much less rosy picture than most politicians. While researching and writing this book, my motto has been *trust the facts; distrust the opinions*. So why on earth should you believe me? You shouldn't – at least not just because you read it here. In these pages, and on the website where more details are given, you'll find the data and the tools with which to make your own informed, independent, reasonable judgement, based on the facts.

By the time you finish reading, I hope that you will not only see the world in a different way but also have confidence that the facts *are* on your side, that a new Golden Age of Abundance *is* attainable – and that, if we act now, we *can* leave behind a better world for those who follow.

Economics – The Five Things You Need to Know

Money is not the only answer but it makes a difference.

Barack Obama

Maybe you have never read a book on the economy. Perhaps it has never interested you, or perhaps you thought that it was too complicated to understand. Actually, I believe that if you have the ability to follow top-level sport, you have the ability to understand all you need to know about economics.

If you already know the definition of GDP and are familiar with all the main measures of inequality, you can safely skip this chapter and get stuck into Part 1, where the story begins. If not, this chapter will give you the tools you need to understand what is happening (economically) to you and to the rest of society.

In one sense, economics *is* complicated. Nobody in the world understands the economy to the extent that they can accurately predict its *future* course. As Simon Wren-Lewis, Oxford Professor of Economics, put it:[1]

Macroeconomic forecasts produced with macroeconomic models tend to be little better than intelligent guesswork.

That is not an opinion – it is a fact. It is a fact because for decades many reputable and long-standing model-based forecasters have looked at their past errors, and that is what they find.

Of course, that's true of football and baseball, as well. Nobody in the world understands them well enough to predict next year's winner of the FA Cup or the World Series. *But that doesn't stop fans from having a detailed grasp of current and past performance.*

And economics is the same. Although it may be difficult to predict the *future* of the economy, you don't need to be a genius to understand the *past* and *present*. As with sport, you just need to understand the score line. Once you understand the scoring system, you can see who is winning and who is losing.

If you follow me through this chapter and come to understand a few basic concepts, you can see for yourself what is working and what is not. And who is benefitting, and who is not. If the economy is not working for you – and in the US and the UK it is *not working for most people* – it is important that you understand why.

And you don't need to be an Oxford don to understand that economics can be more confusing at times than it *needs* to be. In fact, what I'm going to show you in this chapter is exactly that you can understand basic, essential economics no matter your background or interests – that you deserve to understand the concepts I'm about to explain to you and that you *owe it to yourself* to make sure you do.

When you hear politicians talking about the economy, some of what they say is accurate. But much of it is either misleading – facts presented out of context to convey the wrong impression – or simply false. The same thing is true of journalists, and even more so of social media pundits. This chapter will give you the tools you need to sift fact from fiction. And you *need* to know the difference, or you may find that you have just voted to impoverish your own family.

There are five things you *really* need to know.

Thing #1: The economy is the system we have put in place to create and distribute value

When Picasso took a collection of paints and some canvas stretched over a wooden frame and produced an artistic master-piece, he *created value*. The paint and canvas already had some value to start with but the value of the painting Picasso produced is far higher than the value of the inputs (paint/canvas). This is one form of value creation.

For a more conventional example, think about a farmer who produces corn, eggs and milk. A miller adds value to the corn by producing flour. A dairy adds value to the milk by producing butter. Lastly, a baker adds value to the flour, eggs and butter by creating a cake. The cake is more valuable than the corn, eggs and milk that went into it. This is another form of value creation.

The value that has been created is shared between the participants in the value creation process: the farmer receives income for the corn, eggs and milk; the dairy pays for the milk and receives income for the butter; the miller pays for the corn and receives income for the flour; the baker pays for the flour, eggs and butter and receives income for the cake. In this way, a chain of activities carried out by a series of different partici-pants has *created* the value of the cake and *distributed that value* among themselves. This is a system of value creation and distribution.

The economy as a whole is a much larger and more complex system of value creation and distribution, but the principle is the same.

Thing #2: Money is critical

In the economic system in place today, money plays a critical role. It allows us to move beyond bartering and the exchange of goods and services. When the dairy pays for the milk, it pays money (and not, for example, butter). When the miller pays for the corn, she pays money (and not bags of flour). When the baker pays for the flour, eggs and butter, he pays money. Economists would say that money acts as a *'medium of exchange'* in these transactions.

It also acts as a *'unit of account'*: if we want to say *how much* value each has exchanged, the fact that all the transactions took place using money enables us to measure the value (in any unit of currency we wish).

There is a third function of money – it can act as a *'store of value'*: if I like, I can keep some money in the bank or under my mattress to spend later.

The money that we use today is known as a *fiat* currency, from the Latin word meaning *let it be*. The *fiat* money system has been in place since the early 1970s. Before that, the dollar, sterling and most other currencies were backed by gold. This was the 'gold standard' according to which a dollar or a pound could be converted into gold on demand. In 1971, Richard Nixon ended dollar convertibility into gold.[2] A dollar today has value only because the US government says it has value, because there is a legal duty to pay taxes in dollars and therefore – if for no other reason – people need them, and because society as a whole accepts that it has value. The same is true in other countries.

Fiat money is created (almost) out of nothing in a variety of ways:

1. a central bank (e.g. the Bank of England or the US Federal Reserve) can have coins minted and bank notes printed;
2. a central bank can create money electronically;
3. commercial banks can create money electronically by making loans – and *this is how the vast bulk of all money is created.*

As the Bank of England explains:[3]

> In the modern economy, most money takes the form of bank deposits. But how those bank deposits are created is often misunderstood: the principal way is through commercial banks making loans. Whenever a bank makes a loan, it simultaneously creates a matching deposit in the borrower's bank account, thereby creating new money.

You don't need to understand precisely *how* the banks do this[4] – the important point is that they *do* and that this is how most money is created.

The Bank of England goes on to explain that this new money, having been created by lending, can equally be destroyed again by repaying loans – if this does not happen, it will be spent and *create additional demand* in the economy.

Thing #3: Flows and stocks of value are both important to you

In a money-based economy, value created is measured in dollars or pounds (or the currency of the country concerned). But not all value creation involves the exchange of money. If

I pay a landscape-gardening company to mow my lawn, their contribution to value created can be measured because money has changed hands. If I mow the lawn myself, the *same value* has been created (the lawn looks just as good) but it will *not* be measured because no money has flowed.

Despite this flaw in using money flows to measure value created, no better approach has yet been developed. The money-flow-based view of value remains the normal way that economists and politicians look at the economy; it is the way economic statistics are compiled, and it is the view I have adopted throughout this book.

With this money-based view we can think of valuable products and services flowing around the economy in one direction and money flowing in the other. Most people are not allowed to create money – it is a serious criminal offence – and of course most people are careful not to destroy money. Therefore, in most parts of the economy money will be neither created nor destroyed.

If more money flows into part of a system than flows out, the surplus can be stored as a 'stock' of value. A householder could keep surplus cash under the mattress, although in practice it is more likely to be stored in a bank account. In either case, this is a stock of money that has value which can be drawn upon later. Having a surplus usually means that value has been added to a stock. Contrast this with a *deficit*, which will deplete the value of some kind of stock: if I have savings but then spend more than I earn, I dip into my savings – I've depleted the value of my savings.

Your income is a flow; your wealth is a stock: they are different things – and they are both important to you.

Thing #4: Gross Domestic Product is the total flow of value created and available to be consumed

When Picasso painted a masterpiece, the value was created by the act of painting but no value *flowed* through the economy until he sold the painting and received cash in return. Gross Domestic Product is a measure of the total flow of value created in a country during a specific period – usually one year. This includes the value flows generated by artists selling their paintings to collectors, but of course it includes many other things as well.

Since looking at the whole economy at once *is* complicated, let's start with just firms and households and then add banks, governments and the rest of the world.

The diagrams below show how economists normally look at the economy and how Gross Domestic Product (GDP) is defined. To begin with, imagine a simple economy consisting of just households and firms. Households contain wage earners, who work in a firm and receive wages for doing so, property owners who receive rent, and owners of capital who receive dividends as a return on that capital.* (These could all be the same person and not every household has all of these.)

Economists traditionally view the inputs to a firm as being Land and its products, Capital and Labour. The firm pays for these inputs as rent, dividends and wages. With these inputs – and of course possibly intermediate products made by other

---

* If you own a company, or shares in a company, each year you can expect to receive a cash 'dividend' – your share of the profit of the company.

Figure 1: How the economy works – households and firms

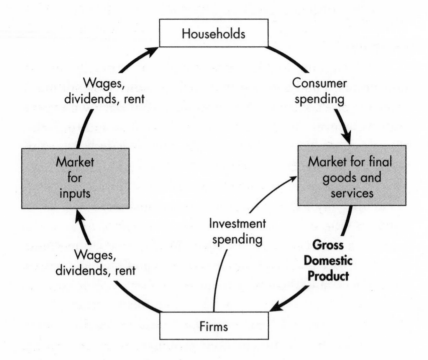

firms – firms can produce the goods and services society re-quires. In our example above, the baker had to buy butter, flour and eggs to be able to bake a cake. The butter, flour and eggs were intermediate products and the cake was the final product. For simplicity, there is no arrow in this diagram representing the purchase of intermediate products since these purchases simply move money between firms and do not directly impact the value of final goods and services.

The households buy final goods and services from firms – this is called consumer spending. The baker might also have needed to buy an oven in which to bake the cakes. The oven is also a final product, but it counts as investment spending by the firm rather than as consumer spending. In this simple economy, consisting of only households and firms, GDP is defined as the sum of the consumer spending and investment spending.

This diagram highlights a couple of critically important points. Firstly, notice that each person's expenditure is someone else's income. We know this from our own experience: whenever we spend money, we pay it to someone else. Nevertheless, the implications of this seemingly obvious point are rather counterintuitive. As an individual or as a single business, it *is* possible for me to boost my income while containing my expenditure (and most businesses aim to do this); for the economy as a whole, *the only way to boost income is for expenditure to rise.* What *is* true for individuals and households is *not* true for the economy as a whole. This is a major cause of confusion for both politicians and voters.

Secondly, there is a circular flow of money. In this simplified world (with no banks or foreign countries or companies), all of GDP ends up back in the hands of households, whether it gets there as wages, as dividends or as rent. In our example, with the farmer, the miller, the dairy and the baker, the GDP represents the value of the cakes produced. In general, GDP represents the total value of goods and services produced in the economy and therefore the total value of goods and services available to be consumed by members of society. If GDP rises, then more value has been created and society as a whole can consume more. It is for this reason that politicians and economists focus so much effort and attention on understanding what will grow GDP.

In the real world, as well as households and firms, we have banks and financial markets in general. Adding them into the picture gives us the following.

Figure 2: How the economy works – households, firms and financial markets

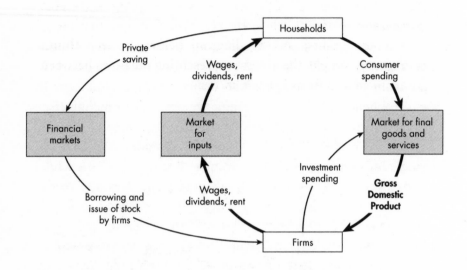

In this slightly more complete picture, households need not spend all their money in the year they earn it – they can also save some. They can, for example, deposit it in the bank or use it to buy bonds or stocks. To be able to pay interest to depositors, banks need to receive interest, and so they need to lend money to others – in particular to firms – to have someone from whom they can receive this interest. For the firms, the existence of banks and capital markets opens up the possibility of investing money that they do not yet have. A baker just starting out, for example, may not have the money to buy a new oven, but can take out a bank loan to get the business started and then repay the bank over time from the proceeds of the bakery. In this version of the economy, as before, GDP is defined as the sum of consumer spending and firms' investment spending.

Another important component missing from these pictures of the economy is the government. Government takes in money in two ways: borrowing in financial markets and taxing households and firms. It also pays out money in two ways: government spending (e.g. on road building) and direct transfers to households (e.g. the state pension) and firms (e.g. government grants). In the diagram below, to keep things manageably simple, the arrows representing the flows between government and firms are not shown.

Figure 3: How the economy works (excluding foreign trade)

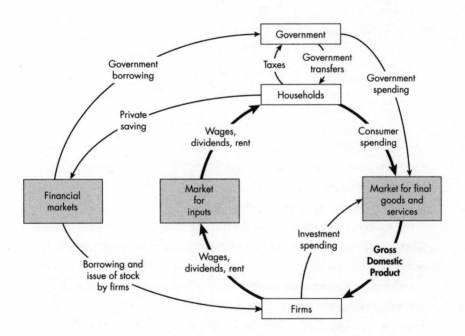

In this now almost complete view of the economy, GDP is defined as being the sum of consumer spending, government spending and investment spending by firms. To complete the picture, we must remember that each country trades with others – so the rest of the world is also important.

Figure 4: How the economy works – complete view

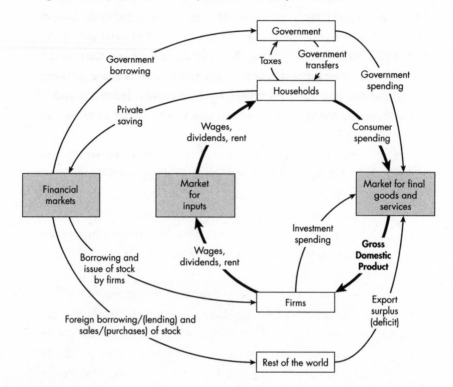

This view of the economy is still simplified – as I mentioned above, not all the arrows are shown – but it is complete in the sense that all economic agents (i.e. anyone who can buy or sell anything) are included in one of the four categories shown in the unshaded boxes.

In the diagram, you will see that I have used the accountants' convention of representing a negative value in parentheses. So lending is negative borrowing; purchases are negative sales; and a deficit is a negative surplus.

Economic agents in the rest of the world can buy or sell goods and services. If they buy more than they sell, our exports exceed our imports and we have a trade surplus. If they sell more than they buy, our imports exceed our exports and we have a trade deficit (this has been the general position in the US and UK in recent years). A trade deficit means that we are *consuming* more products and services than we are *producing*, and we pay for this either by borrowing from abroad or by selling off some of our capital stock – in either case, we are living beyond our means.

If we have a deficit, money is flowing from us to the rest of the world which they then use either to lend back to us or to buy capital in our countries. For example, they could buy property, land or existing businesses – effectively purchasing the wealth of our country, little by little, with our excess spending. It is not government spending that impoverishes a nation but trade deficits.

Now we can finally see the complete definition of GDP: it is the sum of government spending, consumer spending and investment spending by firms plus any trade surplus (or minus any trade deficit). As we saw above, it represents the total flow of value created in the national economy during the period under consideration – typically a year. You can think of GDP as what society as a whole can 'afford'. If GDP is rising, society as a whole can afford more; if GDP falls, we can afford less.

If the economy consisted entirely of farmers, millers, dairies and bakers, GDP would represent the total value of cakes produced during the year – and therefore the total value of cakes that society as a whole could afford to consume. If there are a large number of people to share those cakes, the amount available for each individual will be less than if they are shared between just a few. For this reason, it can be useful to look at the amount of GDP per person in society; this is known as GDP per capita. GDP per capita measures the amount of value created in the year for each person in society – in theory, if each person received the same share of what was produced, this is the amount they would receive. In a society with a fast-growing population, GDP will almost inevitably rise but the experience of the individual members of that society – whether they actually become better off – will be determined by GDP per capita.

Time matters too. GDP (and GDP per capita) is measured in dollars or pounds (or whatever the national currency is). Over a long time period, the value of the dollar or a pound is not constant: inflation will gradually eat away at that value. Roughly speaking, £1 in the year 1900 could buy the same as £75 in the year 2000. Over long time periods, unadjusted figures – known as 'nominal' figures – are *not comparable* and inflation-adjusted figures – known as 'real' figures – are used instead. In this book, because a long time-frame can often provide valuable context, the data will usually be quoted in real terms. We shall look at *real* GDP over time and *real* household income over time.

Thing #5: Understanding who receives what value is critical

There is *another* factor which determines what each individual receives: the way in which the cakes are distributed. In the real world, GDP is *not* shared equally among the entire population so, in this analogy, some people receive several cakes, while others just have a slice of one cake.

Distribution of value is critical to the experience of individual members of society. If I have US$1,000 to distribute among 100 people, I could distribute US$10 to each person – this would be a perfectly equal distribution. At the other extreme, I could distribute US$1,000 to the first person and nothing to the rest – this would be a perfectly unequal distribution.

In practice, the value created by society is neither distributed perfectly equally nor perfectly unequally, but somewhere in the middle. To understand the impact of the distribution of wealth, it is vital to be able to *measure* that distribution.

As a practical example of distribution, let's look at household wealth in the United Kingdom. Household wealth is the stock of value owned by each household. In the UK, the Office for National Statistics (ONS) collects and publishes data on the economy in general and incomes and wealth in particular. Figure 5, below, shows how wealth is distributed in the UK – who owns how much.

Figure 5: Who owns wealth in the UK

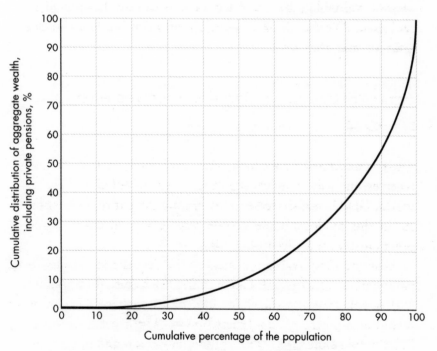

Source: ONS[5]

The chart contains a lot of information but it is difficult to read. On the horizontal axis is the cumulative percentage of the population – ordered from poorest to richest – and on the vertical axis is the wealth of this percentage. The chart shows that *the poorest 20 per cent of the population have almost no wealth at all*. The *bottom 50 per cent of the population own around 10 per cent* of the total wealth; and therefore the top 50 per cent of the population own around 90 per cent of the total wealth. The bottom 90 per cent of the population own 56 per cent of the wealth; and therefore the *top 10 per cent of the population own 44 per cent* of the total wealth. Because it is difficult to read this kind of chart, economists have developed *measures* which encapsulate some of the key information.

In this book, we shall use several different measures to describe how equally or unequally wealth or income is being distributed. These are illustrated in the next few figures using a simple population of 10 people.

Figure 6: Wealth distribution in a population of 10 people

Person	Wealth (£)
1	–
2	–
3	25,000
4	50,000
5	75,000
6	125,000
7	250,000
8	300,000
9	1,000,000
10	2,000,000

Source: Illustrative data

MEAN AND MEDIAN

In the hypothetical population detailed in Figure 6 with total wealth of £3,825,000, persons 9 and 10 have £3 million between them but are clearly not typical of the population as a whole.

Perhaps the simplest measure is the 'average' wealth of the population – total wealth divided by the total number of people (technically, this is one specific kind of average, the arithmetic mean) – in this case, £382,500. It is noticeable that only two members of the population have more than the average wealth, so this type of average does *not* represent the experience of a typical member of the population.

A measure which is more likely to represent the experience of a typical person is the 'median' value. This is the value associated with the person in the middle of the population – in this case between person 5 and person 6, so we say the median value is £100,000. This clearly makes more sense than just quoting the average wealth. Here the ratio of average wealth to median wealth is 3.82:1. This is one measure of inequality: the higher this ratio, the more unequal the distribution of wealth.

The chart overleaf shows the actual data for a selection of countries in 2015.

Of the countries in the sample, the United States is the richest in terms of average wealth per adult, with a figure of over US$350,000. The median wealth – what a typical adult owns – in the US, however, is just under US$50,000. The ratio of average to median in the US is 7.09. In the UK, the average wealth per adult is just over US$320,000 and the median wealth per adult is just over US$126,000, giving a ratio of average to median of 2.53. In practice, this means that *a typical adult in the UK is more than twice as rich as a typical adult in the US* – despite the US being a significantly richer country overall than the UK.

Figure 7: Average and median wealth by country, 2015

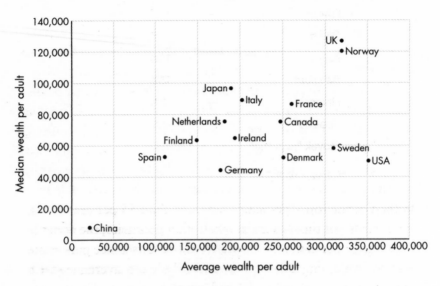

Source: Credit Suisse Wealth Report[6]

Another simple way to look at inequality is to consider the share of the total wealth owned by the top 10 per cent of society, or the top 1 per cent. The figure below shows estimates from the Organisation for Economic Cooperation and Development (OECD) of the proportion of national wealth owned by the top 1 per cent in a selection of leading economies.

Figure 8: Share of total wealth owned by the top 1%, by country

Country	Top 1% wealth share
United States	37%
Germany	25%
Austria	24%
Netherlands	24%
Luxembourg	22%

Portugal	21%
France	18%
Spain	15%
Italy	14%
Belgium	13%
Finland	12%
Greece	8%
Slovak Republic	8%

Source: OECD[7]

In the US, the top 1 per cent own more than 35 per cent of the total wealth of the nation; in most other countries, the figure is between 10 per cent and 25 per cent. This difference goes some way to explaining the large disparity between average wealth and median wealth in the United States.

GINI COEFFICIENT

One of the most widely-used measures of inequality is the Gini coefficient. The Gini coefficient is best understood graphically: Figure 9 overleaf shows the same data as Figure 6 above.

The black line represents a perfectly equal distribution of wealth, and the grey line represents the actual distribution taken from the table above. The gap between the two is a measure of inequality. Perfect inequality would see the line run flat along the bottom until we reach Person 10 at which point it would shoot up vertically. The lines of perfect equality and perfect inequality together make a triangle. This is the concept behind the Gini coefficient, which is defined as the area between the grey cumulative wealth curve and the black equal distribution line divided by the area of the triangle. The

Figure 9: Wealth distribution in a population of 10 people

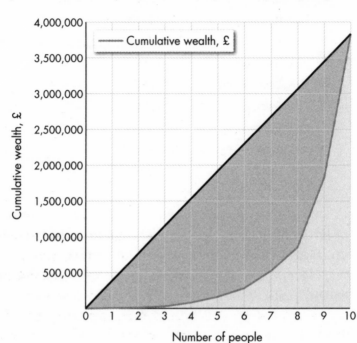

Gini coefficient for a population with perfect equality would be zero, and the coefficient for a population with perfect inequality would be 1.00. The lower the Gini coefficient the lower the inequality and *vice versa*.

The levels of income (as opposed to wealth) inequality, as measured by the Gini coefficient, for some of the leading countries in the world are shown in the table below.

Figure 10: Income inequality by country

Country	Gini Coefficient
USA	0.39
UK	0.351
Greece	0.34

Spain	0.335
Italy	0.327
France	0.306
Germany	0.289
Switzerland	0.285
Sweden	0.274
Finland	0.26
Norway	0.253
Denmark	0.249

Source: OECD[8]

Clearly no country has perfect income equality – which would correspond to a Gini coefficient of zero. In fact, almost all countries have a Gini coefficient of above 0.25. Equally, no country has perfect inequality – which would correspond to a Gini coefficient of 1.0 and mean that one person had all the wealth. Of the countries listed, the US has the highest levels of income inequality, with a Gini coefficient just below 0.4.

ECONOMIC CHOICES

In the US and the UK (and almost every other country), we have a mixed economy, which combines capitalism with state-run activities and uses a *fiat* currency. This is not the only conceivable way to run an economy. If we chose to, we could change our system and step back in time to return to the gold standard – some people do want to turn the clock back in this way – or even to a barter economy. At the futuristic end of the spectrum, we could choose to run a completely planned economy using artificial intelligence to determine what will be produced, in what quantities, and how and where it should be distributed.

Even within the context of a mixed economic system with a *fiat* currency, there are many possibilities (as Chapter 13 explains). An economic system in any society is the result of choices – although not necessarily explicit choices – made by society as a whole or by elements within society and should, in a democracy, be made with the goal of benefiting society as a whole.

PART I

THE BURNING PLATFORM

N obody likes change.

We know and understand the status quo even if we are not happy with it, but we don't know the alternative. Change is difficult in itself and it leads to an uncertain future. As Niccolò Machiavelli pointed out almost five centuries ago:[1]

> ... there is nothing more difficult to take in hand, more perilous to conduct, or more uncertain in its success, than to take the lead in the introduction of a new order of things, because the innovator has for enemies all those who have done well under the old conditions, and lukewarm defenders in those who may do well under the new.

Nevertheless, there are times when we have to change. In the language of change management, the phrase 'burning platform' has a very specific meaning. It refers to the recognition that the status quo is no longer tenable and that, despite our fears, we must find the courage to change. As change management guru Darryl Conner explains:[2]

> At nine-thirty on a July evening in 1988, a disastrous explosion and fire occurred on the Piper Alpha oil-drilling platform in the North Sea off the coast of Scotland. 166 crew members and two rescuers lost their lives in what was (and still is) the worst catastrophe in the fifty-year history of North Sea oil exportation. One of the sixty-three crew

members who survived was Andy Mochan, a superinten-
dent on the rig.

From the hospital, he told of being awakened by the
explosion and alarms. Badly injured, he escaped from his
quarters to the platform edge. Beneath him, oil had sur-
faced and ignited. Twisted steel and other debris littered
the surface of the water. Because of the water's tempera-
ture, he knew that he could live a maximum of twenty
minutes if not rescued. Despite all that, Andy jumped
fifteen stories from the platform to the water.

When asked why he took that potentially fatal leap,
he did not hesitate. He said, 'It was either jump or fry; I
jumped.'

In this first part of the book, I hope to persuade you that for
most people it is now either jump or fry.

We should jump. But we should look before we leap.

CHAPTER 1

The Age of Anxiety

Nothing in life is to be feared; it is only to be under-stood. Now is the time to understand more, so that we may fear less.

Marie Curie[1]

Our age is one of chronic anxiety.[2]

There's more collective fear, I think, in our society than many of us have ever experienced before. Many in the US and the UK are just one pay cheque away from default-ing on our mortgages;[3, 4] others can't cope with the ruinous costs of healthcare.

Even our children are not immune. One in four children will experience an anxiety disorder of some kind before they are eighteen; the suicide rate amongst girls has doubled in the past decade, and the rate for boys is higher still.[5]

And while we may have our own individual reasons for feeling stressed, worried or anxious, there is, I suspect, an increasingly widely-shared feeling that the economic system we currently live under may have run its course. For a growing number of us, it's simply not working the way we expected it to – or the way we need it to.

The future is beginning to hold a particular terror for us. Not long ago, 'futuristic' was a sexy word, full of optimism and promise. No longer. Whatever the future holds, we suspect it isn't going to be pleasant. Fewer jobs, less money, little in the way of prospects, and ever-worse damage to the environment.

I have spent most of my career as a strategist, and whenever someone learns what I do for a living, by far the most common questions begin with '*What do you think is going to happen...?*'

It's part of our professional mystique that strategists, economists and financial analysts can peer through the mists of time into the future. But I'm here to tell you the truth – we cannot. Like astrologers, palmists and crystal-ball gazers, we have a professional jargon that we deliver with an air of authority. And we do have some powerful tools. But our track record on forecasting is less than spotless... and economic forecasting, in particular, is notoriously difficult to get right.

Economics is not like the hard sciences, which deal with accurate data, testable hypotheses and repeatable experiments. If you try to forecast the economy, you grapple not only with inadequate data, but also with obscure human actions, unknown plans, eccentric motivations, and illogical preferences... none of which are documented, and all of which can – and do – change at the flick of a button.

And then we come to technology – the Great Disrupter. In the years ahead, technological developments (in particular, the automation of most jobs) – and the political response to those developments – will have an impact which could be hugely positive... or frighteningly negative. No one in the world can forecast these things.

Where are today's economic policies taking us?

While it's true that I can only guess at what interest rate you'll be paying on your mortgage in five years' time, the price of gas next year or which horse will win the Grand National... I *can* tell you what is known about the world today.

I can also tell you, through historical data analysis, what impact changes in government economic policies have had on their countries' economic performance – and the wealth of their citizens – in the *past*.

And I can tell you what *would* happen, *if* we were to stick with current policies regardless of their effects.

That is the difference between economic forecasting (which has to factor in all manner of unknowable future decisions) and economic analysis (which need not). The first is an attempt to peer into the future and foretell what *will* come to pass. It's a stab in the dark because it has to make so many assumptions about so many factors that are by definition unknown. The second is a much more limited extrapolation of known facts to show what *would* happen in the absence of structural change.

And I'm not dealing with unknowns here. Far from it. Here is what this book is predicated on:

- What are our existing economic policies?
- What effect are they having today?
- What effect will they have in the future – if we stick to them?

In the year 2050

It may appear to be a long way off but 2050 will be upon us all too soon. No one can say whether we'll all be travelling around by jet-packs and flying cars – my hunch is that we won't be – but we can make some pretty clear estimates of how the economy would look, *assuming that today's policies remain in place*.

So, how *will* it look? Fortunately, there are really only two things we need to look at to answer this question. First, how will the economic pie grow? And secondly, how will it be sliced?

In answering this question over the next few paragraphs, I am going to focus on the US. There are two reasons for this. The first is that even though many of the same trends are beginning to be visible in the UK and other countries, they are more clearly visible in the US – because the US is further down the path. The second reason is that the analysis needs high-quality data, and the US has documented them better than many other countries.

Let's start with the first question, that of economic growth. I'm going to assume that economic growth will continue exactly as it has done since 1980. Why 1980? For the period from 1980 to the present day, we've lived predominantly under one particular form of economic policy, the form that we are assuming will remain in place. More on this in the next chapter.

Secondly, we need to consider just how that economic pie is going to be sliced. Again, this is straightforward because the data are available for the past four decades and, in summary, they show that:

- Generally, the highest priority has been to prevent too many of those at the bottom from slipping too far below the poverty line.
- The second priority has been to preserve the growth in incomes of the wealthier segments of society – particularly those segments within the top 1 per cent.
- The lowest priority has been to protect the incomes of those in the middle.

What follows is a quick summary of the impact of these policies. I've kept my workings out of this chapter, to make things clearer, but you can see the detailed methodology and the data on which the calculations are based in Appendix I on the *99-percent.org* website.

The really, really bad news

If these policies continue, the majority of the American population will be living in or near poverty by 2050.

The middle class will have all but disappeared – and with it many businesses whose target market is middle-class consumers. In one of the richest countries in the world.

What does that mean? It means that America in 2050 may be rather like South Africa today. An elite who live luxuriously, protected by intense security from the mass of the population who do not share in the wealth of the country.

As Archbishop Desmond Tutu put it when expressing his disappointment with the progress in South Africa since the end of apartheid:[6]

> We dreamt about a society that would be compassionate, a society that really made people feel they mattered. You can't do that in a society where you have people who go to bed hungry, where many of our children still attend classes under trees.

To put it briefly, US civilization will have failed. And the UK will be on the same track, just not quite so far down the line.

Failure by the numbers

Let's look at the numbers for a minute so that you can see what I mean.

In 2015, there were, according to official statistics, over 40 million Americans living in poverty, out of a population of just over 320 million people.[7] Around one person in eight.

Of those 40 or so million, around 19 million were living in *deep poverty* – their incomes are *below half* of the official US poverty threshold.[8]

In 2015, the official poverty threshold for a family of four was US$24,257, a little over US$6,000 per person.[9] That's about US$17 a day.

Those in deep poverty are surviving on just over US$3,000 per person. That's little more than US$8 a day.

Even worse, as the Nobel Prize-winning economist Sir Angus Deaton points out:[10]

> ... there are 5.3 million Americans who are absolutely poor by global standards. This is a small number compared with the one for India, for example, but it is more than in Sierra Leone (3.2 million) or Nepal (2.5 million), about the same as in Senegal (5.3 million) and only one-third less than in Angola (7.4 million).

If we continue with current policies until 2050, and they continue to have the effects that they have had over the last thirty-five years, by the year 2050, the numbers will look something like this:[11]

- the total US population will be around 390 million people,[12] of whom the bottom 60 per cent will see falling incomes by 2050;
- almost half will be getting by on a household income of around US$27,000 at 2011 prices – that is the same as the bottom 20 per cent today;
- *around 100 million will be living in poverty by today's*

standards. That is a poverty rate of over 25 per cent – comparable to the rate in South Africa today;

- around 45 million people will be in deep poverty;
- and roughly *13 million will be in absolute poverty* by global standards, trying to live on less than US$4 per day.

For the top 1 per cent, things will not be so tough – on the same basis, the average inflation-adjusted income of a household in the top 1 per cent would have risen from around US$1.6 million in 2015 to around US$5 million in 2050.

What this means for you

What does this mean for you, personally, and for your children?

If you are in that bottom 60 per cent (as by definition 60 per cent of people are), the answer is obvious. You will be poorer, possibly much poorer, than today.

But even if you are lucky enough to be in the top 40 per cent, so that on these projections you stand to be better off in 2050 than today, there are two things that may give you pause for thought:

1. If you have children, you can skew the odds to some extent, so that they have a greater than 40 per cent chance of ending up in the top 40 per cent, but you cannot – unless you are seriously wealthy – guarantee it. If you have two children, the chances that both of them will be in the top 40 per cent may be something over 16 per cent. And if *they* each have two children, the probability that all of your grandchildren are in the top 40 per cent will be something over 2.5 per cent – not

great odds. The larger the circle of people that you care about, the greater the chance that at least one of them will be struggling badly.

2. These projections take no account of the likelihood that by 2050, it will be possible to automate almost every job – a machine will do it better and more cheaply than a human. This will put extreme pressure on most people in the top 40 per cent. The projections above, in other words, are probably rosy.

And even if you *are* in the top 1 per cent, this may not be an attractive future for you. Many wealthy people already feel uncomfortable about the plight of those less fortunate than themselves – and if they feel uncomfortable today, they may find the world of 2050 quite unpalatable.

There is a slight possibility that you may both be in the top 1 per cent *and* not be concerned about the plight of your fellow humans. I've heard that such people do indeed exist. Well, even those strangely sociopathic beings won't find 2050 a land of milk and honey.

Because too much concentration of money into too few hands brings a problem even for the beneficiaries: inflation. Although, overall, inflation is today moderate, luxury goods inflation is not. As the hedge fund manager Paul Singer complained in the *Washington Post*:[13]

Check out London, Manhattan, Aspen and East Hampton real estate prices, as well as high-end art prices, to see what the leading edge of hyperinflation could look like.

That household income of US$5 million may not actually buy you more luxury products than US$1.6 million dollars does today. But it will have caused a lot of misery to others.

Is there any good news, then?

The good news is that we have seen nothing that suggests that a future based on this extrapolation is inevitable. If it is *not* to come to pass, however, the policies of the last thirty-five or so years must change.

So, the critical question is what must happen to change these policies for the better?

In order to address this question, we must first be clear about what options we can even consider. Politicians often assure us that *there is no alternative*, that the path we are on represents the best possible path for the economy, and that only minor fine-tuning is possible.

If this is really true, then we should brace ourselves for the possibility of a future similar to (or worse than) the one I described above.

If it is *not* true, then there is everything to play for. Part Two of this book explores in detail whether we should take seriously the pundits and politicians who claim that there are no alternative policies to those in place today.

And most important of all, Part 3 proposes possible solutions.

CHAPTER 2

A Tale of Two Systems

It was the best of times, it was the worst of times,
it was the age of wisdom, it was the age of foolishness,
it was the epoch of belief, it was the epoch of incredulity,
it was the season of Light, it was the season of Darkness,
it was the spring of hope, it was the winter of despair.

Charles Dickens[1]

Although we don't talk about it much these days, it was not so long ago that we were living in a Golden Age.

The seventy years since the end of the Second World War saw enormous change across the world, much of it for the better – and all of it under a mixed economy in which capitalism coexisted with a public sector. There was not – and hopefully will not be – another World War, despite the reality of ongoing conflict and instability in many parts of the world. Technology has progressed enormously. Living standards have risen dramatically in real terms (adjusted for inflation) even in already advanced economies.

But this remarkable progress since the end of the Second World War has *not been uniform*. The post-war period can be split quite neatly into two thirty-five-year eras, driven by different concepts of how society should run. These two concepts have produced markedly different results.

The period from 1945–80 was known in the West as the Golden Age of Capitalism. This was followed, from 1980–2015, by what I shall call the Age of Market Capitalism. As I hope to show you, we have forgotten quite how much better the economy performed during the Golden Age of Capitalism.

In July 1957, the British Prime Minister Harold Macmillan addressed a Conservative party rally saying: 'Go around the country, go to the industrial towns, go to the farms and you will see a state of prosperity such as we have never had in my lifetime – nor indeed in the history of this country.'

And he was right.

The Golden Age of Capitalism

After the end of the Second World War in 1945, both among the victors and in the defeated countries, there was a clear need to rebuild national economies and a determination that the re-building should result in a better world.

Economically, the Great Depression of 1929 (triggered by the Wall Street Crash) was still a living memory, and those in power were determined not to make the same mistakes again. During the post-war period, the revival of trade and general sense of optimism meant that many countries experienced an economic revival.

Globally, governments accepted they had a vital role to play both in driving and directing their economies. This period saw governments funding large infrastructure projects, creating strong social security systems, developing healthcare systems, and investing in education for their populations and in funda-mental research to drive industrial innovation.

Generally speaking, the system seemed to work well until the 1970s, when a succession of unanticipated shocks related to the end of the gold standard and two major oil price hikes – in which the price of oil skyrocketed by over 400 per cent[2] – caused serious problems for the developed economies and resulted in what was known as stagflation (the combination of stagnation in economic growth with price inflation).

The combined result of these events and their economic consequences was a loss of confidence in economic management and a sense of desperation – after thirty-five years of impressive progress – that a radical change was needed to keep the economy growing.

The Age of Market Capitalism

That radical change was not long in coming. In 1979, Margaret Thatcher was elected as Prime Minister of the UK and in 1981 Ronald Reagan became President of the USA. These two leaders were influential in ushering in a new form of capitalism – market capitalism.

Central to market capitalism is the concept that *markets know best*. According to market capitalism, government intervention, no matter how well-intentioned, consumes resources which would be better used in the private sector and therefore inevitably makes matters worse economically. Ronald Reagan summarized this view succinctly: 'Government isn't the solution; government is the problem.'[3]

Free markets, according to this doctrine, while they may occasionally experience painful periods of creative destruction, are the only way to guarantee the best use of resources, the highest levels of economic growth and the fairest distribution of the wealth that they create.

It's a persuasive story: clear, simple and underpinned by a compelling work ethic. For many years I believed it myself.

Institutionally, the biggest change from the Golden Age of Capitalism to the Age of Market Capitalism was that government intervention was no longer perceived as a vital way of alleviating economic woes. Margaret Thatcher and Ronald Reagan both rose to power in the 1970s and both lent their names to their own varieties of market capitalism: 'Thatcherism' and 'Reaganomics'.

Nigel Lawson, the British Chancellor of the Exchequer under Margaret Thatcher, defined Thatcherism as: 'Free markets, financial discipline, firm control over public expenditure, tax cuts, nationalism, "Victorian values" (of the Samuel Smiles self-help variety), privatization and a dash of populism.'[4]

Meanwhile, Republican member of the House of Representatives, Jeff Duncan, summarized Reaganomics like this: 'Limit government, lower taxes, reduce government spending. These were three of the key principles of Reaganomics, principles that brought our country over twenty years of economic growth and prosperity.'[5]

Market capitalism, therefore, has two main objectives:

1. to free-up the private sector
2. to shrink the role of the state

True to these principles, since 1980 in both the US and the UK (as well as many other countries), the direction of policy has been to deregulate (reduce governmental control) wherever possible – and in particular to impose 'light-touch' regulation of financial services; to privatize wherever possible and to contract-out where full privatization is not possible; to reduce rates of income tax; to contain public spending; and to reduce the power of the union movement.

In other words, the government has simply been trying to get out of the way – and get everyone else out of the way – of business.

Yet the Age of Market Capitalism has been punctuated by crises, of which the most recent, and the most serious, was the Global Financial Crisis that began in 2007 and reached its crisis point in September 2008 when Lehman Brothers – the fourth-largest investment bank in the United States – collapsed.

Many financial analysts consider the 2008 crisis to be the worst financial crisis of its kind since the Great Depression in 1929. Some went even further. The Deputy Governor of the Bank of England called it '... possibly the largest financial crisis of its kind in human history'.[6]

Everyone was affected in some way by the 2008 crisis: the housing market crashed; stock markets plummeted; the economy contracted (leading to prolonged unemployment, foreclosures and evictions); companies collapsed amidst high-profile financial scandals (the demise of Lehman Brothers and the near-failure of AIG, in particular, caught public attention); and, in a disaster of almost unprecedented proportions, an entire country almost went bankrupt as the collapse of the banking system in Iceland marked (relative to the size of its economy) the largest such collapse suffered by any single country in history.[7]

The Final Report of the Financial Crisis Inquiry Commission[8] in the US concluded that the causes of the Global Financial Crisis lay – not surprisingly – in the financial system and that the fault was shared between 'captains of finance and the public stewards of our financial system'. In other words, regulation was too light and the financial services industry took advantage of this lack of regulation to maximize its own short-term benefits regardless of the long-term consequences to its shareholders or to society at large. The Commission asked, 'what else could one expect on a highway where there were neither speed limits nor neatly painted lines?' In other words, Market Capitalism had enabled the Global Financial Crisis – the effects of which we continue to feel today.

The narrative I've just laid out is entirely factual. There can be no doubting the events, consequences and timeline. However, at this point you may be thinking that what you've conventionally understood about the post-war period – particularly up to the 1970s – is very different from what I've just said.

And indeed it is.

On both sides of the Atlantic, the generally accepted story is that the post-war period was one of gradual decline – especially for the UK, but also for most other Western countries whose growth lagged behind that of Japan. This so-called decline culminated in the 1970s, a period of dreadful economic performance in which inflation and unemployment ran out of control and growth stagnated.

Then, in the 1980s, a series of market reforms rejuvenated both the US and UK economies, injecting a new sense of dynamism. Growth and prosperity finally began to return. That's the orthodox version of the story, at any rate.

But it's just not true.

Just the facts

We've all heard the story of the economic revival of the 1980s so many times that it seems almost indecent to question it and to dig up the facts. But if we do, the results are startling.

Figure 11 below summarizes the practical results we have seen in the US and the UK during the two different eras.

Figure 11: How Golden Age Capitalism out-performed Market Capitalism in the US and UK

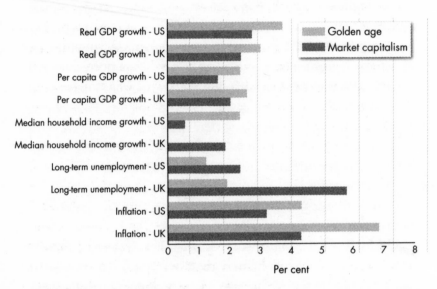

*Source: Data in Appendix II**

It compares a range of generally accepted measurements (household income, GDP and so on) between the two eras – Golden Age in light grey, Market Capitalism in dark grey. If you find the message of this chart hard to believe then take a look at Appendix II on the *99-percent.org* website where you can see the underlying data.

Incontrovertibly, the economy overall – measured by Gross Domestic Product – grew faster in both the US and the UK during the Golden Age than during the subsequent Age of Market Capitalism.

More importantly, because it affects the income available in principle for individuals, per capita GDP also grew much faster in both countries during the Golden Age, too.

---

* Unfortunately, there are no data for UK median household income going back to 1945.

More relevant still, if we look at the growth in real incomes for the typical household – and this is what really matters to *people* – in the US, there is a dramatic difference: each year the typical American household saw its real income grow by 2.3 per cent per annum during the Golden Age; but during the Age of Market Capitalism, this annual growth has been only 0.6 per cent. In other words, even though the pie was still growing at a reasonable rate, the slice available to most households was hardly growing.

Even worse, since the number of wage earners per household has grown since 1980, looking just at household income means that we miss a crucial development – household income has grown slightly but the actual income of the individual wage earners within that household has stagnated. Median wages for individuals in the United States have essentially been flat since 1980 – *virtually no growth at all after adjusting for inflation* – and for some of those below median, wage growth has been negative. If you earned a wage below the median average, in other words, chances are that you actually lost money.

In the US, long-term unemployment has almost doubled from 1.2 per cent during the Golden Age of Capitalism to 2.3 per cent during the Age of Market Capitalism. And in the UK, the picture is even worse: the rise has been from 1.9 per cent to 5.8 per cent.

Many people remember that in 1979 Margaret Thatcher campaigned on the slogan, 'Labour isn't working'. What we have forgotten is that after her election as Prime Minister, rather than falling as promised, unemployment shot up further – more than doubling – and peaked at over 10 per cent, five times the previous norm.

One area where performance *has* improved is in control of inflation: in the US, inflation averaged 4.3 per cent during the Golden Age of Capitalism and has been only 3.2 per cent during market capitalism; and in the UK inflation was 6.8 per cent on average during the Golden Age of Capitalism and averaged only 4.3 per cent during the Age of Market Capitalism.

So, whether it is in terms of overall economic growth or the prosperity of the typical family, the 'twenty years of economic growth and prosperity' that Jeff Duncan, Republican candidate, referred to earlier in the context of Reaganomics are *not* reflected in the data compiled by the Bureau of Economic Analysis, the Census Bureau or the Bureau of Labor Statistics.

The so-called return to growth and prosperity since the 1980s is a myth; it is not a fact.

What the data show is that the period from 1945 up to about 1980 was indeed a Golden Age of Capitalism, but that it has been followed by thirty-five years of poor results on almost every measure.

Even the much-reviled 1970s were better than the ten years from 2007–17. During the 1970s, average real GDP growth in the UK was just over 2 per cent; in the last ten years it has been only just over 1 per cent. If it comes to economic performance – astonishingly – going back to the 1970s would be a *big improvement*.

From 1980–2015, we ran a thirty-five-year experiment with the economy, testing the system of Market Capitalism. And it failed. But instead of learning from the experiment and trying something else, we are at risk of misreporting the results – pretending that the era of Market Capitalism produced growth and prosperity for all – and continuing with the experiment.

And there's more. What the data can't show is that there are important factors that are not picked up in these analyses but which have terrifying real-world consequences: the quality of public services is in a state of near freefall in both the USA and UK as a result of the austerity which has been imposed in response to the downturn in economic performance. Police forces are struggling to respond to emergency calls,[9] while hospitals are struggling to cope with accidents and emergencies[10] and to provide prompt treatment even to cancer patients.[11] Yet few politicians are connecting the dots between the economic stagnation of the Age of Market Capitalism and the public services disaster we are beginning to experience.

It's not too difficult to understand the economic data; they are so clear that it is *astonishing* how easily politicians can slide over the facts. They do it so often that it is *very easy to believe the story* that Market Capitalism successfully reversed a long decline in economic performance.

The truth is precisely the opposite.

A smaller slice of a bigger pie

Politicians often talk as though an increase in the size of the economy is all that really counts: if the pie grows, everyone will naturally get a bigger slice.

That was indeed the case during the Golden Age of Capitalism, but it has not been true in the United States during the era of Market Capitalism; and during the last few years, it has not been true in the UK.

The chart in Figure 12 below compares the size of the US economy (real GDP) with the wages earned by the median worker over the thirty-five years from 1980–2015. (To show the two lines on the same axis, they have both been indexed against their values in 1979. In other words, their values in 1979 have been set at 100, and any growth beyond that point is shown as an increase above 100.)

Figure 12: The disconnect between US GDP and wage growth

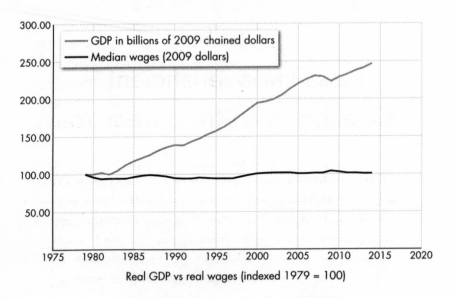

Real GDP vs real wages (indexed 1979 = 100)

Source: BEA/St Louis Federal Reserve[12]

The chart clearly shows that what's good for the economy may not necessarily be so good for regular people. It is demonstrably possible (for example 1987–97 and 2009–14) for the economy to grow while much of the population becomes poorer – and we shall see more about this in the next chapter. Even when the economy is growing, it is increasingly clear that *how* the economy grows, and *who* gets to enjoy that growth, are crucial questions to ask.

It is vital for voters to understand the truth about who really benefits from Market Capitalism. And politicians must not be allowed to get away with policies that are 'good for the economy' without being challenged on whether those same policies are good for the people in that economy, too.

CHAPTER 3

Mass Impoverishment – Coming to a Street Near You

Of the tendencies that are harmful to sound economics, the most seductive, and in my opinion the most poisonous, is to focus on questions of distribution... The potential for improving the lives of poor people by finding different ways of distributing current production is nothing compared to the apparently limitless potential of increasing production.

Robert Lucas[1]

B y now, you know more than most people do about the real economic history of the last seventy years and the worrying disconnect between what we are *told* about the economy, and how wealth is *actually* divided across society.

This isn't an accident. The words of Nobel Memorial Prize-winning economist Robert Lucas quoted above are worth studying closely.

Lucas is one of the leaders of the discipline of economics – which often describes itself, paraphrasing Lionel Robbins, as *the science of allocating scarce resources*.[2] Nevertheless, Lucas and his many followers believe that the focus of economic research and government economic policy should be *entirely* devoted to the consideration of growing the pie. Any discussion of how the pie is distributed – the actual allocation of resources – is poisonous.

This is the sort of sentiment you might expect to hear from a not-too-well-educated layman. Not from 'the most influential macroeconomist of the last quarter of the 20th century'.[3]

His position might be defensible in a world where growing the economy automatically made the poorest richer. But, as you've seen in the previous chapter, the last thirty-five years have demonstrated that is *not* the world we live in. The emergence, extent and duration of mass impoverishment in the real world makes Lucas's insistence that we shouldn't worry about how the pie is divided across society sound almost villainous.

We owe it to ourselves, and to future generations, to find a better way forward.

The system is broken

This chapter delves a little deeper into the causes and effects of mass impoverishment. It confirms that median income – remember, that is the income of a typical family in the middle of the income distribution – is no longer directly linked to the economic growth of the last thirty-five years. In other words, while you once might have expected your wages to rise when the economy grows, for most people this is no longer true.

The largest single factor behind this disconnection between the economy and the median income of a typical family is, quite simply, that *inequality is rising rapidly.*

As long as there is rising poverty in a society where the overall economy is growing, there should be no question that distribution is a factor of vital importance. Why? Because the practical impact on the populations of the US and UK – both of which now suffer from this problem – is that many people now need government support to live. Even if they are working full-time, their 'market price' is now too low for them to survive unaided.

While inequality is a concern in many countries, the US and the UK have a particular problem in this area, so let's focus on these two countries for the moment.

Flatlining

While the US economy has grown almost 150 per cent in real terms since 1980, median wages in the United States have remained static. They've flatlined.

What does this mean? Well, clearly – and rather surprisingly – there is zero connection between economic growth and median wages. But now let's examine the change in a little more detail. The Office of the Chief Actuary, part of the Social Security Administration, has compiled detailed information on wages at different levels, though unfortunately not all the way back to 1980.

The data show that although the richest are better off and the bottom 20 per cent have been protected, *most of the US population are around 20 per cent worse off in real terms today than they were in the year 2000.*

And this is despite the fact that real GDP per capita has grown by 17 per cent over that same period[4] – in other words, most people have received a *less than 0 per cent share* of the benefits of economic growth. When they might reasonably have expected to be 17 per cent better off, they have instead found that they are around 20 per cent worse off. That's a 37 per cent difference over just 15 years.

Politicians of all parties (and in all countries) fixate on GDP growth. The media pretty much agrees, too – it's taken for granted that if a political party can deliver growth in GDP, then they're doing a good job... *for everyone*.

The fact that it is entirely possible for real GDP to display dramatic growth, while *at the same time* most wage earners in the population see no benefit from it – in fact less than none – merits astonishingly little enquiry by the media.

The rising tide of inequality

If growth in a nation's GDP is no longer automatically coupled with growth in typical wages, it's a fair question to ask – *where is this extra money actually going?*

And it's quite a gap that needs explaining: 147 per cent growth in the economy translating into just 1 per cent growth in median wages between 1980 and 2015.

The light grey bars in Figure 13 below explain the gap. In the US, there are two prime causes of mass impoverishment: rising inequality and lower productivity growth.

First, although GDP has grown 147 per cent, that impressive-looking growth has been shared unfairly. Less of it has gone to wages and more of it to corporate profits. In 1980, almost 49 per cent of GDP was paid to employees in the form of wages and salaries; by 2015 only 43 per cent was.[5] This is good for those who make their living from their investments but bad for people who have to work for a living.

Also, wages themselves have become much less equal as CEOs' pay has rocketed while workers' pay has declined. In the 1960s, CEO pay averaged 30 times that of a typical worker; now, the ratio is over 300 times.[6]

Figure 13: What accounts for the lack of wage and income growth in US?

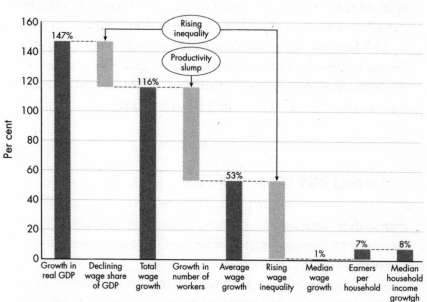

Source: Data in Appendix III

And productivity growth has slumped. Growth in the economy has been significantly fuelled by growth in the working population – which is 42 per cent higher than it was in 1980[7] – rather than by rising productivity. This means that the total wages now have to be shared by 42 per cent more people.

Appendix III on the *99-percent.org* website contains a comprehensive analysis of the figures in both the US and the UK, and even if you're not normally a data geek, I suggest going through the data to make sure of the evidence yourself.

So, the numbers tell a clear story – we *should* all be much better off but, in fact, many people (since 2000 in the US and since 2007) in the UK are worse off. Possibly you are. And if you're not, you probably have friends and relatives who are.

And the biggest single driver of this impoverishment is rising inequality, both because of the falling share of GDP that goes to people who work for a living and because wages themselves have become much less equally distributed.

And that's the way that economists normally look at these issues: using the numbers. Specifically, to an economist, 'demand' is simply the dollar value of products and services that are purchased; there is no qualitative distinction between different *types* of demand.

But there's another way to look at this – a bit less rigorous, but maybe a little more insightful.

We can easily imagine a spectrum of needs. At the left-hand end of the spectrum, demand might be interpreted as 'what people need to stay alive'. At the right-hand end, demand might simply mean 'things people clearly don't *need*, but would like to have'.

At the far left of the spectrum, water, food, shelter – and, when necessary, healthcare – are absolute needs: without them, people will die, quite quickly. Any practical definition of demand must include things that are so fundamental.

Moving further along the spectrum, demand becomes relative rather than absolute. Short-term physical survival does not depend upon these things but without them it is impossible to have a normal life. For example, it is extremely difficult to get a job without a permanent address, some level of education, a phone number and, nowadays, Internet access. It is reasonable to consider this form of demand also as a fundamental need.

In the middle of the spectrum, there is demand for goods and services without which a normal life may be possible but with which life becomes far easier. Being able to take a holiday abroad each year, owning a car and a decent house all fit into this category.

Then there comes a level of demand which is in no sense necessary – owning several houses, luxury cars and private education for the children, for example.

Finally, at the extreme right-hand end of the spectrum there is demand for goods and services of the highest level of luxury – a top-end Swiss watch (which can cost over US$500,000), a house in the Hamptons (US$30–40 million) or a 70-metre yacht (a rule of thumb for super-luxury yachts is that they cost around US$1 million per metre).

We do not have the capacity to provide goods and services at the highest level of luxury to every person on the planet. Not everyone can have a 70-metre yacht or a private island. In this sense, scarcity is real. There is no way around it. At the other end of the spectrum, however, we *could* provide water, food, shelter and essential healthcare to everyone on the planet – though it would require some reallocation of resources to do so.

According to the United Nations, the equivalent of 28 per cent of the world's agricultural area is devoted to production of food that is lost or wasted,[8] while roughly 11 per cent of the world's population is malnourished.[9] In other words, even without increasing production, if we could simply reduce food waste, we could feed the world.

As the Nobel Prize-winning economist Amartya Sen said: 'Starvation is the characteristic of some people not *having* enough to eat. It is not the characteristic of there not *being* enough to eat.'[10]

At the left-hand side of the spectrum, scarcity is *not* inevitable – where it exists (as it does), it is a result of the choices made by society. This is, of course, especially true in rich countries.

Using this spectrum of needs allows us to look at supply and demand in a qualitative as well as quantitative way. We can use the visual metaphor of a target viewed through a telescopic sight. In Figure 14, the bull's-eye represents the absolute needs, and each ring of the target represents increasingly ines-sential, aspirational levels of needs and wants. The field of view of the telescopic sight represents what is actually supplied to meet these needs.

In Figure 14, most but not all people have their absolute needs met (most, but not all, of the bull's-eye is visible through the sight) and the majority (though not a very large majority) are also able to meet their needs for a normal life; it is a minority who have an easy life, or can meet the bulk of their wants and desires; and a still smaller proportion of the population enjoys super luxury.

Inequality, in the qualitative view, is the degree to which supply is off target.

In conventional economics, that part of the target which is not visible within the sight *does not count as demand* – and indeed, to a business, a need that is not backed by money is only hypo-thetical. In this sense, and in this sense only, *poor people have no needs*. On the other hand, rich people have a great many.

Complete equality, which would be represented by aiming the sight into the centre of the bull's-eye, would result in all absolute needs, needs for a normal life and needs for an easy life being met, and everyone would meet some of their wants and desires – but there would be no super luxury. And, of course, intermediate positions are possible in which there is some inequality, but everyone has their fundamental needs met.

As Figure 14 illustrates, the problem in 2015 is *not* that per capita supply – the value that the US can produce per person – has failed to grow over the last thirty-five years. Real per capita GDP is almost 80 per cent higher than it was in 1980,[11] and so the view through the telescopic sight is much wider. The problem is that *supply has drifted further off target*: far more of the resources of society are devoted to production of super-luxury and luxury products and services – the market

Figure 14: Qualitative representation of the development of mass impoverishment in the US

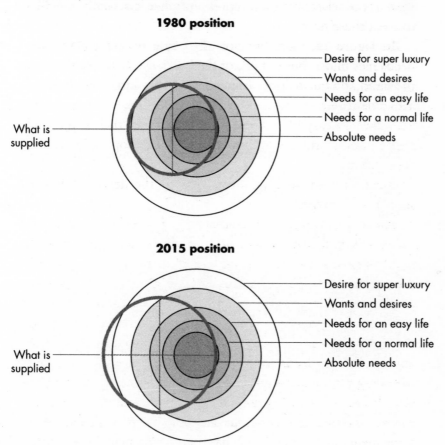

1980 position

Desire for super luxury
Wants and desires
Needs for an easy life
Needs for a normal life
Absolute needs

What is supplied

2015 position

Desire for super luxury
Wants and desires
Needs for an easy life
Needs for a normal life
Absolute needs

What is supplied

has grown by 226 per cent since 1995[12] – while as we saw in Chapter One the fundamental needs of many citizens continue to go unmet.

It is not that the system of Market Capitalism cannot produce *enough* valuable products and services, it is that it produces the *wrong* products and services.

Mass impoverishment in the UK

Mass impoverishment is a more recent phenomenon in the UK than in the US.[13]

But we are catching up. Even the Conservative then Prime Minister, Theresa May, has recognized that, for many people, the economy is no longer working.[14] As she said on becoming Prime Minister:

> But we also need a government that will deliver serious social reform – and make ours a country that truly works for everyone. Because right now, if you're born poor, you will die on average nine years earlier than others. If you're black, you're treated more harshly by the criminal justice system than if you're white. If you're a white, working-class boy, you're less likely than anybody else to go to university. If you're at a state school, you're less likely to reach the top professions than if you're educated privately. If you're a woman, you still earn less than a man. If you suffer from mental health problems, there's too often not enough help to hand. If you're young, you'll find it harder than ever before to own your own home.

Since 2007, despite the Global Financial Crisis, real GDP per capita has grown a little – UK society as a whole is a little richer than it was a decade ago. In fact, taken as a whole, UK society is richer than it has ever been (as is the US). GDP per capita today in both countries is more than 80 per cent higher than it was in 1980 – and in both countries it has risen above the pre-crisis peak.

Figure 15: How the pie is growing – both US and UK are richer than they have ever been

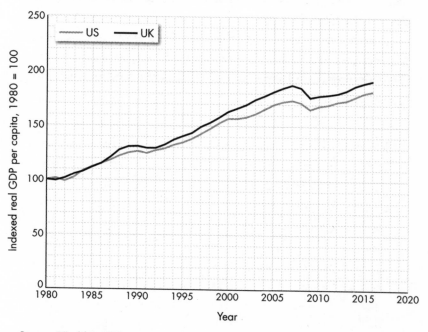

Source: World Bank[15]

But if you were to assume that just because the pie is bigger than it has ever been, *all* members of UK society are richer, you'd be mistaken. The typical wage earner actually takes home less today than they did in 2007;[16] and it is only because there are on average 5 per cent more earners per household that median household income has risen.

This is because, in the UK, the increase in the workforce has been approximately equal to the increase in GDP – like the US, productivity growth has stagnated – and the share of GDP which goes to wages has declined (and the share to profit has grown), so the average wage has also fallen.

The two key factors driving mass impoverishment in the UK are again rising inequality (but principally because of the falling wage share of GDP rather than wage inequality) and stagnant productivity.

Without welfare many working people would not survive

THE US PICTURE

Since 2004, Amy K. Glasmeier of the Massachusetts Institute of Technology has been compiling data on the costs of living in different regions of the United States. Her team has calculated the gross salary needed to meet the basic requirements of life for a range of household types.

The data make grim reading. But the facts are undeniable: many of the working population would be unable to survive without some level of government support.

Each cell in the table below is colour-coded. A *light grey* cell means that a typical adult – or a couple – in the occupation listed on the left would very comfortably be able to support the type of household described in the column headings. Conversely, a *dark grey* cell means that an adult – or a couple – would be *una*ble to support that type of household, without support of some kind. And a *mid grey* cell means that they are above the minimum threshold but not by much.

In a healthy society, most of the table would be shaded light, or at least mid grey. In reality, as you can see, the table is almost half dark grey.

For single adult wage-earners, the data show that 79 per cent of them would be able to survive unaided (nevertheless, the remaining 21 per cent represents around 28 million people).

Figure 16: Salaries needed in the US for different household types

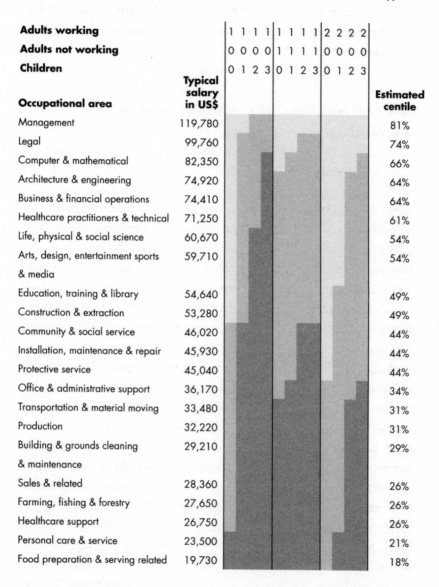

		Adults working				1 1 1 1	1 1 1 1	2 2 2 2
		Adults not working				0 0 0 0	1 1 1 1	0 0 0 0
		Children				0 1 2 3	0 1 2 3	0 1 2 3

Occupational area	Typical salary in US$	Estimated centile
Management	119,780	81%
Legal	99,760	74%
Computer & mathematical	82,350	66%
Architecture & engineering	74,920	64%
Business & financial operations	74,410	64%
Healthcare practitioners & technical	71,250	61%
Life, physical & social science	60,670	54%
Arts, design, entertainment sports & media	59,710	54%
Education, training & library	54,640	49%
Construction & extraction	53,280	49%
Community & social service	46,020	44%
Installation, maintenance & repair	45,930	44%
Protective service	45,040	44%
Office & administrative support	36,170	34%
Transportation & material moving	33,480	31%
Production	32,220	31%
Building & grounds cleaning & maintenance	29,210	29%
Sales & related	28,360	26%
Farming, fishing & forestry	27,650	26%
Healthcare support	26,750	26%
Personal care & service	23,500	21%
Food preparation & serving related	19,730	18%

Source: Glasmeier[17]

But what if those same wage earners want to have a child?

At that point, the proportion who could survive unaided falls to 51 per cent. That's just over half the adult wage-earning population. 49 per cent are unable to have a child without state support.

'Get married,' the politicians may say, 'then you'll have two incomes, and you can afford to have a child!' And yes, that would be an obvious solution to this problem. Unfortunately, this *still* leaves a large proportion of the American population unable to afford to have a child without state support. If only one parent works, so that there is only one income but no childcare costs, then 56 per cent of the population could survive unaided; if both parents work, then 74 per cent could afford to have one child. And if you can't form a couple – or don't wish to – this option isn't available to you.

To maintain a stable population, of course, the average family needs to have *two* children. For a couple with two kids and one working partner, 51 per cent of the population could survive unaided; for a couple with two working partners, 66 per cent could survive unaided. In both cases, this is a *long* way short of 100 per cent. We are talking about millions of people unable to provide basic sustenance and amenities for their families.

In other words, with income distribution as it is, and without government support, America cannot have a sustainable population. That is, of course, not the same thing as saying that America cannot *afford* a sustainable population – demonstrably it can – only that unless it tackles its income distribution issues, government support will be necessary for a large proportion of the population.

THE BRITISH PICTURE

In the UK, similar research has been carried out by the Centre for Research in Social Policy (CRSP) and their findings are very similar. Without at least some support from government, many working people could not survive.

Again, we see that the table is roughly half dark grey, when it should be largely light grey.

Figure 17: Salaries needed in the UK

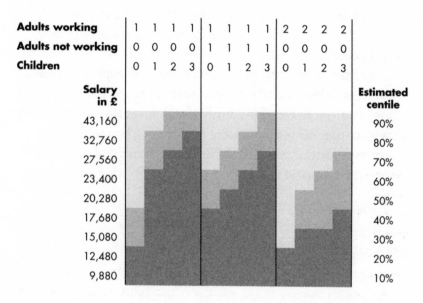

Adults working	1	1	1	1	1	1	1	1	2	2	2	2
Adults not working	0	0	0	0	1	1	1	1	0	0	0	0
Children	0	1	2	3	0	1	2	3	0	1	2	3

Salary in £		Estimated centile
43,160		90%
32,760		80%
27,560		70%
23,400		60%
20,280		50%
17,680		40%
15,080		30%
12,480		20%
9,880		10%

Source: CRSP[18]

All but the bottom 20 per cent of the population in the UK could survive unaided as a single adult but as soon as children form part of the household, only around 30 per cent of single adults could survive unaided. Forming a couple is again helpful if both partners are working, in which case 60 per cent would be able to afford a single child, and about 50 per cent could afford to have two children. In the UK, also, a sustainable population would not be possible without government assistance – unless something happens to change income distribution.

And for many people, even with government assistance, it has become difficult or impossible to make ends meet. As British nurse Danielle Tiplady wrote in the *Independent*, explaining the practical consequences of the fact that over the previous six years, nurses' salaries had fallen by 14 per cent in real terms:[19]

At the end of last month, I had £1.10 left in my bank account, and for many nurses it's worse than that. A friend of mine had to choose between eating and paying her mortgage. After a year of eating beans on toast she conceded defeat, sold her flat and moved back with her parents. When [the UK Health Secretary] was confronted by Andrew Marr [BBC interviewer] last week with the reality that nurses were using food banks, he said that the reasons for this were 'complex'. They aren't complex. We aren't being paid enough.

As Warren Buffett remarked in an interview with Bloomberg, commenting on the problems of rising US inequality and the need for government to take action to address it:[20]

I was born in 1930. There's now six times as much real output per capita in the United States than there was, in real terms – six times. If you'd told my parents that under these circumstances, there would be millions and millions of people living in poverty, they would have said it was impossible... The real problem isn't the people who fit in well... It's the people whose skills just don't command much of a market price.

In both the US and the UK, the problem is that the 'market price' of around half of the working population is now too low for them to survive without some form of government assistance.

What should the 'price' of a nurse really be? Or a firefighter, or a police officer? There are two ways of looking at this question. If we believe that people exist to meet the needs of markets, then a large and rising proportion of the population now cost more to keep alive than they are worth – and very quickly we will start to categorize people in a very disturbing and dystopian way.

Alternatively, if we view markets as existing to serve society, we'll have to understand why the needs of many go unmet under our present system. This is a major challenge to our current form of capitalism.

The US and the UK have a particular problem of inequality

Figure 18 below shows the distribution of income for a selection of developed countries, as measured by the Gini coefficient. As you may remember, this is a number used by economists to measure inequality: perfect equality – everyone getting exactly the same – would correspond to a Gini coefficient of 0; perfect *in*equality – one person getting everything and the rest getting nothing – would correspond to a Gini coefficient of 1.

While the US and the UK are not alone in having an unequal distribution of income, they do stand out as having a particular problem in this area.

Figure 18: Inequality of disposable income by country

Country	Gini Coefficient (income)
USA	0.39
UK	0.351
Greece	0.34
Spain	0.335

Italy	0.327
France	0.306
Germany	0.289
Switzerland	0.285
Sweden	0.274
Finland	0.26
Norway	0.253
Denmark	0.249

Source: OECD[21]

You may find it hard, as Warren Buffett does, to believe that, in the twenty-first century, we can live in such a grossly unbalanced society. If the economy as a whole – on both sides of the Atlantic – is growing ever richer, why are we allowing so many people to become poorer?

That is the question we should be asking ourselves.

CHAPTER 4

An Alternative Morality

Cecil Graham: What is a cynic?

Lord Darlington: A man who knows the price of every-thing, and the value of nothing.

Oscar Wilde[1]

In Chapter 1, I posed the question, 'Where are today's economic policies taking us?'

We saw that the data suggest we are moving into a world in which mass impoverishment will directly blight the lives of tens of millions of people. The knock-on effects will impact even more.

For most people, this is simply not an acceptable future. But for some – and sadly, many of them are in positions of power and influence – this outcome would be nothing more or less than natural justice at work. Many successive governments have implicitly accepted this argument. Since our lives, and those of our children, are shaped by these people, we should be concerned.

Market fundamentalists have an alternative morality

The Oxford Dictionaries define *morality* as follows:[2]

Morality (noun)

1. Principles concerning the distinction between right and wrong or good and bad behaviour. 'the matter boiled down to simple morality: innocent prisoners ought to be freed'

    1.1 A particular system of values and principles of conduct. 'a bourgeois morality'

    1.2 The extent to which an action is right or wrong. 'the issue of the morality of the possession of nuclear weapons'

For most people, this definition makes sense. Morality has to do with right and wrong, with good and bad. It is connected with values and principles. A moral person makes judgements – sometimes difficult ones – about what is right and wrong, based on values and principles.

But not everyone sees it this way.

Cecil Graham replied to Lord Darlington by saying: 'And a sentimentalist, my dear Darlington, is a man who sees an absurd value in everything and doesn't know the market price of any single thing.' Graham is not alone in thinking that any value other than the market price is absurd. Many proponents of free markets think this way.

This line of thought has an engaging clarity and simplicity: if a willing buyer and a willing seller agree on a price, what right has anyone else to say that this is not the fair value?* Why bring subjective notions of right and wrong, good and bad into the question? Why complicate matters with systems of values and principles? Why not simply say that the market price *is* the moral price?

As soon as this point is accepted, often as a near-religious tenet, most of morality can happily be left to the market. In the words of George Soros:[3] 'This idea was called *laissez faire* in the nineteenth century... I have found a better name for it: market fundamentalism.'

Is Mark Lore, the CEO of Walmart, really worth US$236 million per annum?[4] Let the market decide. Should there be more low-cost housing? Let the market decide. How much should a nurse be paid? Let the market decide!

This line of thinking produces results that most people find bizarre. In the US, an oncology nurse can expect to earn between US$74,000 and US$118,000.[5] But each of the key executives of the tobacco company Philip Morris is paid more than US$5 million.[6] If we accept that the market price truly reflects their moral value, we must conclude that each one of these executives does more good for society by producing, marketing and selling (carcinogenic) cigarettes than fifty oncology nurses do in tending those with cancer.

Most people would reject that explanation and say that, while the nurses clearly do far more good for society, their skills are not so scarce, their bargaining power is lower and so they are paid less.

---

* In the real world, this story does not stack up. By no means all transactions are between willing buyers and sellers. Many smokers buy cigarettes, not because they consider the price a fair one for the benefits they get from the cigarettes, but because they are addicted to them. Most people have to sell their labour whether they consider their wages fair or not, because they have no other way to live. In most transactions, bargaining power is not equal.

Market fundamentalists view this rejection as absurd sentimentalism. If the nurses really were worth more, they would be paid more; if the executives really were worth less, they would be paid less. When these people say, 'markets are the best way to allocate resources', they don't simply mean best as in easiest: they mean best as in most moral.

Market fundamentalists view taxation as theft

A fundamentalist defines a market transaction as one between a willing seller and a willing buyer. By this definition, therefore, there is no coercion. Tax, on the other hand, is often *not* willingly paid: people pay only when they are legally obliged to do so (and not always even then).

For a market fundamentalist, this is *simply wrong*: it doesn't matter how much good the taxes will do – even how many lives they will save – or how frivolous the taxpayer's alternative use of the money might be, the fact is that the money was effectively taken by force. That is theft.

And they believe that far too much is taken. As the American investor James Dale Davidson and William Rees-Mogg, the former editor of *The Times,* explain in their book, *The Sovereign Individual*:

> ... with the top 1% of taxpayers paying 30.2% of the total income tax in the United States (1995), it is not a question of the rich failing to repay any genuine investment the state may have made in their education or economic prosperity. To the contrary. Those who pay most of the bills pay vastly more than the value of any benefits they receive.[7]

Market fundamentalists believe that, like a business, governments *should* view their taxpayers as customers, and charge them only for the services they receive, in a non-coercive transaction. As Davidson and Rees-Mogg put it:

> Yet when you think about it, when customers really are in the driver's seat it would be considered outrageous that they should not get what they want. If you went into a store to buy furniture and the sales people took your money but then proceeded to ignore your requests and consult others about how to spend your money, you would quite rightly be upset. You would not think it normal or justifiable if the employees of the store argued that you really did not deserve the furniture, and that it should be shipped instead to someone whom they found more worthy... The terms of progressive income taxation, which emerged in every democratic welfare state during the course of the twentieth century, are dramatically unlike pricing provisions that would be preferred by customers.

The answer, they believe, is for government to start acting like any other business. Of course, this will mean that taxation will fall dramatically, and with it, public spending.

Market fundamentalists view normal people as a burden

We saw in Chapter Three that with income distribution at current levels, roughly half of the working population in both the US and the UK would be unable to survive without external help. Most people regard this as a sign that the system isn't working properly, and they view providing the help as an intrinsic part of a civilized society.

To a market fundamentalist, though, these people are simply not worth what it costs to keep them alive. Their existence is not cost-effective, and being forced to sustain them is an unjustified burden. Market forces, they say, are meritocratic – and the problem is that these people have too little merit.

Ira Sohn, Professor of Economics at Montclair State University, has pointed out that with technological advances, many of these people (i.e. people who have to work for a living) will no longer be needed at all:[8]

The prospects for adopting labour-saving technologies in many of the labour-intensive sectors in the economy are improving annually: self-checkout at supermarkets, self-check-in and -out at hotels, self-ordering and bill settlement in restaurants, self-administered health diagnostic tests and so on all translate into a reduced need for workers per dollar of gross domestic product on the one hand, and fewer total workers along with higher levels of GDP on the other. Horses were used extensively on the farm and in transport in eighteenth- and nineteenth-century America and Europe, but once mechanization and electrification were implemented, and the railroad, automobiles and buses became commercially viable as transport alternatives, owning horses became a hobby of the rich, and the horse population declined quickly and dramatically. The same can probably be said about humans in the 21st century: we just don't need that many of them – and, in the rich countries, they are expensive to 'produce' (prenatal and postnatal care), 'assemble' (nurture and educate), and 'maintain' (from adolescence to death). As technology continues to become ever more capable and most humans, frankly, do not, there is less and less need for workers to produce the goods and services required by society.

Most people today, Sohn believes, are like horses at the end of the nineteenth century. There will shortly be no need for them. And Chapter 5 shows that he may well be right. This should give us all pause for thought.

For the market fundamentalists, there is a choice here: the more hard-nosed think that the redundant people should simply sink or swim; the more compassionate think that the most deserving should receive (voluntary) support from charities or wealthy individuals – but not, of course, at the levels that they have been used to.

And only if they appear deserving.

Mitt Romney, the US presidential candidate, explained to his potential donors his view that 47 per cent of Americans take no personal responsibility and make no contribution to society – and so his job is not to worry about those people:[9]

> There are 47 per cent of the people who will vote for the president no matter what… These are people who pay no income tax. Forty-seven per cent of Americans pay no income tax… And so my job is not to worry about those people – I'll never convince them that they should take personal responsibility and care for their lives.

Davidson and Rees-Mogg explain their thoughts on what should replace government support for the roughly half of the population who depend on it:[10, 11]

> The collapse of coerced income redistribution is bound to upset those who expect to be on the receiving end of the

trillions in transfer programs. Mostly these will be 'the losers or left-behinds', persons without the skills to compete in global markets.

When the hope of aid for those falling behind is based primarily upon appeals to private individuals and charitable bodies, it will be more important than it has been in the twentieth century that the recipients of charity appear to be morally deserving to those voluntarily dispensing the charity.

The only barrier to making this happen is that the law would have to change, and both the UK and the US are democracies, at least for now.

Market fundamentalists view democracy as tyranny

Peter Thiel, the billionaire co-founder of PayPal, stated in 2009: 'I no longer believe that freedom and democracy are compatible.'[12]
He explained his reasons:

The higher one's IQ, the more pessimistic one became [after leaving college] about free-market politics – capitalism simply is not that popular with the crowd... For those of us who are libertarian in 2009, our education culminates with the knowledge that the broader education of the body politic has become a fool's errand. Indeed, even more pessimistically, the trend has been going the wrong way for a long time... Since 1920, the vast increase in welfare beneficiaries and the extension of the franchise to women – two constituencies that are notoriously tough for libertarians – have rendered the notion of 'capitalist democracy' into an oxymoron.

Davidson and Rees-Mogg agree:

> Mass democracy leads to control of government by its 'employees'. But wait. You may be saying that in most jurisdictions there are many more voters than there are persons on the government payroll. How could it be possible for employees to dominate under such conditions? The welfare state emerged to answer exactly this quandary. Since there were not otherwise enough employees to create a working majority, increasing numbers of voters were effectively put on the payroll to receive transfer payments of all kinds. In effect the recipients of transfer payments and subsidies became student employees of government who were able to dispense with the bother of reporting every day to work.[13]

The answer, of course, is to do away with mass democracy. Davidson and Rees-Mogg set out to show how to become a Sovereign Individual: one who can dictate to government, rather than being dictated to. (Their answer is principally through aggressive tax avoidance, playing off multiple tax havens against one another to get an acceptable deal.) Once enough wealthy people have become sovereign individuals, coerced redistribution will have to end. At this point, governments will have no choice but to dismantle the welfare state.

Tyler Cowen, Economics Professor at George Mason University, set out his vision of a free market 'hyper-meritocracy' in which poor people will be forced to move to low-cost housing and to accept vastly reduced support, pacified by computer games and digital media:

> The American polity [political system] is unlikely to collapse, but we'll all look back on the immediate post-war

era as a very special time. Our future will bring more wealthy people than ever before, but also more poor people, including people who do not always have access to basic public services... we will allow the real wages of many workers to fall and thus we will allow the creation of a new underclass. We won't really see how we could stop that. Yet it will be an oddly peaceful time with the general ageing of American society and the proliferation of many sources of cheap fun. We might even look ahead to a time when the cheap or free fun is so plentiful that it will feel a bit like Karl Marx's Communist utopia, albeit brought on by capitalism. That is the real light at the end of the tunnel.[14]

Of course, we are not there yet. We have not yet attained Tyler Cowen's utopia. But already, the work of creating a hostile environment for the less well-off is underway. In the UK, for example, benefits for working people have been 'frozen' since 2015[15] – that means that they have been falling in real terms, and they will continue to do so – and the government plans to roll-out Universal Credit, a so-called reform of the benefits system, despite the evidence that it causes enormous hardship to the most vulnerable and has forced many to turn to food banks to survive.[16]

The Conservative MP, Jacob Rees-Mogg commented that this growth in food banks was rather uplifting:

[The State] provides a basic level of welfare, but on some occasions that will not work and to have charitable support given by people voluntarily to support their fellow citizens I think is rather uplifting and shows what a good, compassionate country we are.[17]

And there is a growing movement to criminalize homelessness:

> Despite updated Home Office guidance at the start of the year, which instructs councils not to target people for being homeless and sleeping rough, the *Guardian* has found over fifty local authorities with public space protection orders (PSPOs) in place. Homeless people are banned from town centres, routinely fined hundreds of pounds and sent to prison if caught repeatedly asking for money... Local authorities in England and Wales have issued hundreds of fixed-penalty notices and pursued criminal convictions for 'begging', 'persistent and aggressive begging' and 'loitering' since they were given strengthened powers to combat antisocial behaviour in 2014 by then home secretary, Theresa May.[18]

In the US, the unemployed already face strict constraints on the support they can receive, and President Donald Trump has declared his intention to let states tie eligibility for Medicaid to work:

> Benefits under welfare programmes – including temporary cash assistance to needy families and food stamps – can [already] be linked to work. But to date conservative hopes of tying Medicaid benefits to employment have failed to bear fruit. Under current law states are not allowed to impose work requirements... The Trump White House has been signalling for some time that it wants to change course... Hannah Katch, a senior policy analyst at the Center on Budget and Policy Priorities, called the guidance a 'drastic change' that would not help people's health outcomes. She said the majority of people

with Medicaid coverage who can work are already work-ing – some eight in ten adult beneficiaries are living in working families.[19]

We have become used to the narrative in which market price is the same thing as value. As a result, we are already beginning to accept that the less well off are simply lower-value people – and not just the poor, but about half the population.

We have already accepted years of budgetary constraint for public services despite evidence that even the most vital are struggling to perform. And we have become accustomed to the idea of continuing tax cuts, which favour the wealthiest in society. Taken together, and pursued to their logical conclu-sion, these ideas lead to a world like that of Chapter 1.

There is power behind these ideas

Some of my friends, on reading this, commented, 'But nobody serious thinks like that.'

Unfortunately, they are wrong. There is a considerable free-market literature, from Hayek and Ayn Rand through Milton Friedman and Davidson and Rees-Mogg to Tyler Cowen.

Distinguished followers of these writers include some of the wealthiest and most powerful people on the planet:[20] Jeff Bezos, the founder of Amazon; Alan Greenspan, former Chairman of the US Federal Reserve; Steve Jobs, former CEO of Apple; the Koch brothers, one the chairman and the other the EVP of Koch Industries, the second largest privately owned company in the US[21]; Rupert Murdoch, executive chairman of News Corp; Politicians Donald Trump,[22] Rex Tillerson, Ron and Rand Paul, and Paul Ryan in the US, and Daniel Hannan and Sajid Javid in the UK; Pay-Pal co-founder, Peter Thiel and

Wikipedia co-founder Jimmy Wales. These are serious people. And they wield untold influence.

Politicians respond to this influence. It is easy for a politician to attack people on benefits; it is very risky for them to attack wealthy tax-avoiders. It is easy to propose cuts in public spending; it requires enormous courage to propose an increase. It is easy to privatize a public-sector activity; nationalizing a private-sector business, even a failing monopoly, is described as communism.

The direction of travel is clear: ever smaller government, and ever lower taxes. And the endpoint is the failure, before 2050, of our current civilization.

CHAPTER 5

The Fork in the Road

The fundamental challenge is that, alongside its great benefits, every technological revolution mercilessly destroys jobs and livelihoods – and therefore identities – well before the new ones emerge. This was true of the eclipse of agriculture and cottage industry by the industrial revolution, the displacement of manufacturing by the service economy, and now the hollowing out of many of those middle-class services jobs through machine learning and global sourcing.

Mark Carney, Governor of the Bank of England[1]

I t is no exaggeration to say that we are entering the most exciting, yet most ominous period of technological development in human history.

If we are prepared to reinvent our economic system, we could be looking at a future of abundance for the entire population. If we fail to reinvent, most people will have no way to live. If you were born after 1980, unless you have been saving very effectively, you will still need a job in the 2040s in order to survive. But there may not be a job for you. And if you were born before 1980, unless you are extremely wealthy, your children will face this problem.

Technology is rapidly bringing us to a fork in the road. If we choose the right path, a very attractive future awaits. If we make the wrong choice, we shall end today's civilization prematurely – before the year 2050.

Technology has been advancing quickly

Technology has transformed our lives over the last thirty-five years. In 1980, few homes contained a computer – the first mass-market computer was the Commodore PET, launched in 1977. Mobile telephones had not yet reached the market – it was not until 1983 that the first mobile phones went on sale in the US (at almost US$4,000 each). Sir Tim Berners-Lee invented the World Wide Web only thirty years ago.

Now, almost every home has at least one computer; almost every adult has a mobile phone; and we all use the Internet and mobile networks for entertainment, for shopping and for social interaction. In the UK, adults now spend more than eight hours a day interacting with technology.[2]

The world of business has been transformed. In the US, over 8 per cent of retail sales are now online[3] and in the UK, the figure is more than 20 per cent.[4] Entire categories of job have disappeared and some new categories have been created. Typing pools are a thing of the past; web design is big business.

Given the speed and scope of advancement over the past three decades, and the number of exciting technologies that have already reached the prototype stage, it is reasonable to predict that over the next thirty-five years, technology will drive – for good or ill – fundamental change to our lives.

On the upside, these technologies have the *potential* to solve some of humanity's most serious problems. But we have not yet put in place an economic system that can accommodate the changes they will bring. If we do so, our civilization will be transformed for the better; and if not, it will be changed out of all recognition for the worse – the impact of these new technologies will therefore be either *hugely beneficial* or *hugely destructive*.

Without reinvention of our economic system, they will be hugely destructive, as you will see.

Important new technologies will become mainstream

In terms of scientific and technological progress, thirty-five years is a long time. But much of today's sunrise technology is already having a growing impact on our lives. I would pick out the following technologies for special attention, because they seem to me to be harbingers of what is just around the corner:

- additive manufacturing – for example, 3-D printing;
- nanotechnology – for example, new processes like genetic editing and new materials like graphene;
- new computing approaches – for example quantum computing, new applications of narrow artificial intelligence (AI) such as self-driving cars, and even full artificial intelligence (AI) capable of solving any problem a human can solve;
- clean energy – possibly even nuclear fusion.

Most of these technologies will have entered the mainstream by 2040, so over the next thirty-five years, you can expect to feel their impact.

ADDITIVE MANUFACTURING

Traditionally, to manufacture a complex structure, you would start with a block and machine away the material you didn't want. Additive manufacturing works the other way: you build up complex structures by adding material. Additive manufacturing is already well established in specialist areas and has even become available to consumers. You can buy a 3-D printer for under £400.

Additive manufacturing has four main advantages over conventional manufacturing techniques:

1. it enables short production runs to be undertaken economically – and customized products can be mass-produced;
2. lead times from concept to product can be substantially reduced;
3. for some applications, costs of production can be reduced;
4. certain types of design – for example, lattices – become feasible with additive manufacturing which would just be too expensive using conventional techniques.

Initially, the main application of additive manufacturing was in rapid prototyping, reducing a design process which might have taken weeks to days or even hours. As the technology progressed, it became possible to produce working parts using additive manufacturing, initially in polymers and later in metals. 3-D printing has now entered the mainstream.

What does this mean in practice? In the short term, it means that some manufactured products will become cheaper – in particular, customized products. When you need spare parts for your car or washing machine, they will no longer come from a warehouse but will be printed locally.

In the medium term, your next house might be 3-D printed rather than built. If you would rather have curved walls than straight ones, that will be feasible. Within the next few years, we are likely to see an explosion of applications in the medical world, and by 2030 it is possible that additive manufacturing will allow new body parts to be built.[5] For those with money, 3-D printing (and some of the other technologies in the pipeline) could be a lifeline. But not, perhaps, for those without.

NANOTECHNOLOGY

The term nanotechnology refers to any technology that is extremely small: of the order of a few nanometres in size. (1 nanometre equals 10^{-9} metres – i.e. 1 billionth of a metre). Two areas where nanotechnology looks set to become extremely important are in the development of new materials and in the construction of extremely small machines that can be either mechanical or biological, such as the CRISPR technology used in gene editing (see below).

New materials such as graphene

In 2004, Professors Andre Geim and Kostya Novoselov of the University of Manchester, discovered how to extract from graphite (the form of carbon found in pencil lead) an atom-thick, two-dimensional crystal called graphene.[6] In 2010, they were awarded the Nobel Prize in Physics for their work.

Graphene has properties that makes it extremely attractive. It is extraordinarily light and immensely tough – it is 200 times stronger than steel and very flexible. It is the thinnest material possible (being only one atom thick, roughly 1 nanometre) but it can act as a perfect barrier – not even the lightest gas, helium, can pass through it. As well as being transparent, it is a superb conductor of heat and electricity.

These properties open a wide range of applications in areas ranging from sports (it is possible that you already play with a graphene tennis racket) and automotive and aerospace (lighter, faster cars and aeroplanes) to medicine (wearable sensors and new drug delivery systems) and electronics (the world's smallest transistor has been produced at the University of Manchester using graphene).

Genetic editing

Genetic editing is a type of genetic engineering in which DNA is inserted, deleted or replaced in the genome of a living organism, rather in the way that a film is edited.

For genetic editing, 'molecular scissors' are used and there are currently four distinct types of these scissors, of which perhaps the best known is CRISPR. CRISPR was co-discovered in 2012 by molecular biologist Professor Jennifer Doudna, whose team at Berkeley, University of California, was studying how bacteria defend themselves against viral infection.[7] They found that when a bacterium comes under attack it produces a strand of genetic material that matches the genetic sequence of the invading virus. This strand, in tandem with a key protein called Cas9, can lock on to the DNA of the virus, break it and disable it. Scientists are now able to deploy the same process to insert, delete or repair DNA.

The potential applications of CRISPR, and of genetic editing more generally, are widespread – particularly in the fields of genetic modification of plants and in medicine. Genetic disorders may become treatable, immune systems can be rebuilt, resistance to, for instance, malaria can be engineered, and disease-resistant strains of important crops can be developed.

Of course, there is the potential for misuse too. At one end of the spectrum there is the possibility of designer babies – stronger, more attractive children with higher IQs for those who can afford them. And at the other, there is the risk of biological warfare:

> The scientific community engaged in this research is developing ways to potentially mitigate or reverse unintended harmful effects... Nonetheless, we need to carefully consider the possibility of irreversible ecological damage. This is especially worrisome when it comes to 'dual-use concerns' – essentially the possibility that gene drives could be used for both peaceful and military purposes, such as driving a harmful gene through a country's food crops. There are numerous examples of good technology being used badly and little reason to think gene drives would be an exception.[8]

NEW COMPUTING APPROACHES

The world of computing is highly innovative, and there are many emerging technologies that may prove influential over the next thirty-five years. These range from distributed ledger technology (block chain) as used by Bitcoin and other digital currencies, through virtual reality and the Internet of Things to cerebral interfaces.

Two areas which may prove to be fundamental are quantum computing and the development of AI: first narrow AI – the use of artificial intelligence to solve tightly defined problems such as image recognition – and, ultimately, full AI.

Quantum computing

Whereas conventional computing is based on the idea of a 'bit' (short for 'binary digit') that takes either the value 0 or the value 1 at any time, quantum computing takes advantage of the fact that, according to quantum mechanics, particles can be in multiple, superimposed states at the same time. A quantum bit or 'qubit' is not restricted to the values 0 or 1 – it can also simultaneously take all the values in between.

For certain types of problem, where many possibilities need to be tested, a conventional computer would need to test them sequentially, whereas a quantum computer can test in parallel. For some problems, such as factorizing numbers that are the product of two extremely large primes, quantum computing may make a solution feasible in practice – i.e. within a reasonable timescale – where a conventional computer might take thousands of years. Being able to solve problems of this type is particularly relevant to code-breaking and computer security. The security of your Internet banking could be made or broken by quantum computing.

Other problems which may benefit from this kind of high-power computing include mapping of entire proteins in the way that genes can be mapped today – or even entire genomes – and, of course, the development of full AI.

Narrow AI for applications such as autonomous vehicles

Proof of concept studies on self-driving cars have been underway for almost a decade and large-scale trials are now in progress. Google, for example, has more than twenty autonomous vehicles in the US, and NuTonomy has trials of taxis underway in Singapore.

Many commentators believe that the first commercially available self-driving cars will hit the market before 2020.[9] The heads of automakers General Motors and Nissan have both confirmed that they expect driverless cars on the roads by 2020.

Widespread adoption is harder to predict but the CEO of Uber has said that he expects his entire fleet to be driverless by 2030.[10] Initially, like many other innovations in the automotive sector, driverless cars may be more expensive but the costs are likely to fall over time until – like automatic gearboxes, electric windows and in-car entertainment systems – they become commonplace.

So commonplace that sometime in the 2020s, you will find yourself riding in a driverless car.

Full AI

As Professor Nick Bostrom of Oxford University has written:

> ... expert opinions about the future of AI vary wildly. There is disagreement about timescales as well as about what forms AI might eventually take. Predictions about the future development of artificial intelligence, one recent study noted, 'are as confident as they are diverse'... A series of recent surveys have polled members of several relevant expert communities on the question of when they expect 'human-level machine intelligence'... The combined sample gave the following (median) estimate... 50% probability by 2040.[11]

If this is correct, then by 2050 artificial intelligence will surpass human intelligence, possibly by a large margin. Furthermore, the rate of progress will then accelerate as the level of intelligence being brought to bear to produce that progress increases. Problems which are intractable to human intelligence will become solvable – the upside is literally unimaginable (to us).

On the other hand, human beings will no longer be the most intelligent and powerful entities on the planet. We will no longer be in control. The downside is unthinkable.

CLEAN ENERGY

Most countries have embarked on plans for dramatic reductions in greenhouse gas emissions from energy production. The German Advisory Council on the Environment, for example, has stated that by 2050, 100 per cent of its electricity supply could come from renewable sources.[12] These sources include wind, solar, biomass and geothermal energy, nuclear (fission) power, and fossil fuel power generation using carbon capture and storage technology.

One of the most significant changes which may be in place by 2050 or shortly afterwards is the commercial availability of power from nuclear fusion. Fusion is attractive as a power source because it is constantly available (unlike solar power or wind power, which suffer from the so-called intermittency problem), uses widely available raw materials and does not produce either greenhouse gases or long-lasting radioactive waste (unlike nuclear fission).

Its big downside is the formidable technical complexity of maintaining very high temperatures (hundreds of millions of degrees Celsius), sufficient plasma particle density (to increase the frequency with which collisions occur) and sufficient confinement time to hold the plasma within a defined volume.

Because of these technical challenges, accurately costing

a fusion plant is still impossible. But thirty-five nations – China, the twenty-eight states of the European Union plus Switzerland, India, Japan, Korea, Russia and the United States – have sufficient confidence in the concept that they are collaborating to build the world's largest tokamak, a magnetic fusion device that has been designed to prove the feasibility of fusion as a large-scale and carbon-free source of energy. The project, known as ITER (International Thermonuclear Experimental Reactor), is on schedule to produce the first plasma by the end of 2025.[13] This represents a technical proof of concept rather than a commercially viable plant, but it will (if successful) demonstrate the ability to produce 500 MW of fusion power – enough for a small city.

Once the scientific and engineering systems have been tested on ITER, the next stage will be to build a demonstration fusion power plant. Designs are already advanced for this prototype machine, known as DEMO. DEMO will produce two gigawatts of electrical power to the grid, a similar output to a standard electrical power plant, and will be online by 2050.[14] If successful, DEMO will lead to the first generation of commercial fusion power stations.

If we get it right, we can solve many human problems

Individually, these technologies are exciting. Collectively, their potential is mind-boggling. In combination, these new technologies give us the power to create an improvement in human lives over the next thirty-five years at least comparable to that during the Golden Age of Capitalism.

A huge range of high-value products and services, and indeed new business models, will become feasible. The total cost to the world – *including environmental cost* – will fall dramatically. And, economically, the size of the pie could expand enormously.

Autonomous vehicles alone will have a huge impact on society: people who are not mobile because they cannot drive or cannot afford a car will become mobile; fewer people will feel the need to own a car since one could arrive at their doorstep when they need it; roads lined with cars that spend most of their lives immobile will be a thing of the past; the total number of cars needed will be far fewer and congestion may even reduce; and people whose jobs today involve driving buses, taxis, lorries and trucks will no longer be employed in those areas.

The medical applications of products created by additive manufacturing and using new materials, genetic editing and advanced computing to solve complex problems relating to these other technologies will transform the treatment of many serious diseases.

There is already research underway in Canada on using CRISPR to target a rare form of blindness, as well as ovarian, brain, retinal and colorectal cancers and Duchenne muscular dystrophy.[15] Propensity to contract Alzheimer's disease, diabetes and many other serious conditions is also genetic and therefore potentially addressable using CRISPR. CRISPR technology is also being researched in the US as a potential treatment for HIV.

Outside of medicine, new materials, clean energy and advanced computational power will improve the performance – and the environmental footprint – of many forms of transport and distribution. Even recreation will be changed out of all recognition: sports clothing and equipment will improve dramatically; musical instruments will be 3-D printed at low cost and high quality; and virtual reality will transform the experience of playing computer games.

These new technologies also enable a wide range of services to be automated – from care of the elderly[16] to manning the telephones in call-centres.[17] In Japan, there is already a hotel staffed almost entirely by robots.[18] Perhaps even more importantly, new business models become possible. Smart cities, for example, which aim, in the words of the Smart Cities Council, to improve:

1. Liveability: Cities that provide clean, healthy living conditions without pollution and congestion. With a digital infrastructure that makes city services instantly and conveniently available anytime, anywhere.
2. Workability: Cities that provide the enabling infrastructure – energy, connectivity, computing, essential services – to compete globally for high-quality jobs.
3. Sustainability: Cities that provide services without stealing from future generations.[19]

Even more fundamentally, the concept of a 'closed-loop' or 'circular' economy offers the potential to minimize waste, to reduce costs, to prevent harmful pollution such as greenhouse gas emissions and degradation of the natural world, and to safeguard supply of finite resources such as rare earth metals. There need no longer be a trade-off between economic growth and sustainability.

The diagram below, from the Ellen MacArthur Foundation, illustrates the biological and technical cycles in the circular economy as well as the three key principles:[20]

1. **preserve and enhance** natural capital by controlling finite stocks and balancing renewable resource flows;
2. **optimize** resource yields by circulating products, components and materials in use at the highest utility at all times in both technical and biological cycles;
3. **foster system effectiveness** by revealing and designing-out negative externalities.

Figure 19: The key cycles in the circular economy

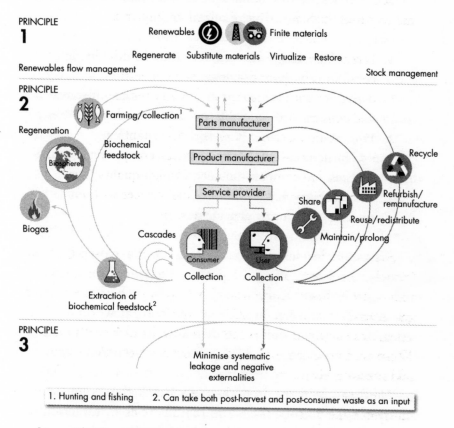

1. Hunting and fishing   2. Can take both post-harvest and post-consumer waste as an input

Source: The Ellen MacArthur Foundation

Taken together, these technologies and business models will have some extraordinary impacts, not the least of which is that the total cost to the world could fall dramatically.

The principal *financial* costs of a product or service are those of labour, energy, raw materials and land. The innovations that we have discussed above should reduce many of these costs. Currently missing from our accounting but critically important nevertheless, are the costs of externalities such as pollution, destruction of natural habitats and exhaustion of finite resources. A world using clean energy in a closed-loop economy would have lower *total* costs: the financial cost as we can currently measure it plus the cost of externalities. Such a world would be far more sustainable.

Our current – financial only – definition of profit *makes it harder* for companies to migrate towards a circular economy. Correctly charging them for their externalities – what Margaret Thatcher called the 'polluter pays' principle – brings their incentives in line with the needs of society at large.[21]

At the same time as the costs fall, we could see a dramatic expansion in our ability to provide new products and services. Our ability to provide valuable products and services will not be constrained by lack of labour, energy or raw materials and therefore the size of the pie has the potential to grow enormously – *if demand is visible.*

In a market-based economy, supply 'sees' demand which is backed by money; it does not 'see' demand which is not expressed financially. In this sense, *poor people have no (visible) needs.*

Our economic future therefore does not depend so much on our ability to supply the products and services populations will require – this ability will expand rapidly. It does not depend on unexpected sources of demand developing – an ageing population and the need to develop a sustainable model for the economy both create enormous demand. It *does* depend on whether supply can 'see' the demand – whether the demand is backed by money.

As more and more jobs become possible to automate, we face a challenge – will these new technologies create a demand for new and higher added-value jobs for all as some predict, or will they produce a new underclass?

What happened last time

British people have been through this sort of transformation before, although none of us can remember it. Last time, we called it the Industrial Revolution.

The Industrial Revolution was a period of unprecedented technological change which transformed almost every aspect of society. With the benefit of hindsight, we can see whether, and over what timescales, benefits accrued to ordinary members of society.

The historical perspective suggests that the Industrial Revolution caused a thirty-year stagnation in average wages. It was a more-than-a-generation-long period of mass impoverishment.

The United Kingdom was one of the first countries to industrialize. The process of industrialization began in about 1760 and ran until around the 1830s. Many sectors of activity were affected: textile manufacture, agriculture, iron and steel, chemical industries and transportation were all revolutionized during this period. *And GDP grew rapidly.*

Yet not everyone was happy: many craft workers in Britain lost their jobs and the Luddite movement was formed. Luddites attacked factories and destroyed machines, trying to prevent further destruction of jobs. Nowadays, the word 'Luddite' is almost always used in a pejorative sense, to mean someone who is unable to see the benefits of technological progress. It is interesting to look at the facts to see whether the Luddites had a point.

Robert C. Allen of Oxford University has studied the economic effects of the Industrial Revolution, and, in particular, its impact on ordinary workers. He concludes:

The prime mover was technical progress beginning with the famous inventions of the eighteenth century including mechanical spinning, coke smelting, iron puddling and the steam engine. It was only after 1800 that the revolutionized industries were large enough to affect the national economy... and the purchasing power of wages stagnated... Hence, the upward leap in inequality.[22]

In a separate paper, he carried out a detailed analysis of wages during the Industrial Revolution.[23] His work, details of which you can see in the Appendix on the *99-percent. org* website, shows that the initial period of mass industrialization (1801–30) interrupted real wage growth in the UK – despite the additional demand for manpower from the military (this was the time of the Napoleonic wars). For more than a generation, during which time the UK was leaping forward in terms of growth and competitiveness, real wages remained essentially flat. It was not until 1833 that real wages again reached the level they had attained in 1798, *thirty-five years earlier.*

Even in the subsequent period, after 1830, when the process of industrialization was largely complete and wages began to rise again, the rate at which they did so was still lacklustre compared with the overall growth in the economy. Real wage growth from 1830 to 1869 averaged around 1 per cent per annum; in that same period, real GDP grew at over 2 per cent per annum – more than twice as quickly.

The Industrial Revolution, then, *was* a revolution for the economy as a whole but, especially for the first thirty years or so, all the benefits went to the rich. Although the new technology *did* create new jobs, these were often less skilled and less well-paid than the jobs they destroyed. It was not until the process of industrialization was essentially complete, and the 'creative destruction' was finished, that wages could resume their upward progress.

This is *not*, of course, an argument that ordinary people never benefitted from the Industrial Revolution – of course, *over the very long-term*, we have all benefitted enormously and our standard of living today is vastly higher than any prior period in history – which it would not be had the world not industrialized.

But it does demonstrate that technological progress, even if ultimately beneficial, can lead to a generation or more of mass impoverishment if its introduction is not managed well.

The next industrial revolution will be worse

We are on the brink of another Industrial Revolution as artificial intelligence, coupled with a range of other technologies, begins to make it possible for machines to do jobs which currently require people.

As Klaus Schwab, founder of the World Economic Forum that meets annually at Davos, put it:

> There are many challenges in the world today, and I feel that one of the most intense and impactful will be shaping the 'Fourth Industrial Revolution' – driven by the speed, the breadth and the complete 'systems innovation' of technological change underway. The challenges are as daunting as the opportunities are compelling. We must have a comprehensive and globally shared understanding of how technology is changing our lives and that of future generations, transforming the economic, social, ecological and cultural contexts in which we live. This is critical, in order to shape our collective future to reflect our common objectives and values.[24]

Among the agenda points for the meeting at Davos 2016 was the following question: 'How can technology be deployed in ways that contribute to inclusive growth rather than exacerbate unemployment and income inequality?'

Currently, for example, around 13 per cent of the US population are employed in the Retail and Transportation industries.[25] There are signs that many of these jobs will not exist in a few years' time – we have self-service checkouts in supermarkets; some fast food restaurants have introduced screen-based ordering; driverless trains are a reality today; driverless cars have already reached a high level of technical proficiency, and cars with some degree of autonomy (e.g. motorway driving) are already on the market; warehouses increasingly use automated picking and packing technologies. In these areas alone, we could see tens of millions of jobs disappear. But this is just the beginning.

Another team at Oxford has been taking a close look at the possibilities for automation in the US. Carl Frey and Michael Osborne examined over 700 occupational categories and for each one assessed the probability that jobs in that sector would be automated within the next twenty years. Their conclusion was that 47 per cent of US jobs are in high-risk categories, with more than a 75 per cent chance of being computerized in the next two decades.[26] Only 33 per cent of jobs have less than a 25 per cent chance of being computerized by 2033 – and by 2050 the process will have advanced much further. You can see more details of their work in the Appendix on the *99-percent.org* website.

High-risk categories of jobs include sales and related areas, many service jobs, much office and administrative support work, as well as construction and extraction, production and – as mentioned above – transportation and material moving. In the high-risk categories alone, some 67 million jobs (out of a

:

total of 142 million) stand to be lost. These are the people that Ira Sohn referred to in his metaphor with the horses.

If you work in one of these areas, you should be concerned. And even if you don't, even if you're an upper-middle-class professional – like a doctor, banker or lawyer – there are recent developments that might worry you. As Vivienne Ming, one of America's most celebrated speakers on artificial intelligence, pointed out in a *Financial Times* interview:

> What we really need to worry about is AI-related labour market disruption, not just for factory workers, but for brain workers too. I think the global professional middle class is about to be blindsided.[27]

She cites a recent competition at Columbia University between human lawyers and their artificial counterparts, in which both read a series of non-disclosure agreements with loopholes in them.

> The AI found 95 per cent of them, and the humans 88 per cent. But the human took 90 minutes to read them. The AI took 22 seconds.

The optimistic view would be that this represents capitalism at its best: new technology enabling a leap forward in productivity; creative destruction releasing resources currently tied up in inefficient old approaches to providing products and services, and freeing them up to provide newer, higher added-value products and services.

It is certainly true that there will be new jobs created – at least in the short term – for people to design, program, commission and service all the new machines. It is also likely that these jobs will, by and large, be well-paid. There will not, however, be a need for 67 million people to do these things.

Some recent reports suggest that, nevertheless, there will be no shortage of jobs, at least not by 2030 – the extra wealth created by the robots will generate enough demand to employ everyone.[28] This might be true if a) the extra wealth were to be spread amongst the entire population so that they could all contribute to increased demand, and b) the extra demand cannot be met by automated supply. Neither of these assumptions sounds robust, especially when we start looking out as far as 2050.

As Erik Brynjolfsson, an economist at the Massachusetts Institute of Technology and co-author of *The Second Machine Age*, has pointed out:

There's no economic law that says, 'You will always create enough jobs or the balance will always be even', it's possible for a technology to dramatically favour one group and to hurt another group, and the net of that might be that you have fewer jobs.[29]

It is more plausible that tens or even hundreds of millions of people will be unable to find work – and unless we change the system, they will be workless in a very hostile environment.

By the year 2050, new technology will have progressed well beyond what was envisaged in Frey and Osborne's analysis. It is at least a highly plausible scenario that almost every job will be able to be done better and more cheaply by machines than by humans. And if jobs are the way that most people will live, then most humans will not have a way to earn a living.

We need to rethink the system now to avoid disastrous social outcomes

This is an enormous policy challenge, which no major party has even touched on. And thirty-five years is not long to prepare.

The more pessimistic view would see Frey and Osborne's projection playing out over the next twenty years without any radical rearrangement of society, adding tens of millions to the 80 million who are currently of working age but not economically active in the US (and similar proportions in other countries). In this view, most of those who stay in work will see falling wages – although a few will see massively higher earnings – and the lives of the majority of people will have to change fundamentally.

Tyler Cowen, author of the book *Average is Over*, suggests that poorer Americans will need to move away from their current homes to much lower-cost housing, to be much less 'wasteful' in their spending, and to accept lower standards of healthcare:

This process of economizing won't always do so well when it comes to poor women... children don't help single mothers' incomes. Taking care of one's children can be thought of as a very expensive preference. Younger women in the lower end of the income distribution will probably be some of the biggest losers, especially if they have a strong 'baby lust' that induces or compels them to have lots of children early in life... The disparities of healthcare access, across classes of income and education, will increase. The world will look much more unfair and much less equal and indeed it will be. That sounds pretty bad and maybe it is. There will however be some compensating factors. The first, as I've already noted, is that more people will get more aid than ever before, even though the quality of that care – and how long many will have to wait for it – is anyone's guess.[30]

With our current economic system, technology will accelerate the move towards a dystopian world like that of Chapter One. A more optimistic view would say that we are on the brink of an explosion in productivity that could, over the next twenty years, enable our society to produce double the value of goods and services with the same number of people. If we manage it correctly, therefore, we could all be roughly twice as well off in twenty years' time. The world might in some ways begin to resemble the utopian pictures of families of the future presented in comic books of the 1960s and 1970s in which ordinary families led lives of luxury, waited on hand-and-foot by robots.

The problem with this more optimistic view is that it is very hard to see a government – or indeed any significant political party – with any kind of policy to steer us towards this destination. The policy challenge was summarized by Professor Dwight D. Murphey:

The astonishing technology of computers, robotics, materials sciences, and biotechnology is such that the future offers the prospect of a near-utopia, while at the same time there will be a move to a near workerless economy. Both aspects will shake societies to their core. When work is largely replaced as a source of income, a catastrophe will result in less-developed economies, where income from work is almost the sole source of support. In the more-advanced economies, the high incomes of those who own or manage the technology and of those who possess high skills may be enough to provide auxiliary service employment for everyone else, but the level of inequality will become so great that a free society will not be able to accept it.[31]

There is enough evidence to conclude that the coming industrial revolution – if we do not change our economic system – poses an unprecedented threat to millions of people. Over the next twenty years, almost half of jobs currently existing will be automated which will, at the very least, mean wrenching change. By 2050 we could be in a near-workerless economy.

We need to rethink our social and economic system fundamentally if we are to avoid disastrous social outcomes. If we do not change it, although we shall have almost limitless potential for supply, much of the demand will be invisible. Many people's needs will simply not be met.

CHAPTER 6

Wealth, Power and Freedom

"People feel like the system is rigged against them. And here's the painful part: they're right."

Elizabeth Warren[1]

Most developed nations are democracies. They operate on the principle of one person, one vote – each adult, regardless of wealth or status, has (at least in principle) an equal opportunity to determine how the country will be governed and the policies that it will adopt. Each person, in principle, regardless of wealth or status, is equal under the law. No system is perfect, but as Winston Churchill said: 'Democracy is the worst form of government – except for all those other forms that have been tried from time to time.'[2]

The rapid increases in inequality that we have seen in earlier chapters have resulted in an enormous concentration of wealth and power. This has caused some to question whether our democracy itself risks being undermined by a conspiracy of the wealthy. In fact, there is no need for a conspiracy. In very natural ways, we have put in place a set of dynamics that have begun, and will continue until they are challenged, to transfer ever more wealth to the already wealthy and to undermine the democratic freedoms of the rest of the population:

- without any need for a conspiracy, the dynamics of wealth concentration naturally lead to an undermining of democratic equality;
- not only power but also freedom risks being concentrated into very few hands; and therefore
- preserving democracy and freedom requires these dynamics to be challenged – but it must be done intelligently if we are to achieve positive results and avoid painful conflict.

Excessive wealth concentration undermines democracy

Excessive concentration of wealth naturally leads to a set of social, financial and political dynamics that undermine the democratic ideal.

Making very large amounts of money is about playing a game: the game of capitalism. Like any game, of course, ability to play the game depends on skill and effort. Unlike most other games, ability to play the game of capitalism is also heavily determined by the social circles you move in and by the amount of money you have available as you start the game. It is also strongly influenced by whether or not you are in a position to rewrite the rules of the game in your own favour. These dynamics are summarized in the diagram overleaf.

Making money from business investments requires a) that you are aware of an investment opportunity and have access to the individuals who control it, b) that you have capital to invest, and c) that you either have the skill to manage the investment yourself or can buy these skills in. Starting with a large amount of capital is a big advantage in playing this game. It helps you with all three requirements.

Figure 20: How wealth and power reinforce each other

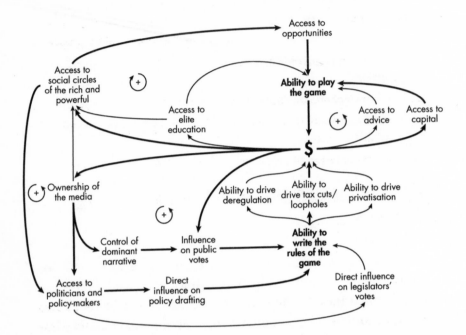

The top part of the diagram illustrates these dynamics and shows that there are two critical self-reinforcing chains of cause and effect. These dynamics – although they *are* self-reinforcing and tend to lead to the phenomenon of the rich getting richer faster than the poor can hope to – do not pose any direct threat to democracy.

The extent to which they are self-reinforcing can be seen in the chart below, from the work of Thomas Piketty who, as part of his research for his book *Capital*, looked at returns achieved by university endowment funds and discovered the strikingly different rates of return on capital available to those with different – though in all cases considerable – amounts of capital to invest.

Figure 21: Impact of wealth on rates of return

Endowments	Number of universities	Average real rate of return
Harvard, Yale and Princeton (higher than US$10 billion)	3	10.2%
Endowments higher than US$1 billion	60	8.8%
Endowments between US$500m and US$1 billion	66	7.8%
Endowments between US$100m and US$500m	226	7.1%
Endowments less than US$100m	498	6.2%

Source: Piketty[3]

The bottom part of the diagram in Figure 20 is perhaps less obvious and is where the challenges to the democratic ideal arise. Mixing in the social circles of the rich and powerful gives access to politicians and policymakers and enables one – especially if one is also a major political donor – to have a direct influence on policy drafting as well as on the way that legislators will vote on draft bills. With extreme wealth comes the option to own major media outlets, which strengthens access to politicians and policymakers but also gives the owner control of the dominant narrative in society and therefore the ability to influence the votes of millions.

This enables the wealthiest individuals to shape policy in the interests of their own businesses, for example by encouraging the government to sell public assets at below intrinsic value, by creating tax breaks and perpetuating loopholes and by reducing regulation – or indeed by introducing regulation favourable to the leading players in an industry.

Without even setting out to do so, they can rewrite the rules of society in their own interests. Ben Stein illustrated in the *New York Times* in 2006 how the tax code benefits the very rich, using some analysis carried out by Warren Buffett, one of the world's richest men:

> Mr Buffett compiled a data sheet of the men and women who work in his office. He had each of them make a fraction; the numerator was how much they paid in federal income tax and in payroll taxes for Social Security and Medicare, and the denominator was their taxable income... It turned out that Mr. Buffett, with immense income from dividends and capital gains, paid far, far less as a fraction of his income than the secretaries or the clerks or anyone else in his office. Further, in conversation it came up that Mr Buffett doesn't use any tax planning at all. He just pays as the Internal Revenue Code requires. 'How can this be fair?' he asked of how little he pays relative to his employees. 'How can this be right?'[4]

There are four key levers of power that are easier to pull if you are extremely rich:

1. Access to elite education
2. Access to social circles of the rich and powerful
3. Ownership of major media outlets
4. Access to policymakers and politicians

There are many examples of individuals who found ways to pull some of these levers without great wealth – but they are the exceptions. Martin Luther King may have been able to meet with the president[5] but most members of the population of the United States cannot.

Being a billionaire, however, is helpful in this respect: Bill Gates, for example, has met President Barack Obama of the United States,[6] President Xi Jinping of China[7] and President Nelson Mandela of South Africa,[8] among others.

The most accessible of the four levers is access to elite education – the top schools and universities in each country, from which a high proportion of the future elite are drawn. The power of this lever is surprising. In the UK, for example, 35 per cent of members of Parliament were educated in private schools, against 7 per cent of the population as a whole.[9] Even more strikingly, David Cameron, the former Prime Minister of the UK, and four of his most trusted aides all attended the same school, Eton College, and more than half of the Cabinet were privately educated and attended either Oxford or Cambridge University.[10] As with meeting the president, it is not impossible to attend these schools without a privileged background – they all offer scholarships – but it does require exceptional ability. For the vast majority of the bottom 99 per cent of the population, elite education is out of reach. For the top 1 per cent, the chances are much higher.

Access to the most exclusive social circles can be more or less guaranteed for anyone possessing hundreds of millions of dollars and, if they are prepared to splash their money about a little, probably for anyone with tens of millions – as can access to policymakers and politicians. Without such wealth, it is extremely unlikely. In other words, it is not the top 1 per cent but the top 0.1 per cent who enjoy this privilege. For the bottom 99.9 per cent of the population, such access requires exceptional talent and tenacity.

The most exclusive of all is ownership of major media outlets. The most popular television channels and newspapers are the preserve of billionaires and multibillionaires.

The media empire of Rupert Murdoch, for example, has

included the UK newspapers the *Sun* (which has a circulation of almost 2 million readers, making it the UK's best-selling newspaper), the *News of the World*, *The Times* and the *Sunday Times*, as well as a large shareholding in the dominant satellite broadcaster, BSkyB. In the United States, he has controlled, among others, the *New York Post*, 20th Century Fox (including *Fox News*), DirecTV, Intermix Media and Dow Jones, which owns the *Wall Street Journal*, *Barron's Magazine* and *SmartMoney*.

These media outlets have not been shy of trying to influence political outcomes. On Saturday, 11 April 1992, the *Sun* famously claimed to have determined the result of the then recent general election in the United Kingdom.

If you are in the bottom 99.9 per cent of the population, you cannot expect to have such control of the media. Nonetheless, in some countries – such as the United States, since the Supreme Court decided in 2010 in the case of *Citizens United vs Federal Election Commission* that there should be no limits imposed on corporations' political spending or communication – business owners can exercise direct influence on the votes of the population as well as on those of legislators.[11] Wealthy individuals and corporations essentially have unfettered power to lobby, to advertise, to fund political parties and even to instruct their employees on how to vote.

The *New York Times* has reported that major companies such as Georgia-Pacific, Koch Industries and Cintas wrote to their employees suggesting – or even recommending – how they should vote.[12] At least one CEO, David A. Siegel of Westgate Resorts, went so far as to threaten redundancies if Obama were to be re-elected:

The economy doesn't currently pose a threat to your job. What does threaten your job, however, is another four years of the same presidential administration. If any new taxes are levied on me, or my company, as our current president plans, I will have no choice but to reduce the size of this company.

Mr Siegel denied that he was pressurizing his employees into voting in line with his own views and likened his guidance to good parenting:

There's no way I can pressure anybody, I'm not in the voting booth with them. I really wanted them to know how I felt four more years under President Obama was going to affect them. It would be no different from telling your children: 'Eat your spinach. It's good for you.'

In fact, of course, his comment on job losses makes no business sense: if new taxes were levied on him personally, he would be mad to reduce the size of his company in response. His comment makes sense only when considered as a threat. We cannot know for sure, as Mr Siegel points out, whether this threat influenced their behaviour in the privacy of the voting booth but he would not have made it if he didn't believe there was a chance.

There are other important areas where the power of the wealthy to shape mass opinion is clear. Climate change is such an example. As NASA points out:

Multiple studies published in peer-reviewed scientific journals show that 97% or more of actively publishing climate scientists agree: climate warming trends over the past century are very likely due to human activities.[13]

This near-unanimity on the part of the experts has not resulted in a comparable consensus among the public at large – at least not in all countries.

Figure 23: Climate change attitudes by country

Country	Agree that climate change is largely the result of human activity
China	93%
Argentina	84%
Italy	84%
Spain	82%
Turkey	80%
France	80%
India	80%
Brazil	79%
Belgium	78%
South Korea	77%
South Africa	76%
Sweden	74%
Germany	72%
Canada	71%
Japan	70%
Poland	68%
Russia	67%
Australia	64%
UK	64%
USA	54%

Source: Ipsos MORI[14]

One of the key reasons for the outlying position of the United States is its Climate Change Counter Movement, 'a deliberate and organized effort to misdirect the public discussion and distort the public's understanding of climate change'.[15] As *Scientific American* reported in 2013:

> The study, by Drexel University environmental sociologist Robert Brulle, is the first academic effort to probe the organizational underpinnings and funding behind the climate denial movement. It found that the amount of money flowing through third-party, pass-through foundations like DonorsTrust and Donors Capital, whose funding cannot be traced, has risen dramatically over the past five years. In all, 140 foundations funnelled US$558 million to almost 100 climate denial organizations from 2003 to 2010. Meanwhile the traceable cash flow from more traditional sources, such as Koch Industries and ExxonMobil, has disappeared.[16]

The example of the Climate Change Counter Movement does sound rather like conspiracy: a small number of powerful actors coordinating their activities and attempting to cover their tracks as they do so. Jane Mayer and Owen Jones in their books, *Dark Money*[17] and *The Establishment*,[18] chart in some detail how some of the wealthiest in society have used covert means to increase their influence over recent decades.

Recent revelations about the role of companies such as Cambridge Analytica in the US presidential election campaign and in the UK's Brexit vote make the risk to democracy even clearer.[19] But in general, there is no need for conspiracy. Simply behaving naturally will activate the dynamics in Figure 20 above. What could be more natural than to keep in touch with school friends? What could be more natural than to mix with others in the same social class? What could be more natural than to bounce ideas off one's friends? What could be more natural, if one owns a newspaper, than to want to see it voice opinions which one believes to be correct – i.e. one's own opinions? What could be more natural, if one owns a company, than to wish to see legislation favourable to that company? What could be more natural than to express these wishes as clearly and forcefully as possible, especially if one is a major donor to a political party and its elected members?

In other words, even without any conspiracy, the natural behaviour of the rich and powerful will tend to rewrite the rules of the game in their favour. Over time, this constant rewriting of the rules results in an ever-greater concentration of wealth and power – it can be seen as the fundamental cause of the emergence of mass impoverishment. The process of manipulating public policy or economic conditions as a strategy for increasing profits is sometimes called 'rent-seeking' by economists because it enables one to appropriate the benefits of someone else's work in the same way that a landlord can raise farm rents if farmers become more successful.

There are so many different forms of rent-seeking – from exploiting tax loopholes to ensuring favourable privatizations; from creating monopolies to weakening the bargaining power of employees; from externalizing the costs of one's business to society to capturing control of regulators; and, of course, literal rent on land or property – that it would be difficult to produce a comprehensive list. But if rent-seeking continues unchecked, so will mass impoverishment.

Individuals with extreme wealth are able, if they choose, to have an impact on the dominant narrative in society disproportionate to their numbers but perhaps proportionate to their wealth, shaping public perceptions of reality in line with their own wishes and influencing the votes of thousands or even millions of their compatriots.

They do not literally have more than one vote at the ballot box but they are able to influence the votes of millions. We have preserved the appearance of democracy but undermined the reality. Metaphorically, though not technically, we have started to move from *one person, one vote* to *one dollar, one vote*. Or perhaps, more precisely, *one dollar, one unit of political influence*.

How excessive wealth concentration undermines freedom and justice

Defenders of the status quo sometimes argue that tackling the dynamics implied by any of the natural behaviours described above would amount to an infringement of freedom of speech. In the case of *Citizens United vs Federal Election Commission*, referred to above, the United States Supreme Court held that the First Amendment (specifically, that part dealing with the right to free speech) prohibited the government from restricting political expenditures by corporations.[20]

There are, however, two distinct types of freedom: *freedom to* and *freedom from*. The two concepts need to be kept in balance. My freedom to say and write what I like must be balanced against your freedom from being libelled. My freedom to go where I like must be balanced against your freedom from trespassers on your property. My freedom to sell tobacco products must be balanced against your child's freedom from exposure to harmful and addictive substances. This need to balance *freedom to* and *freedom from* was highlighted by Franklin D. Roosevelt in his 1941 State of The Union address:

In the future days, which we seek to make secure, we look forward to a world founded upon four essential human freedoms. The first is freedom of speech and expression – everywhere in the world. The second is freedom of every person to worship God in his own way – everywhere in the world. The third is freedom from want – which, translated into world terms, means economic understandings which will secure to every nation a healthy peacetime life for its inhabitants – everywhere in the world. The fourth is freedom from fear – which, translated into world terms, means a world-wide reduction of armaments to such a point and in such a thorough fashion that no nation will be in a position to commit an act of physical aggression against any neighbour – anywhere in the world.[21]

While billionaires are free to speak with 1 million voices when ordinary people have just one, then it takes only 330 billionaires to drown out the voices of the rest of the US population. It is perilously close to formalizing a move away from *one person, one vote* and towards, *one dollar, one unit of influence*. We are, in effect, experimenting with moving away from democracy and towards wealth-based government or plutocracy.

This move has greatly reduced the freedom of the bottom 99 per cent of the population – both because their *freedom to* be heard politically and to self-determination have been diluted in the ways described above; and because the legislative changes of the last thirty-five years and the process of mass impoverishment that these changes have ushered in have reduced their *freedom from* poverty. Appendix IV shows that their *freedom to* achieve high levels of educational attainment is lower, their *freedom from* ill-health is less, their *freedom from* violence is decreased and even their *freedom to* live as long as their compatriots is less. As Isaiah Berlin put it, 'Freedom for the wolves has often meant death to the sheep.'[22]

Perhaps most shocking of all in the US and the UK, two countries that pride themselves on their entrepreneurial spirit, their *freedom to* better themselves is dramatically reduced. Despite their rhetoric, the US and the UK have lower levels of social mobility than countries such as France, Germany, Sweden, Canada, Norway, Finland and Denmark.[23]

The chart below illustrates what a move from *one person, one vote* to *one pound, one unit of influence,* if it became a *de facto* reality, would mean in the United Kingdom.

Figure 23: Impact of moving from one person, one vote to a wealth-based system in the UK

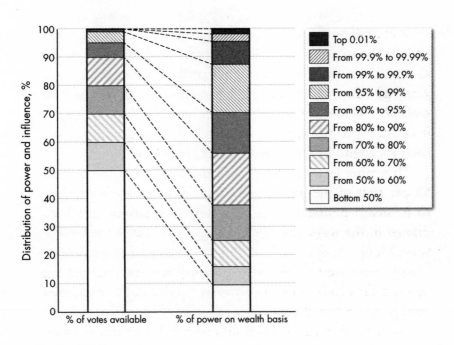

Source: ONS[24]

If the UK were to move to a system in which political power was proportional to wealth, then the bottom 50 per cent of the UK population would have less than 10 per cent of the influence – even collectively they would be negligible. The bottom 80 per cent of the population could be comfortably outgunned by the richest 20 per cent. The UK does not yet have a wealth-based system: it is still closer to a democracy than to a plutocracy, but it is moving perceptibly in the plutocratic direction.

In the US, wealth concentration is greater, so the effect would be even more pronounced as Figure 24 below illustrates.

Figure 24: Impact of moving from one person, one vote to a wealth-based system in the US

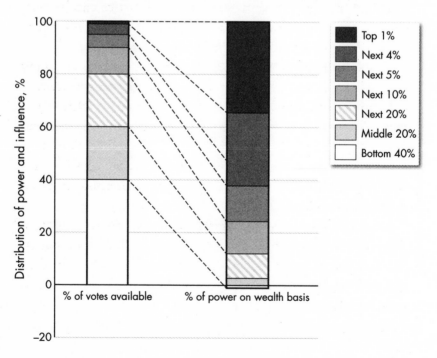

Source: Wolff[25]

In the United States, the bottom 80 per cent of the population has only about 11 per cent of the wealth, so on a *one dollar, one unit of influence* basis they would be collectively negligible. Even the bottom 95 per cent has significantly less than 50 per cent of the wealth – if power were strictly proportional to wealth, the top 5 per cent would be comfortably in control of the country. The vast mass of the population would have essentially no say in how it was run.

The other key tenet of democracy is equality under the law. Unfortunately, good lawyers are expensive, so equality under the law has sometimes been more of an aspiration than a reality. The *Economist* cites the ironic remark of Sir James Matthew – 'Justice in England is open to all – like the Ritz hotel' – and suggests that the UK is again returning to a society in which those who can afford justice can have it, while the rest must take their chances by representing themselves or even by conceding that justice is out of reach.[26]

Seeking redress against unfair dismissal, for example, now costs an individual £1,200. Since this charge was introduced, the number of cases brought has fallen by 70 per cent – but, as the *Economist* points out, the rate of success has remained unchanged, which suggests that the fall is not simply down to a decline in weak claims. In other words, 70 per cent of those who believed they had a case simply could not afford to bring it. Justice is no longer for them.

And the way laws are drafted often seems to constrain the poor far more than the rich. As Anatole France put it, 'the law, in its majestic equality, forbids the rich as well as the poor to sleep under bridges, to beg in the streets, and to steal bread'.

How the dynamics can be challenged

There are only two possibilities: either we will challenge these dynamics, or we will not. If we do not, then we risk a continuation of current trends, which as Chapter One showed is undesirable in the short term and unsustainable in the medium and long term.

The interesting question, then, is *how* these dynamics can effectively be challenged. It is certainly not easy to challenge them. Although it is relatively straightforward to take decisions which concentrate wealth and power (as each of the losers loses a relatively small amount while each of the gainers gains a tremendous amount), it is much more difficult to reverse the process. Indeed, some people strongly oppose even discussion of such issues as amounting to class war. As Warren Buffett remarked in 2006, however, 'There's class warfare, all right, but it's my class, the rich class, that's making war, and we're winning.'[27] The statistics that we saw in Chapter One confirm that he is right.

It is unlikely that a solution will be found that involves the poor defeating the rich in a class war. As highlighted by Figures 23 and 24 above, the top 20 per cent probably have more power than the rest of society combined. If it comes to any kind of war, there is a good chance that the bottom 80 per cent will lose decisively. Even if such an approach were to be successful, it is likely that any struggle would be bitter and painful for both sides, leaving a deeply divided society in which many of the wealthy would be seeking their revenge.

More optimistically, a coalition of the concerned, spanning the spectrum from the poor to the ultra-rich, could gradually develop an effective set of policies and bring public opinion behind them. Ending these dynamics does not require impoverishment of the rich – indeed, as we shall see in Part 3, in the very long-term it may even make them richer – nor does it require a move to some kind of communist society, *but it does require action.*

There are already many members of the super-rich concerned about inequality and mass impoverishment who have begun proposing policy solutions. Warren Buffett, for example, has suggested an expansion of the earned income tax credit as a way of ensuring that those whose market value has fallen below what it takes to enjoy a decent life can still have one.[28] Paul Tudor Jones II, a hedge fund manager whose personal wealth is estimated at around US$5 billion, has set up the Just Capital Foundation[29] to encourage corporations to act in the interests of society as a whole rather than to focus on short-term profit maximization. George Soros has suggested that he personally should be paying more in taxes[30] and has set up the Institute for New Economic Thinking. And they are not alone.[33] A suitably powerful and coherent coalition is still a long way off – but it is no longer fanciful to believe that it could be created.

CHAPTER 7

Eight Scenarios

Prediction is very difficult, especially about the future.

Often attributed to Niels Bohr

We have seen that over the thirty-five years from 1980 to 2015 the phenomenon of mass impoverishment began to take hold in several developed economies – notably in the US and, more recently, in the UK.

An extrapolation of current trends would see a generalized failure of society before the next thirty-five-year period is over, in 2050. But extrapolation is not the same as a forecast – and the record of economic forecasts in general is poor. In the face of such uncertainty, what can we actually say about where society is heading?

Despite the intrinsic difficulty of forecasting, it is undeniable that the answers to these three simple questions will determine our future:

1. **Will the pie grow?** Or in economic terms, will real per capita GDP grow over the next thirty-five years?
2. **Will most people's slices grow?** Will real median incomes grow over the next thirty-five years?
3. **Will we have a peaceful transition** to our future state?

For each of these questions, the answer may be *yes* or *no*. The combinations of these three answers give us eight scenarios for the future. There are no other possibilities. These eight scenarios are illustrated in Figure 26 below.

Figure 26: Eight scenarios for the world of 2050

		Will the pie grow?		Will we have a peaceful transition to our future state?
		Pie grows	Pie does not grow	
Will the median slice grow?	Median slice grows	Scenario 1: Revolution	Scenario 2: Eat the Rich	Violent transition
		Scenario 3: Solidarity and Abundance	Scenario 4: Philanthropy ++	Peaceful transition
	Median slice does not grow	Scenario 5: Accepting Impoverish-ment	Scenario 6: Sharing Decline	
		Scenario 7: Neo-feudalism	Scenario 8: Collapse	Violent transition

Scenario 1: Revolution

At the top left of the diagram is the scenario titled *Revolution*. In this scenario, the size of the pie continues to grow and the median slice also grows – both of which are positive outcomes – but the route to this state is not by a peaceful transition. Even if the end state is acceptable, the route is not – it still represents a (violent) failure of our current civilization and the construction of a new one.

Scenario 2: Eat the Rich

At the top right is the scenario *Eat the Rich*. This scenario is still less pleasant and it does not even have the virtue of being sustainable. In this scenario, the pie as a whole is not growing but the median slice is growing – in other words the masses are becoming wealthier, but only by confiscating income and wealth from the rich by force. This scenario cannot be sustained indefinitely because with a shrinking pie, eventually there will be no more income and wealth to be confiscated from those who used to be rich.

Scenario 3: Solidarity and Abundance

The next scenario, *Solidarity and Abundance*, is by far the most attractive. The pie as a whole continues to grow, and the median slice grows with it. Furthermore, the transition is a peaceful one – society has united to implement the policies which bring about this shared growth in income and wealth.

Scenario 4: Philanthropy++

Philanthropy++ seems an implausible scenario. It is broadly similar to *Eat the Rich*, except that, for this scenario to materialize, the rich must peacefully agree to have their wealth and income confiscated.

Scenario 5: Accepting Impoverishment

Accepting Impoverishment may also not be a stable scenario. It assumes that the mass of the population is prepared to tolerate indefinitely shrinking incomes, even in the face of continuing growth in the economy. Their experience will be of increasing scarcity and decreasing support from the rest of society. Whether a world of scarcity and isolation will be tolerated is not clear. We have already seen rising anger on the part of those left behind: there is growing evidence of the radicalization of the working class; and race and religious hate crime have started to rise. Maintaining a peaceful democracy in the face of another thirty-five years of mass impoverishment seems unlikely.

Scenario 6: Sharing Decline

The plausibility of *Sharing Decline* is also questionable. For this to happen, both the rich and the mass of the population would have to acquiesce in the decline of their living standards rather than struggle to preserve their own at someone else's expense. The experience of the last thirty-five years makes this seem unlikely – but it is, of course, not impossible.

Scenario 7: Neo-feudalism

Neo-feudalism represents a world which has been seized by the wealthy. The economy continues to grow but most people continue to grow poorer. And there is nothing they can do about it.

Scenario 8: Collapse

The final scenario, *Collapse*, represents a failure of Neofeudalism. The wealth has been so concentrated that demand begins to fall. Even the rich begin to get poorer.

Which of these scenarios will come to pass? Probably not those on the right: economies do tend to grow over the medium term. In the UK, for example, since 1700 there has not been a thirty-five-year period over which the economy has shrunk.[1]

Of the scenarios on the left, only *Solidarity and Abundance* can be described as representing the survival of our current civilization – even *Accepting Impoverishment* would be a (peaceful) transition from a representative democracy to a *de facto* plutocracy, and the other two possibilities both involve regime change by force.

Using the diagrammatic representation, we can compare these two scenarios – *Solidarity and Abundance* and *Accepting Impoverishment* – qualitatively.

This representation makes it clear that it is a political rather than an economic challenge that confronts us. The total value of what is supplied is the same in both cases; it is the targeting of that supply which differs. In the case of *Solidarity and Abundance*, supply is targeted first on meeting the most fundamental needs (absolute needs, needs for normal life and needs for an easy life), and indeed these are entirely met for the entire population. Most people also have some of their wants and desires met, and quite a few people – as at present – enjoy super luxury.

Figure 26: The world in 2050 – two scenarios

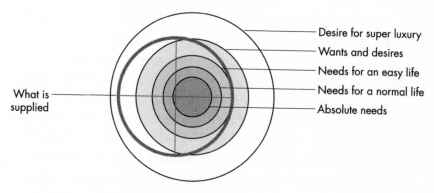

Solidarity and abundance

Desire for super luxury
Wants and desires
Needs for an easy life
What is supplied
Needs for a normal life
Absolute needs

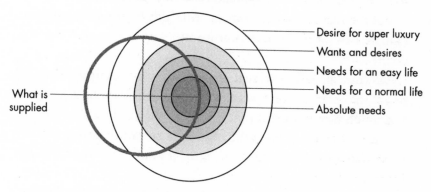

Accepting impoverishment

Desire for super luxury
Wants and desires
Needs for an easy life
What is supplied
Needs for a normal life
Absolute needs

In the case of *Accepting Impoverishment*, supply is not so well targeted, and we see more people whose most fundamental needs are not met as well as significant numbers who cannot enjoy a normal life, let alone an easy one. On the other hand, there is a far greater supply of super luxury.

Current policy is not directing us towards the desirable outcome

It is easier to speak about the direction of policy in the UK than the US, because one party, the Conservative Party, has been in power since 2010. Although there have been changes in the leadership of this party, and policy has changed slightly, the overall direction is largely unchanged.

When the new government set out its 2016 Autumn Statement, the Institute for Fiscal Studies (IFS) was able to compare its policies with those of its predecessor. In summary, while the policies of the May/Hammond government represented an improvement on those of the Cameron/Osborne government, their likely impact is still a continuation of the process of mass impoverishment. Analysis by the IFS[2] paints a grim picture of the near-term future:

> On these projections, real wages will, remarkably, still be below their 2008 levels in 2021. One cannot stress enough how dreadful that is – more than a decade without real earnings growth... We have certainly not seen a period remotely like it in the last 70 years.[3]

The Resolution Foundation looked in detail at the impact of government policy by income level and concluded: 'Overall the Chancellor reversed only 7 per cent of the inherited policy-related hit to the poorest half of families.'[4] In other words, Hammond's predecessor's policies were set to perpetuate the process of mass impoverishment; Hammond has improved things somewhat, but not greatly. At this point, you may be thinking, 'yes, there is pain, but that is necessary to put the economy on a sound footing for the long term.' As we shall see, the facts do not support this line of argument.

On their projections, not only will average wages perform extremely poorly but the pain will also be disproportionately borne by the lower-income segments of the population. This is, of course, a relatively short view. Unfortunately, the longer term will pose additional challenges because of the automation, described in Chapter 5, of most jobs and the inability (under current policies) of society to cope with this phenomenon.

In the US, of course, the election of Donald Trump represents a more significant change in the direction of travel. His most significant legislation has been his Tax Bill which, according to the Institute on Taxation and Economic Policy (ITEP), will result in a total reduction in tax of US$205 billion in 2027.[5] Of this US$205 billion, over US$98 billion (or 48 per cent) will go to the top 1 per cent, and only US$3.9 billion (or 2 per cent) to the bottom 20 per cent of the population.

US$205 billion represents around US$640 for every man, woman and child in the US. If it were actually distributed that way, so that all Americans benefitted equally from the bill, only around US$2 billion would go to the top 1 per cent and US$41 billion would go to the bottom 20 per cent. Instead, the Tax Bill is 480 times more generous to those at the top than to those at the bottom.

Even worse, if the tax cut has to be paid for by reducing public services and benefits, it will be the mass of the population that does the paying. In the US, it seems reasonable to conclude that current policies will, if anything, accelerate mass impoverishment.

The governments of both countries are, even if unconsciously, steering us towards Scenario 5: *Accepting Impoverishment*.

Without more significant policy changes, the future will not be pretty

The Resolution Foundation's analysis also illustrates the relatively narrow range of policies that are currently being considered. Of course, the two sets of policies illustrated are both those of Conservative chancellors. But even between parties, the policy space is small. No party in any major developed nation currently:

- has made a commitment to ending mass impoverishment using the full range of policy options;
- measures its performance according to how well it succeeds in improving the lives of ordinary people;
- formulates trade and immigration policy in such a way as to share the benefits of globalization with the mass of the population;
- has any policy to deal with the mass unemployment that will result from automation over the next thirty-five years.

Without more significant change in policy, we are headed, at best, towards the scenario of *Accepting Impoverishment*. If this scenario does materialize, that will be bad enough; and if not, we may end up either with a *Revolution* or in the world of *Neo-feudalism*.

None of these outcomes represents a successful continuation of our civilization to the year 2050. We are heading in a very bad direction.

But there are things we can do to change this. In Part 2 of this book we shall explore the barriers 'preventing' governments from addressing the policy points above, and in Part 3, we shall look in more detail at what action we must take to ensure that we build a future of *Solidarity and Abundance*.

PART 2

WHY WE DON'T ACT

It ain't what you don't know that gets you into trouble.
It's what you know for sure that just ain't so.

Attributed to Mark Twain

P art Two of this book sets out a case that the barriers to action lie in our mind. We are imprisoned not by any features of the external world but by what we *think* we know. It is not reality that imprisons us, it is a post-fact description of the world.

The notion of going post-fact has become mainstream in the wake of the 2016 US presidential election campaign and the UK's EU referendum campaign in the same year. But post-fact politics is not new and history shows that it can be very dangerous. While it is heartening that sections of the Establishment are beginning to wake up to this risk, there are no grounds for complacency as there is a natural tendency for media and politicians, as well as ordinary people, to go post-fact.

When politicians and journalists talk about the economy, they routinely resort to myths and metaphors. These myths and metaphors are widely used, even by those who are supposedly experts in the area, and naturally lead us to the conclusion that the way we are running the economy today is the best way. These myths and metaphors, however, bear no relation to the facts about the real world as recorded in official government statistics.

Even economic models tend, unfortunately, to form part of this post-fact world. Because of the underlying assumptions on which they are based and the structures on which they are built, the most commonly used economic models give us no insights into the most important and fundamental economic questions that we are wrestling with, such as mass impoverishment or financial crises. They do not represent the real world in any important way – they represent a sophisticated form of post-fact thinking. There are, however, new types of economic model being developed that may enable us to better explore these important questions.

Possibly even more dangerous is the use of rhetoric, building on these models, myths and metaphors, to distort and even to reverse our perception of the facts. These models, myths, metaphors and rhetoric combine into an enormously plausible – but completely unfounded – narrative that to do anything differently would be unaffordable. Politicians are even able to fool themselves. As Philip Alston said of the UK:

> ... the full picture of low-income well-being in the UK cannot be captured by statistics alone. Its manifestations are clear for all to see. The country's most respected charitable groups, its leading think tanks, its parliamentary committees, independent authorities like the National Audit Office, and many others, have all drawn attention to the dramatic decline in the fortunes of the least well off in this country.
>
> But through it all, one actor has stubbornly resisted seeing the situation for what it is. The government has remained determinedly in a state of denial.[1]

While we continue to accept the rhetoric, our ability to think clearly and accurately about our problems remains very limited. And governments' ability to formulate sound policy remains negligible. In other words, the narrative of unaffordability implies that there is no alternative. The facts say that there are many alternatives.

CHAPTER 8

Going Post-Fact

Everyone is entitled to his own opinion, but not to his own facts.

Daniel Patrick Moynihan[1]

Post-truth *(adjective): Relating to or denoting circumstances in which objective facts are less influential in shaping public opinion than appeals to emotion and personal belief.*

Oxford Dictionaries[2]

Oxford Dictionaries made *post-truth* its word of 2016, noting that there was increasing use of it during the year – in particular in the lead-up to the UK's referendum on whether to remain within the EU and on the American presidential election campaign.

Traditional media have covered – and in some cases given credence to – many post-truth utterances, like the claims that President Obama was born in Kenya and that, by leaving the EU, the UK could recoup £350 million per week to fund the National Health Service (NHS).

Over the past year or so, as Oxford Dictionaries noted, mainstream media have begun to comment on the post-truth phenomenon itself. The impression they often give is that going post-fact is a relatively recent phenomenon, mainly affecting and promulgated by the less-educated strata of society. Until very recently, it is implied, it was not considered a serious problem.

In reality, going post-fact is *not* new, does *not* involve just the less-educated and it *is* very dangerous. Although the elite are waking up to these dangers, it will be hard to reverse the trend as there are powerful incentives to drift towards the post-fact end of the spectrum.

Going post-fact is not a new phenomenon

Some of the most unsavoury episodes in history have been enabled by post-fact politics – think of Hitler's Third Reich or Joseph McCarthy's 'red scare' in the United States. Post-fact argument has also been prevalent in more moderate times, such as in the debate in the UK as to which of the two main parties has a better record on unemployment.

Adolf Hitler's chief propagandist, Joseph Goebbels, clearly understood the distinction between effective propaganda and intellectual truth:

> To attract people, to win over people to that which I have realized as being true, that is called propaganda. In the beginning, there is the understanding; this understanding uses propaganda as a tool to find those men that shall turn understanding into politics. Success is the important thing. Propaganda is not a matter for average minds, but rather a matter for practitioners. It is not supposed to be lovely or theoretically correct... It is not the task of propaganda to discover intellectual truths.[3]

The cost to the world of Goebbels's successful propaganda is hard to overstate.

After the Second World War, fear of communist influence abroad and infiltration at home was widespread in the United States. This fear provided a platform from which Senator Joseph McCarthy could launch his 'red scare' campaign. In February 1950, McCarthy gave a speech that caught the national mood and made him a household name. Showing the crowd a piece of paper he held in his hand, he declared that he was in possession of a list of 205 known members of the Communist Party who were 'working and shaping policy' in the State Department. Shortly afterwards, a Senate subcommittee launched an investigation into this allegation that found no proof of subversive activity in the State Department. Many of his colleagues disowned his methods.

On the face of it, his list had been discredited. Nevertheless, buoyed by popular support, McCarthy continued his campaign. When he was put in charge of the Committee on Government Operations, he launched investigations of the alleged communist infiltration of the federal government. In a series of hearings, he aggressively interrogated witnesses. Despite the lack of any proof of subversion, more than 2,000 government employees lost their jobs and their reputations because of McCarthy's investigations, in what many saw as a violation of their civil rights.

His downfall came when he turned his attention from civil servants to members of the military. His targets now enjoyed more popular support and were better able to defend themselves:

In April 1954, Senator McCarthy turned his attention to 'exposing' the supposed communist infiltration of the armed services. Many people had been willing to overlook their discomfort with McCarthyism during the senator's campaign against government employees and others they saw as 'elites'; now, however, their support began to wane. Almost at once, the aura of invulnerability that had surrounded McCarthy for nearly five years began to disappear.

First, the Army undermined the senator's credibility by showing evidence that he had tried to win preferential treatment for his aides when they were drafted. Then came the fatal blow: the decision to broadcast the 'Army–McCarthy' hearings on national television. The American people watched as McCarthy intimidated witnesses and offered evasive responses when questioned. When he attacked a young Army lawyer, the Army's chief counsel thundered, 'Have you no sense of decency, sir?' The Army–McCarthy hearings struck many observers as a shameful moment in American politics.[4]

The wounds caused to American society by McCarthy's five-year campaign took many years to heal.

The use of post-fact argument is not limited to tyrants and demagogues. Apparently respectable politicians also find that going post-fact can be extremely useful sometimes. The election of Margaret Thatcher as UK Prime Minister in 1979 was at least partly due to a powerful message encapsulated in the slogan 'Labour isn't working', illustrated in an iconic poster (shown in Appendix II). In 1979, this was a fair point: unemployment had doubled under the Labour government, and a promise to tackle the problem was therefore politically powerful.

The course of UK unemployment in the post-war period is shown in the figure below:

Figure 27: UK unemployment rate

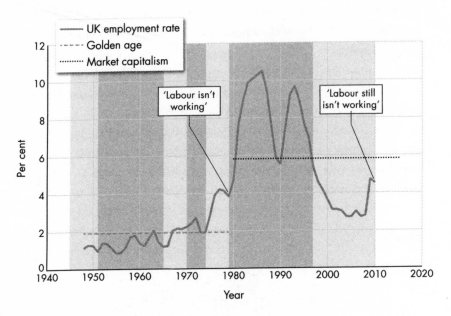

Source: ONS,[5] Political Science Resources[6]

The shading indicates which party was in government for each time period: dark grey for the Conservative Party and light grey for the Labour Party. As the chart shows, however, rather than *tackling* the problem of unemployment, the Tory party *more than doubled* it between 1979 and 1986. Unemployment then declined until 1990 – though it still did not reach as low a level as the Conservatives had inherited in 1979 – and then rose again until 1992, after which it again declined. The Conservatives never managed to return unemployment to the level that they had inherited.

It was not until 1999 – under the Labour government of Tony Blair – that unemployment finally recovered to the level that Margaret Thatcher had inherited. And it continued to decline until the Global Financial Crisis of 2008 caused the

Great Recession. Over the period 1981–2009, *every* year that unemployment was above the average was a year when the Conservative Party was in power and almost every year when unemployment was below the average was a year when Labour was in power. Even after the impact of the Global Financial Crisis, the rate of unemployment in 2010 was lower than Labour had inherited from the Conservatives.

Fact-based discussion of unemployment would suggest that the Conservative Party had no case in 2010 to criticize Labour on their record, but in the post-fact world they did so rather effectively, with the poster shown below.

Figure 28: Poster from the 2010 election campaign

Source: The Conservative Party Archive / Getty[7]

Had the electorate been aware of the facts shown in Figure 28 and understood the two parties' records on unemployment over the previous thirty years, this line of campaigning would have been ineffective.

It is not just the less-educated who engage in post-fact discussion

Much recent discussion in the media on going post-fact has focused on readers of the *Daily Mail*, viewers of Fox News and consumers of the sorts of social media posts cited below. The impression given is that the less-educated sections of society have gone post-fact and have stopped listening to the experts (who know what is going on). The vote for Brexit and the election of Donald Trump, according to this narrative, shows a large group of people voting against their own interests and against the advice of those who know better.

But this story is too simplistic and too convenient. While it is true that getting one's information from the *Daily Mail*, Fox News, Facebook or Twitter makes it very hard to stay in touch with reality, the elite have tended to live in their own information bubble – they have also gone post-fact.

The dominant narrative among the elite before, during and after the Global Financial Crisis highlights this bubble clearly. Before the crisis, most members of most sections of the Establishment, whether left wing or right wing, believed that, in general, the global economy was being well-run. Very few people warned of the problems inevitably growing because of the scale of global imbalances (trade surpluses and deficits between countries) and rising inequality within countries – although Wynne Godley did so and was generally ignored.[8] Very few warned about the dangers of house price bubbles – although Dean Baker did so and was generally ignored.[9] Very few accepted that there was a downside to globalization that needed to be managed – though Dani Rodrick did so and was generally ignored.[10]

Bankers, and those who regulated them, wanted to believe that modern approaches to risk management were sophisticated and robust – especially within the large banks – and that banks could safely be trusted to assess for themselves what level of capital buffer was required to keep them safe. In other words, markets know best and regulation should be kept to a minimum. As Alan Greenspan, the former Chairman of the US Federal Reserve, said after the crisis materialized:

> I made a mistake in presuming that the self-interest of organizations, specifically banks and others, were such that they were best capable of protecting their own shareholders. I have been dealing with the American economy for sixty years. That premise always worked and I was shocked into disbelief that what unfolded was a complete breakdown of that premise.[11]

In the UK, Hector Sants – who became Chief Executive of the then UK regulator the Financial Services Authority (FSA) in July 2007 – commented:

> The prevailing climate at the time and indeed right up till the crisis commenced was that the market does know best... The FSA didn't really look forward and didn't make judgments... if there's a risk of your business model running into difficulty we won't come and say to you 'you shouldn't be doing that'. The FSA was not a forward-looking organization in respect of business model risk.[12]

Politicians and economists generally believed that the growth in the economy was sustainable – many talked about the Great Moderation or the NICE decade.[13] Gordon Brown, then the Chancellor of the Exchequer in the UK, explained how the Labour Party had put an end to economic instability:

> Now, the essential first stage of our journey since 1997 has been to end damaging economic instability – to tackle the Tory boom and bust which served the interests of a privileged few but left millions insecure and worse off.[14]

During the early stages of the Global Financial Crisis, there was a strong tendency to view what was later described as 'the largest financial crisis of its type in human history'[15] as merely a little local difficulty which would soon be resolved. Ben Bernanke, then Chairman of the Federal Reserve, put it this way:

> … we believe the effect of the troubles in the subprime sector on the broader housing market will likely be limited, and we do not expect significant spill-overs from the subprime market to the rest of the economy or to the financial system.[16]

After the peak of the crisis, when such denial was no longer possible, Alan Greenspan explained that his free-market view of reality had been flawed:

> Well, remember what an ideology is, it is a conceptual framework with the way people deal with reality. Everyone has one. You have to – to exist, you need an ideology. The question is whether it is accurate or not. And what I'm saying to you is, yes, I found a flaw. I don't know how significant or permanent it is, but I've been very distressed by that fact.
> [I found a] Flaw in the model that I perceived as the critical functioning structure that defines how the world works, so to speak.[17]

This was remarkably honest – but it did not take long for the old narrative to reassert itself. Free-market economists started to rewrite the history of the crisis and banks began to push back hard against any attempt to regulate them more tightly. Eugene Fama, the Chicago economist, denied that there had been a housing bubble in the United States and suggested that the Great Recession (which followed the Global Financial Crisis) was caused by government efforts to save the banking sector, without which the knock-on effects of the crisis would only have lasted a week or two:

> The experiment we never ran is, suppose the government stepped aside and let these institutions fail. How long would it have taken to have unscrambled everything and figured everything out? My guess is that we are talking a week or two. But the problems that were generated by the government stepping in – those are going to be with us for the foreseeable future. Now, maybe it would have been horrendous if the government didn't step in, but we'll never know. I think we could have figured it out in a week or two. [The government should have] let them all fail. We let Lehman fail. We let Washington Mutual fail. These were big financial institutions. Some we didn't let fail. To me, it looks like there was not much rhyme or reason to it.[18]

In the real world, the insolvency process for Lehman Brothers was still not complete in 2015 – seven years after its failure.[19]

Bob Diamond, then chief executive of Barclays Bank, expressed his desire to get back to business as usual at a Parliamentary hearing in 2011:

> There was a period of remorse and apology [on the part of the Bankers]; that period needs to be over. We need

our banks willing to take risks, to be confident and to work with the private sector in the UK to create jobs and improve economic growth.[20]

Diamond warned MPs that any attempt on their part to constrain bankers' bonuses would lead the banks to relocate outside the UK: 'The other option is that you don't have investment banks located in the UK.'

We tend to think of post-fact in terms of outright falsehood, like the 'tweets' from the Mayor of Rayne cited below. Seeing these falsehoods peddled as truth makes the dangers of going post-fact obvious, but the subtler forms employed by the elite are at least equally dangerous. An elite that has gone post-fact and believes that markets always know best and bubbles never happen, that banks are overregulated, that globalization is an unalloyed good with no casualties, is dangerously out of touch with reality and with the suffering of significant numbers of its own population. And an elite that is out of touch with its own population has effectively gone rogue. The subtler forms of post-fact discourse pave the way for the gross forms.

A post-fact world is extremely dangerous

Good decisions depend on facts. A post-fact world is therefore extremely dangerous: rational political discussion becomes difficult, society becomes polarized and extremism can flourish.

RATIONAL POLITICS BECOMES DIFFICULT IN A POST-FACT WORLD

In Senator Moynihan's world, it is always possible to have a discussion with a political opponent: one agrees about the facts and then begins to discuss their implications. Where a difference of opinion emerges, more facts can be sought to help clarify the situation. Ultimately, the truth can prevail even if both sides must modify their positions. In this world, civil discussion is the norm, rational politics can be expected, and some degree of consensus is possible. In the absence of agreed facts – for example, when one side claims that globalization is the root of all problems while the other keeps repeating that it is good for the economy – this kind of rational debate is far more difficult.

Developments in the media, in particular social media, increase the risk of individuals constructing their own set of 'facts'. According to Caleb Gardner:

Forty-four per cent of US adults get news on the [Facebook] site, and 61 per cent of millennials… if that doesn't frighten you, you don't know enough about Facebook's algorithm. If you have a parent who's a Trump supporter, they are seeing a completely different set of news items than you are.[21]

The algorithm that worried Gardner also worried Eli Pariser, author of *The Filter Bubble: What The Internet Is Hiding From You*. As Pariser put it:

Democracy requires citizens to see things from one another's point of view, but instead we are more and more enclosed in our own bubbles. Democracy requires reliance on shared facts; instead we are being offered parallel but separate universes.

My sense of unease crystallized when I noticed that my conservative friends had disappeared from my Facebook page. Politically, I lean to the left, but I like to hear what conservatives are thinking, and I've gone out of my way to befriend a few as Facebook connections. I wanted to see what links they post, read their comments and learn a bit from them. But their links never turned up in my top news feed. Facebook was apparently doing the math and noticing that I was still clicking my progressive friends' links more than my conservative friends'... So no conservative links for me.[22]

Meanwhile, Hannah Kuchler, writing in the *Financial Times*, noted:

Facebook has long said it is a technology company, not a media company, using engineers to write algorithms that encourage people to read posts via its platform – rather than editors to curate stories with any traditional notion of balance and accuracy. It went even further this year when it closed the one team that exercised some editorial judgment, following pressure from right-wing commentators who accused the network of repressing conservative news.[23]

But it is not just Facebook: since 2009, Google's search engine has returned personalized search results. If you and I both search for the same term, we will not see the same results. We will not base our opinions on the same facts.

It now requires considerable personal effort *not* to live in a bubble, seeing only the opinions of those with whom we agree already. Furthermore, the ranking of search results does not reflect reliability, only popularity. At the time of writing, if I type 'did the' into the Google search engine, it suggests as the completion of my search, 'did the Holocaust happen?' If I then select this suggestion, the first search result shown is 'Top 10 reasons why the Holocaust didn't happen' on a neo-Nazi website called Stormfront.

Figure 29: Search results suggested after typing in 'did the'

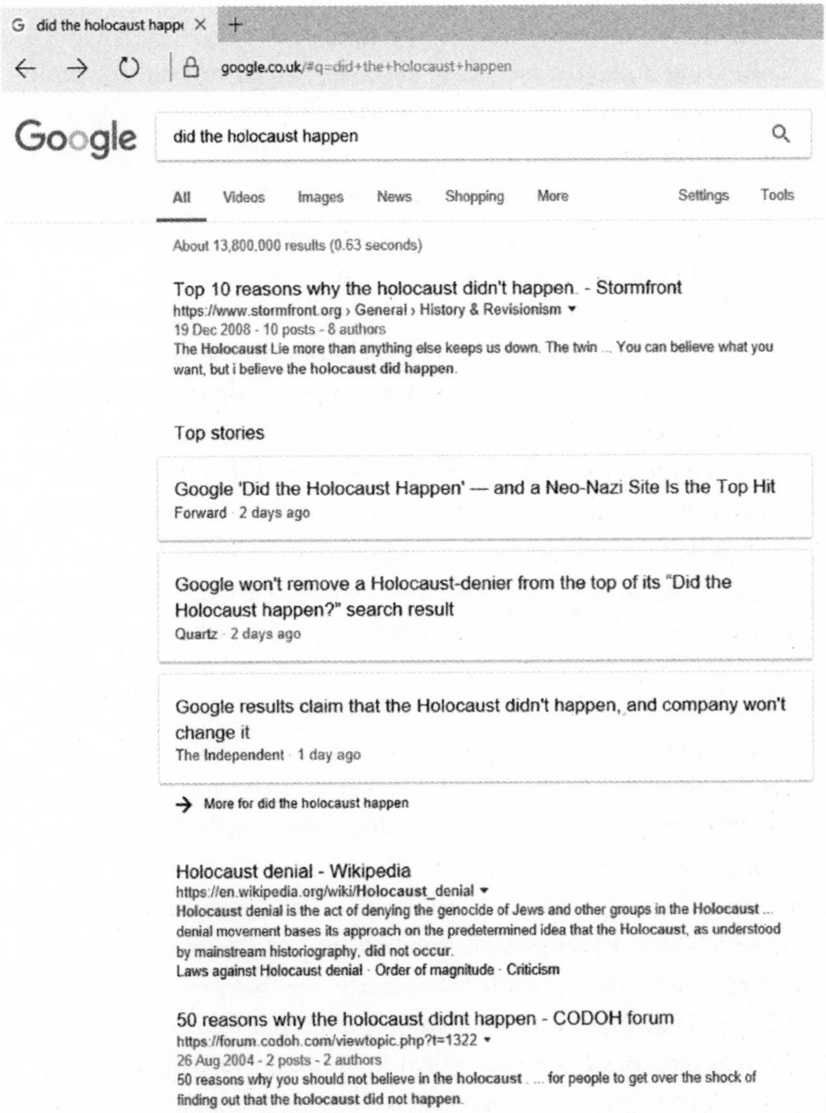

Source: Author's Google search

SOCIETY CAN BECOME DANGEROUSLY POLARIZED IN A POST-FACT WORLD

Without an agreed basis of fact, it is far harder to find common ground on which to begin any form of constructive discussion. As rational politics becomes more difficult, the points of consensus become fewer and further between. In a post-fact world, discussions across political divisions become a rarity and trading insults becomes the norm.

In this world, members of an opposing camp may be seen not as well-meaning people with different opinions, but as the enemy – and possibly even as criminal, evil or subhuman. The calls for Hillary Clinton to be jailed, which became loud and more strident during Donald Trump's 2016 presidential campaign, shocked many people (and delighted others) but they are a natural manifestation of a post-fact world.

The rise in religious and race hate crimes in the UK after the Brexit result[24] was equally shocking but may simply be a manifestation of the demonization of others that can so easily take place in a post-fact world.

EXTREMISM CAN MORE EASILY FLOURISH IN A POST-FACT WORLD

The historical examples of the persecution of the Jews under Hitler and the persecution of innocent US citizens during Joseph McCarthy's anti-communist campaign in the US illustrate what can happen when, in the words of Oxford Dictionaries, 'objective facts are less influential in shaping public opinion than appeals to emotion and personal belief'.

Post-fact politics thrive when a large group are left behind

2016 saw two political events that shocked large parts of the Establishment:

- the UK referendum on EU membership; and
- the US presidential election.

In both cases – regardless of the view that one takes on the respective outcomes – it is undeniable that mass impoverishment created a large class of people dissatisfied with the status quo, while post-fact political discussion was highly influential in directing their votes.

THE UK REFERENDUM ON EU MEMBERSHIP SHOWED THE POWER OF POST-FACT ARGUMENT WHEN THE ELITE ARE DIVIDED

A significant loss of confidence in traditional institutions manifested during the campaign leading up to the referendum on UK membership of the European Union. Possibly the most powerful argument made by the Leave campaign was encapsulated in their slogan, 'We send the EU £350 million every week. Let's fund our NHS instead.' After many commentators pointed out that leaving the EU would *not* free up £350 million per week for the NHS, and the Leave campaign nevertheless continued to stick to their claim, the UK Statistics Authority felt obliged to go on record in an attempt to debunk the assertion:

> Given the high level of public interest in the European Union referendum debate, it is vital that official statistics

are used accurately, with important caveats and limitations explained. The UK Statistics Authority is disappointed to note that there continue to be suggestions that the UK contributes £350 million to the EU each week, and that this full amount could be spent elsewhere... The continued use of a gross figure in contexts that imply it is a net figure is misleading and undermines trust in official statistics.[25]

But misleading arguments did not only come from the Leave side. Discussion on immigration has for many years focused on the impact on the economy as a whole (the size of the pie) rather than considering the impact on individuals (the way the pie is sliced). These points from the OECD are typical:[26]

Benefit or burden – what's the reality? To answer this question, it can be helpful to look at migration's impact in three areas – the labour market, the public purse and economic growth:

Labour markets:

- Migrants accounted for 47 per cent of the increase in the workforce in the United States and 70 per cent in Europe over the past ten years.
- Migrants fill important niches both in fast-growing and declining sectors of the economy.
- Like the native-born, young migrants are better educated than those nearing retirement.
- Migrants contribute significantly to labour-market flexibility, notably in Europe.

The public purse:

- Migrants contribute more in taxes and social contributions than they receive in benefits.
- Labour migrants have the most positive impact on the public purse.
- Employment is the single biggest determinant of migrants' net fiscal contribution.

Economic growth:

- Migration boosts the working-age population.
- Migrants arrive with skills and contribute to human capital development of receiving countries.
- Migrants also contribute to technological progress.

These points are true but, as a summary of the impact of migration, they are incomplete to the point of being misleading. In December 2015, Stephen Nickell and Jumana Saleheen of the Bank of England published a working paper that concluded:

We find that the immigrant-to-native ratio has a small negative impact on average British wages. This finding is important for monetary policy makers, who are interested in the impact that supply shocks, such as immigration, have on average wages and overall inflation. Our results also reveal that the biggest impact of immigration on wages is within the semi/unskilled services occupational group.[27]

In other words, while it may be true that immigration is good for the economy, it is *not* true that it is good for everybody working within that economy and, in particular, not for those within the semi/unskilled services occupational group.

Many people in this group felt that the elite was ignoring their predicament, and they were prepared to vote for radical change on that basis. This tendency to deny the issue of mass impoverishment has created a large group distrustful of the elite, resentful of their policies, desperate for change and prepared to vote in ways that might have seemed beyond the pale even a decade ago.

Michael Gove, who was at the time Secretary of State for Justice in the Conservative government and a prominent member of the Leave campaign, was asked how he could be confident that Brexit would be a success in the face of so many countries, institutions and individuals warning that Brexit would damage the British economy. The list included India, China, the US, the Bank of England, the International Monetary Fund, the Confederation of British Industry, the Institute for Fiscal Studies, the chief executive of the National Health Service and leaders of several trade unions.[28] Gove simply dismissed them *en masse*: 'I think the people in this country have had enough of experts... from organizations with acronyms saying that they know what is best.' The results suggest that Michael Gove may have been right on this point – a significant proportion of the population no longer believed the messages coming from the elite.

THE US PRESIDENTIAL ELECTION SHOWED THE POWER OF POST-FACT ARGUMENT EVEN IN THE FACE OF A UNITED ELITE

The election of Donald Trump as President of the United States was a shock to many people, even in the Republican Party. One aspect of the campaign that was particularly surprising was that despite fact-checkers in mainstream media pointing out that many of Trump's claims were unfounded, and despite a clear majority of these mainstream media and indeed several senior Republicans declaring their support for Hillary Clinton, Trump emerged as the winner. As Joshua Benton, head of the Nieman Journalism Laboratory at Harvard, pointed out:

> A clear indicator of the breadth of negative coverage of Trump is the distribution of newspaper and magazine endorsements of both candidates. Hillary Clinton was endorsed by 229 dailies and 131 weeklies, including news organizations that historically have not been identified with either party and others clearly representing a conservative ideology normally linked to Republican candidates. By contrast, Trump received the endorsement of 9 dailies and 4 weeklies. That's a 27-to-1 difference.
>
> Although counterfactuals are always difficult to evaluate, I think it's reasonable to argue that, for instance, during the second half of the twentieth century, even a fraction of this negative coverage would have been enough to seriously damage the chances of a presidential candidate, and maybe even derail the candidacy altogether. [29]

Clearly, mainstream – traditional – media did not swing the US election. But maybe social media did. Joshua Benton hails from Rayne, a small town in Louisiana whose mayor posted on Facebook in the last forty-eight hours of the presidential campaign: 'Hillary Clinton Calling for Civil War if Trump Is Elected'; 'Pope Francis Shocks World, Endorses Donald Trump for President'; 'Barack Obama Admits He Was Born in Kenya'; and 'FBI Agent Who Was Suspected of Leaking Hillary's Corruption Is Dead'.[30] The story of the Pope's endorsement had been shared 868,000 times on Facebook, notes Benton, while the relevant debunking article on the fact-checking website, Snopes, had at the time been shared only around 33,000 times.

In America, even more than in the UK, a large group who have been left behind by the policies of both main national parties and ignored by mainstream media showed that they were prepared to vote in ways that defied most predictions. But their votes made perfect sense in the context of their desperation with the status quo and the information available within their bubble.

As Mark Carney, Governor of the Bank of England put it when describing the effects of globalization:

> Despite such immense progress, many citizens in advanced economies are facing heightened uncertainty, lamenting a loss of control and losing trust in the system. To them, measures of aggregate progress bear little relation to their own experience. Rather than a new golden era, globalization is associated with low wages, insecure employment, stateless corporations and striking inequalities.[31]

In other words, observing that the pie is bigger matters little to people whose own slices have become smaller.

The elite are waking up to the dangers of a post-fact world

Recent events in the US and the UK have caused ripples well beyond their national borders. The French ambassador to the US, already shocked by the Brexit decision, responded to the US presidential election result by tweeting: 'After Brexit and this election, everything is now possible. A world is collapsing before our eyes. Dizziness.'[32] He was not alone in his concern. Many senior politicians are worried about the implications of going post-fact, as are leading academics and, indeed, even social media outlets too.

POLITICIANS ARE CONCERNED

In both the US and Europe, politicians are becoming increasingly concerned about the post-fact world in general and, in particular, the tendency to create information bubbles that give individuals a very partial view. The German Chancellor, Angela Merkel, has expressed her concerns about the role of search engines and related algorithms in creating information bubbles:

> This is a development that we need to pay careful attention to... The big internet platforms, via their algorithms, have become an eye of a needle, which diverse media must pass through to reach users... These algorithms, when they are not transparent, can lead to a distortion of our perception. They narrow our breadth of information.[33]

President Obama commented, in the wake of the 2016 US presidential election and in the context of the role of the media:

> If we are not serious about facts and what's true and what's not, and particularly in an age of social media when so many people are getting their information in sound bites and off their phones, if we can't discriminate between serious arguments and propaganda, then we have problems.[34]

ACADEMICS ARE CONCERNED

Cambridge University has recently announced the formation of a new Centre for Risk and Evidence Communication, to be hosted within the Faculty of Mathematics. The aim of the centre is to ensure that relevant facts on important issues are presented accurately and transparently. Professor Sir David Spiegelhalter – Winton Professor for the Public Understanding of Risk, and Chair of the new Centre's Executive Board – said:

> We reject claims that we live in a 'post-truth' society, and that people are fed up with experts. We do acknowledge, however, that the public, professionals and policy-makers are often ill-served by the way in which evidence is communicated. We hope to work with others to improve how this is done, and empower people to make informed decisions that reflect both existing scientific evidence and their personal values.[35]

If anything, he underestimates the scale of his challenge.

SOCIAL MEDIA OUTLETS THEMSELVES ARE CONCERNED

The prevalence of fake news stories has itself become big news. As Gardiner Harris and Melissa Eddy wrote in the *New York Times*, both Facebook and Google have announced that they plan to take steps to address the issue:

> Facebook and Google, which has also faced mounting criticism over distribution of fake stories on its platforms, said this week that they would take aim at the fake news sites' online sources of revenue.[36]

Meanwhile, Google's chief executive, Sundar Pichai, has committed to driving up the quality of news his company provides:

> I don't think we should debate it as much as work hard to make sure we drive news to its more trusted sources, have more fact checking and make our algorithms work better, absolutely.[37]

This widespread concern and, even more so, evidence of action is heartening. It will, however, take concerted efforts on a range of fronts to address the underlying problem. There is a natural tendency to drift towards becoming post-fact and reversing direction will be difficult.

There are powerful incentives to drift to the post-fact end of the spectrum

Being post-fact or being factual is not a binary choice: there is a spectrum of reliability. Unfortunately, this makes it easy to drift towards the post-fact end of the spectrum – especially since there are forces operating both on commercial media and on politicians that tend to encourage a move in that direction. Furthermore, it is difficult to reverse the process of going post-fact at the individual level – once people have adopted a post-fact mindset, they tend to reject evidence that might change their minds.

THERE IS A SPECTRUM OF RELIABILITY

Figure 30, below, illustrates a spectrum of reliability from absolute truth on the left-hand side to unfounded falsehood on the right-hand side.

Figure 30: The spectrum of reliability

Fact		
	Absolute truth	Approximate truth
Definition	True without reservation and demonstrable by experiment or logical reasoning	Broadly true and not misleading – but there will be exceptions
Example	'The world is not flat' 'There are no integers a,b for which $a^2/b^2 = 2$'	'Immigration is good for the economy as a whole, but for unskilled and semi-skilled workers there is a small negative impact'
	Research in hard sciences and mathematics	Research in soc

		Post-fact
Spin	Deliberate misrepresentation	Unfounded falsehood
Does not contain outright falsehoods, but facts are presented in such a way as to be misleading	Comment may be based on real-world events but reporting is not factual and is deliberately misleading	No real-world basis – simply an attempt to manipulate opinion without regard to truth
'Migration has a positive impact in three areas – the labour market, the public purse and economic growth'	'Every week we send the EU £350 million which could be used to fund our NHS instead'	'Pope Francis shocks world, endorses Donald Trump for President'

ences and economics

Mainstream media

Political discussion

Social media

THERE ARE COMMERCIAL REASONS FOR MASS MEDIA TO MOVE TO THE POST-FACT END OF THE SPECTRUM

The left-hand end of the spectrum – absolute truth – is difficult to find outside of mathematics and the hard sciences. Even there, it requires great skill and enormous effort to unearth a new truth.

As soon as the behaviour of people comes into question, the best that can be done – again with great skill and enormous effort – is to find approximate truth. One also has to struggle against one's own biases and prejudices to remain at this end of the spectrum. The result is that approximate truth is often complex, drily worded and heavily caveated – and has little rhetorical power.

The right-hand end of the spectrum, by contrast, requires neither research nor checking. It enables one to give full rein to one's own biases and prejudices, and has far greater emotional appeal (at least to the target audience). In short, it is rhetorically enormously powerful. It seems that Yeats was right: the worst *are* full of passionate intensity, and the best do lack all conviction.[38]

Since rebutting falsehoods requires those who wish to rebut to operate at the left-hand end of the spectrum, they will struggle to put in the effort to rebut large numbers of false claims. And even if they do so, the appeal of their rebuttal will be limited. This alone makes it difficult for mass or social media to operate successfully at the left-hand end of the spectrum.

THERE ARE ALSO STRONG INCENTIVES FOR POLITICIANS TO GO POST-FACT

The ability of those who operate towards the right-hand end of the spectrum to appeal to emotions is extremely seductive to politicians. Very few people vote after a painstaking analysis of policies and their likely impact; many more vote according to their feeling about a particular politician or party. As Ron Suskind put it in the *New York Times*:

> That was explained to me in late 2002 by Mark McKinnon, a long-time senior media adviser to Bush... He started by challenging me. 'You think he's an idiot, don't you?' I said, no, I didn't. 'No, you do, all of you do, up and down the West Coast, the East Coast, a few blocks in southern Manhattan called Wall Street. Let me clue you in. We don't care. You see, you're outnumbered 2 to 1 by folks in the big, wide middle of America, busy working people who don't read the *New York Times* or *Washington Post* or the *L.A. Times*. And you know what they like? They like the way he walks and the way he points, the way he exudes confidence. They have faith in him. And when you attack him for his malaprops, his jumbled syntax, it's good for us. Because you know what those folks don't like? They don't like you!' In this instance, the final 'you', of course, meant the entire reality-based community.[39]

Being fact-based, for a politician, has the minor advantage that they will not be held to account by fact-checkers (and the ability of both the Brexit campaign and the Trump campaign to shrug off criticism by fact-checkers demonstrates quite how minor this advantage is). The huge *dis*advantage is that it makes it more difficult to connect to large segments of the population. Putting on a good show and connecting with the voters is a far better bet than being painstakingly correct.

It is hard to reverse direction

Moreover, at the individual level, it is not easy to reverse direction. Paradoxically, once someone has committed to a belief that runs counter to the facts, the act of being exposed to these facts typically does not prompt them to change their views but tends to *reinforce* their belief. Presenting the facts, in other words, can backfire. Research by Brendan Nyhan and Jason Reifler – of the University of Michigan and Georgia State University, respectively – found that:

> In each of the four experiments, which were conducted in fall 2005 and spring 2006, ideological subgroups failed to update their beliefs when presented with corrective information that runs counter to their predispositions. Indeed, in several cases, we find that corrections actually strengthened misperceptions among the most strongly committed subjects.[40]

In other words, fact-checkers will have little or no impact on a population which has gone post-fact.

We are not living in a completely post-fact world, nor even in a world where the facts are difficult to obtain. We are, however, in a world in which much political discussion, and media reporting of that discussion, takes place at or near the post-fact end of the spectrum. Many voters – and indeed policymakers – are exposed to post-fact versions of the truth and, as a result, many important decisions relating to politics and economics are not based on the facts.

CHAPTER 9

Myths and Metaphors

Science must begin with myths, and with the criticism of myths.

Karl Popper[1]

This chapter explores the extent to which our thinking about the economy is constrained by myths and metaphors with no basis in fact. If we internalize them, it becomes easy to confuse them with reality – and extremely difficult to evaluate or even to see alternatives. Indeed, some of these myths and metaphors are so well established that it can feel rather shocking even to consider that they might not be true.

Myths are all around but we often take them as fact

There are statements that we have all heard so often that we assume they must represent reality, and therefore form safe ground on which to base our economic judgements. Unfortunately, many of these are simply not factually based.

Seven of the most commonly circulated myths are:

- the private sector is always more efficient than government;
- America is the land of opportunity;
- only the private sector can create jobs;
- money can't just come from nowhere;
- governments should follow the same economic guidelines as households and businesses;
- if your wages are falling, it is because you don't have the right skills;
- there simply isn't enough to go around (the myth of scarcity).

These myths are so widespread that it is difficult to entertain even the possibility that they might not be true – and it takes a certain amount of intellectual courage to be guided by the facts.

MYTH #1: THE PRIVATE SECTOR IS ALWAYS MORE EFFICIENT THAN GOVERNMENT

It is a commonplace observation that large government departments are highly bureaucratic, often slow-moving and that inefficiency lurks in every corner.

This is probably true: almost all large organizations are highly bureaucratic, slow-moving and, to some extent, inefficient. In the UK, for example, the NHS is often criticized for inefficient practices, and there is constant effort to modernize and increase efficiency. This is quite correct and constant effort to improve is required. It would be quite wrong, however, to conclude that the NHS is inefficient relative to other large healthcare systems, and in particular relative to the essentially private sector healthcare system of the United States.

The OECD compiles data on healthcare expenditures per person in a range of countries, comparing them with healthcare outcomes such as life expectancy at birth.[2] On this basis of comparison, the most efficient healthcare system in the world is that of Japan, which gets very good healthcare outcomes for less than US$5,000 per head. The majority of developed countries get good to very good outcomes for about US$4,000 to US$6,000 per head. The UK spends around US$4,000 per head but the US achieves relatively poor outcomes for a cost of over US$10,000 per head.

Most other bases of comparison show a similar result: the NHS always comes out as at least a reasonable performer – and occasionally a very strong performer – whereas the US system almost always comes out as a very poor performer. This does not prove that the public sector is always – or even usually – more efficient than the private sector, but it is conclusive evidence that it *can* be, even in large and important industry sectors such as healthcare. It is simply not the case, in other words, that the private sector is always more efficient than government.

MYTH #2: AMERICA IS THE LAND OF OPPORTUNITY

The American Dream was defined by James Truslow Adams in his book, *The Epic of America*, as:

> ... that dream of a land in which life should be better and richer and fuller for everyone, with opportunity for each according to ability or achievement. It is a difficult dream for the European upper classes to interpret adequately, and too many of us ourselves have grown weary and mistrustful of it. It is not a dream of motor cars and high wages merely, but a dream of social order in which each

man and each woman shall be able to attain to the fullest stature of which they are innately capable, and be recognized by others for what they are, regardless of the fortuitous circumstances of birth or position.[3]

This vision, of a meritocratic society in which attainment is based on innate capabilities rather than the fortuitous circumstances of birth and position, has been a powerful motivating force. The promise of upward mobility is one of the reasons why people have, for so long, been keen to immigrate into the United States, and it continues to be held by politicians to be one of the great strengths of the USA. The table below shows the facts relating to upward mobility in a selection of OECD countries.

Figure 31: Upwards mobility in different countries

Country	Earnings mobility
Denmark	85%
Australia	84%
Norway	83%
Finland	82%
Canada	81%
Sweden	73%
Germany	68%
Spain	68%
France	59%
United States	53%
Italy	52%
United Kingdom	50%

Source: OECD[4]

Of the selected countries, the lowest level of earnings mobility is to be found in the UK. In other words, in the UK your parents' income has a bigger impact on your own ability to earn than in any of the other countries. A vastly higher level of mobility exists in Denmark, Austria, Norway and Finland. Canada is very close to these highly mobile countries, whereas the United States has almost as little mobility as the UK.

The American dream is alive and well, but is now living in Denmark.

MYTH #3: ONLY THE PRIVATE SECTOR CAN CREATE JOBS

There is a widely held belief that 'government cannot create jobs'. While no one would deny that there are such things as government jobs, those who hold this belief typically argue either that they are not proper jobs, or else that for every job created in the public sector, one or more will be lost in the private sector.

The first argument relies on the power of the market to determine what constitutes a proper job. As the conservative economist Tyler Cowen put it:

> People who work in government, healthcare and education just aren't that worried about foreign competitors or even outsourcing.
>
> That security in these non-tradable sectors is nice for many of us, but it also means that people in most newly created jobs in the United States aren't facing so much of a daily market test. Most of our job growth is coming in what I call low accountability sectors. People get paid to produce things, or offer services, and we are never quite sure how much value they are putting on the table. The

value they produce, or the lack thereof, is never subject to much of a market test. Of course that may not augur well for our ability to upgrade our future productivity, even if today a lot of these workers are producing fairly valuable goods and services.[5]

The implication is that jobs that face a daily test of market value are proper jobs, while those that don't are not. Specifically, he says civil servants, doctors, nurses and teachers are not really subject to a daily test of market value – and implicitly, therefore, we should doubt whether they really are providing value to society.

Conversely, although he does not say this, those who worked in banks packaging subprime mortgages and finding clever ways of persuading the rating agencies to grade them triple-A so that they could be bought by pension funds did face a daily test of market value. Similarly, those who find creative new ways to market tobacco products in the face of ever more stringent government regulation face the same daily test, as do pornographers. You may feel that teachers, doctors, nurses, firefighters and police officers do more good for society than reckless financiers, tobacco marketers and pornographers. But those who apply the sophisticated tests of modern economics apparently know better.

The second argument is subtler but more plausible. One could accept that government is capable of creating valuable jobs but still believe that it should not do so because if it did not, the private sector would more than fill the gap. This is a specific case of the more general argument that government spending 'crowds out' private sector spending. This crowding-out can either be direct, or indirect. An example of direct crowding-out might be, for example, when the government hires someone into the civil service, and consequently that person cannot be hired by the private sector for any other purpose, however beneficial. At times of full employment, this crowding-out could be a real phenomenon. At times of mass unemployment or underemployment, it is far less plausible.

Indirect crowding-out (sometimes known as Ricardian equivalence) happens when individuals or businesses observe increased government spending (which inevitably results from increased hiring) and deduce that, sooner or later, the additional spending will be recouped via higher taxes. As a result, they cut back on expenditure as a precautionary measure.

The IMF looked at this very issue in 2013 in a working paper by its chief economist, Olivier Blanchard, and his colleague, Daniel Leigh.[6] Their research investigated the relationship between austerity and growth forecasting. The key finding related to 'fiscal multipliers'. (A fiscal multiplier determines the impact of change in government spending on GDP. If the multiplier is 1.1, then GDP will increase by $1.10 for every additional dollar of public spending. Conversely, a $1 dollar decrease in public spending will result in a $1.10 decrease in GDP.) If these multipliers are zero or below, that would support the argument for indirect crowding-out: public sector austerity results in a more-than-offsetting loosening of private sector purse strings. If the multiplier is between zero and 1, there is a partial off-setting from the private sector but the total impact of reduced spending is still negative. If the multiplier is greater than 1, then reduced public spending can actually damage private sector spending.

Further work at the IMF concluded, after an extensive review of research in the area, that in time of recession the multipliers are in fact greater than 1, especially if interest rates are close to zero.[7] In other words, increased public sector spending actually boosts the private sector, while austerity harms the private sector – the reverse of Ricardian equivalence.

The evidence is clear: at least in recessionary times, crowding-out (both direct and indirect) is a myth. Government *can* create jobs.

MYTH #4: MONEY DOESN'T COME FROM NOWHERE

In 2013, the British Prime Minister, David Cameron, rejected calls from his Business Secretary, Vince Cable, for increased government spending to kick-start the UK's struggling economy with the argument that 'there is no magic money tree'.[8]

Of course, in the strictly literal sense that there is no tree on which money grows, what David Cameron said was true. On the assumption, however, that he was speaking figuratively, and that what he meant was that money can't simply be created out of nothing, then his comment bore no relationship to the reality of the economy over which he presided.

First, and most obviously, the Bank of England has the power to create money out of nothing and indeed has done so – in the form of so-called quantitative easing – to the tune of £375 billion.[9] That is over four times the total budget of the NHS. As the Bank of England explained:

> The Bank of England electronically creates new money and uses it to purchase gilts from private investors such as pension funds and insurance companies... Quantitative easing [QE] was first used by the MPC [Monetary Policy Committee of the Bank of England] in March 2009.

In other words, the Bank of England absolutely has the power – and exercised its power when it wanted to avoid under-shooting the inflation target – to create money out of nothing (and without even the expense of printing banknotes). In fact, the then Governor of the Bank of England, Mervyn King, explained in 2009 in the aftermath of the Global Financial Crisis:

> The sheer scale of support to the banking sector is breath-taking. In the UK, in the form of direct or guaranteed loans and equity investment, it is not far short of a trillion (that is, one thousand billion) pounds, close to two-thirds of the annual output of the entire economy.
>
> To paraphrase a great wartime leader, never in the field of financial endeavour has so much money been owed by so few [the banks] to so many [the UK population].[10]

The Bank of England could and did – quite quickly and easily – create almost £1 trillion when it wished to save the banking system. However, politicians of all parties continue to assure us that there is no money available for hospitals and flood defences. But government and Central Bank money-creation is only the first and most obvious way that money can be created out of nothing. There is also a less obvious, but far more important, way: private sector banks create money.

As Michael McLeay, Amar Radia and Ryland Thomas of the Bank of England's Monetary Analysis Directorate explained, in a society like the UK that operates a *fiat* currency:

> In the modern economy, most money takes the form of bank deposits. But how those bank deposits are created is often misunderstood: the principal way is through commercial banks making loans. Whenever a bank makes a loan, it simultaneously creates a matching deposit in the borrower's bank account, thereby creating new money.[11]

As their paper makes clear, 97 per cent of the money in circulation is in the form of bank deposits – which are essentially IOUs from commercial banks to households and companies; only 3 per cent are in the form of currency. Most of this 97 per cent is created by the banks themselves, and as the Bank of England explains, it is created out of nothing.

The idea that money cannot come from nothing is therefore not only technically incorrect but also bears *no relationship* to the practical day-to-day reality of a modern economy. Of course, the fact that it is *possible* to create money out of nothing – and indeed that we have done it in the UK and the US when it was needed to give a boost to the economy – does not imply that it would *at all times* be the right policy. At some level of money creation, inflation would become a problem, so unlimited creation of money is not a panacea. But it is shocking for the head of the UK government to assert that money creation is impossible and that there is no alternative to a programme of austerity during a deep recession.

MYTH #5: GOVERNMENTS SHOULD FOLLOW THE SAME ECONOMIC GUIDELINES AS HOUSEHOLDS AND BUSINESSES

What every Swabian housewife knows has famously been used by Angela Merkel as a basis for determining how to run a major international bank or to formulate economic policy in the Eurozone.[12] Many others have used households as a convenient and easily communicated analogy for a national economy. Unfortunately, while it may be convenient – especially for those looking for arguments to slash government spending – it is not a good analogy.

There are numerous differences between a national government and a household or business. Of these, some are truly fundamental. The first is, of course, that governments – at least those that still have their own central bank such as the US and the UK – can create money out of nothing when appropriate. Households and businesses cannot. Even Swabian housewives might manage their budgets somewhat differently if they had a printing press in the basement.

The second relates to the applicability at the national level of popular rules-of-thumb associated with household budgeting. That you should cut your coat according to your cloth, or live within your means, for example. The idea, in short, that when times are tough the solution is to cut expenditure and reduce borrowing. Unfortunately for fans of such rules-of-thumb, national and global economies are more complex than household finances.

This can be demonstrated relatively simply. Any financial transaction has two ends, and the values at the two ends cancel out. If I pay you US$100, that is +$100 for you and -$100 for me and the total is zero. One person's expenditure is another person's income and *vice versa*.

From a householder's perspective, cutting expenditure may be a sensible and effective policy when managing the household finances. The household does not feel the pain of the external party who loses income as a result. But if society collectively decides to 'cut our spending' – sensible as it may sound – society loses overall as income is cut overall by exactly the same amount (although, of course, there are inevitably some winners and some losers from such a policy).

For society as a whole, the *only* way incomes can rise is if expenditures also rise. As economists say, 'each person's expenditure is someone else's income'. In fact, all economic activity is nothing more than a series of financial transactions. The two sides of each transaction add up to zero. Therefore, the total amount of economic activity in any economic system will add up to zero (considering both sides of each transaction).

We can think of a national economy as having three main sectors. Two domestic sectors – the government and the private sector – and one foreign sector, representing trade with the rest of the world. Taken together, the total economic activity must add up to zero. It is, however, possible for individual sectors to be positive or negative (i.e. to be in deficit or surplus), providing the total still adds up to zero.

A surplus means that a sector is spending less than its income and is using the difference to increase its savings (or pay down debt). A deficit indicates that a sector is spending more than its income by eating into its savings (or by borrowing more, if it is already in debt). So, for example, if the government sector is running a deficit (i.e. government spending is greater than government revenue in the form of taxation – a budget deficit) and the foreign sector is running a surplus (i.e. imports are greater than exports), the private sector may be running a surplus or deficit depending on the relative size of the other two deficits, as long as the total of the three balances (surpluses/deficits) sums to zero.

Usually, we consider the foreign sector from the perspective of our own domestic economy. So a foreign surplus (from the foreign party's perspective) is a trade deficit from *our* domestic perspective. Since the total of the three balances must sum to zero, if the government is running a surplus and there is a trade deficit (which is the same as a foreign surplus), then there *has* to be a private sector deficit.

This is borne out by historical data from the US economy, as shown below. Remember, in all years the sum of the three balances equals zero. There have been years in which the private sector has been in surplus, and there have been years in which the private sector has been in deficit. There have been years in which the government has been in surplus, and years when it has been in deficit. There have been years when the current account balance (i.e. foreign trade) is in surplus, and years of deficit. What has *never* happened, because it cannot happen, is a year in which both the government sector and the private sector are in surplus while the current account is in deficit.

Figure 32: Sectoral balances in the US over time

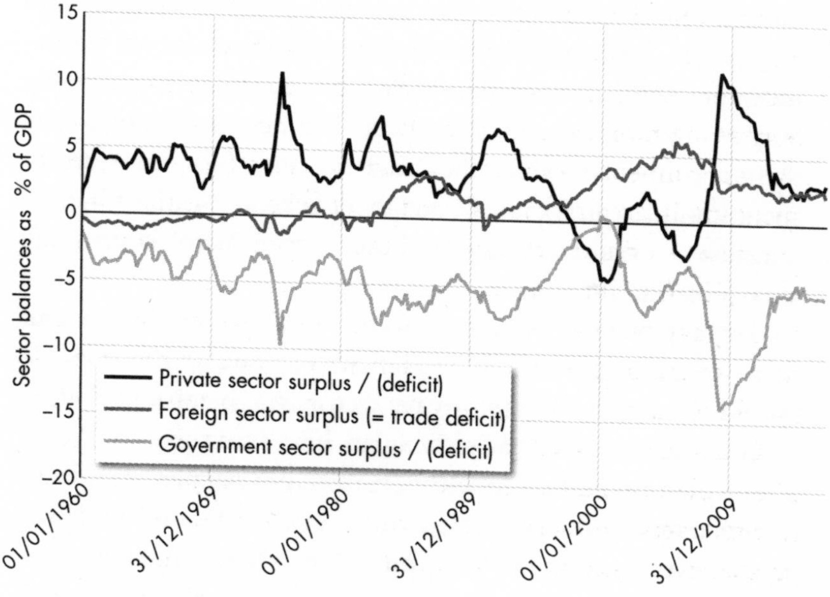

Source: FRED[13]

As you can see, the private sector is usually in surplus and the government sector usually in deficit – they roughly mirror each other. In recent years the US has run a trade deficit – i.e. the foreign sector has run a surplus with the US. And the three sectors always sum to zero. These observations are also true of the UK economy.

For the global system – since we do not have interplanetary trade – there is no foreign trade element. Therefore, the private sector and government sector must balance each other if they are to add up to zero. If we assume the private sector runs as prudently as the Swabian housewife would like (i.e. in surplus), governments must necessarily run a deficit.

Taking the national economies of the US and UK, a stubbornly persistent trade deficit means that running a budget surplus would condemn the private sector to a persistent deficit. Yet, politicians and economic policymakers still propagate the myth that we should run the economy in the same way as a household should manage its finances. Householders should only spend what they earn so, therefore, the government should similarly avoid budget deficits and aim for budget surpluses – even though such a policy acts against establishing a sustainable economy.

For national governments – such as those of the US and UK – to set policy on the basis of what a Swabian housewife would do condemns the private sector to a persistent deficit, with all the results that a Swabian housewife would expect from running a deficit. For this reason, government surpluses are relatively rare and are usually swiftly followed by slowdown or recession. The diagram below shows this reality in post-war Britain – there were recessions in 1975, 1980 and 1990, while the dot.com bubble burst in 2000 causing a serious slowdown.

Figure 33: UK history of government borrowing

Source: ONS[14]

Of the 234 quarters shown in the graph above, the government borrowed in 200 of them (85 per cent of the time). In Margaret Thatcher's 46 quarters in power, the government borrowed in 39 (85 per cent of the time). The reality is that government borrowing is not an anomaly, it is the norm. And it is so for a very good reason – for the government to run a persistent surplus, unless there is also a trade surplus, the private sector will have to run a deficit. As every Swabian housewife knows, that is no way to run an economy.

MYTH #6: YOU JUST NEED THE RIGHT SKILLS

'It is a truth universally acknowledged that the UK is facing a technical skills shortage,' claimed Madeline Bennett, writing in the *Daily Telegraph* about the UK's supposed STEM (Science,

Technology, Engineering and Mathematics) skills shortage. It is a claim that is so often repeated that it *seems* universally acknowledged – and it might be tempting to assume that it is the truth.[15]

Apparently, the US has the same problem:

> It should be well-accepted that the US economy could use more workers with high levels of knowledge in science, technology, engineering and mathematics. The shortage of these skilled STEM professionals eased during the recession, but by any conventional definition, now it appears to have returned.[16]

But let's just take a moment to look at the facts. If it were really true that there was a desperate shortage of people with STEM skills, it would be reflected in their wages. Even if waiters and bar staff might have to accept falling wages, we would see scientists, IT professionals and engineers enjoying healthy wage growth. But in reality, we do not see this.[17] What we do see is that those with STEM skills have seen their real wages declining more slowly than bar staff – but decline they have.

Having the 'right' skills is better than having the wrong ones but it is no defence against the threat of mass impoverishment.

MYTH #7: THE MYTH OF SCARCITY

We hear and read so much about scarcity that it is difficult to remember that society as a whole is continuing to get richer. As we saw in Chapter 0, the value of goods and services that have been created and are available to be consumed by society as a whole in any given year is measured by GDP. The 'size of the pie' – the amount available for each person to consume –

is measured by GDP per capita. Despite constant talk of the need for government cuts and the reality that many people are becoming poorer year after year, the fact is that the pie continues to grow (as we saw in Figure 15). In both the US and the UK, the pie is almost twice as big as it was in 1980. Despite the enormous damage to the economy caused by the Global Financial Crisis, both countries have recovered and – per person, if it were shared that way – they are *richer now than they have ever been.*

Money has not become scarce. Most people are just not seeing any of it. Incredibly, if we sliced the pie in the same way as we did in 1980, most people would be almost twice as well off today (even after adjusting for inflation) as they were in 1980. The myth of scarcity is a post-fact masterpiece. It makes it feel inevitable that government cuts should continue indefinitely and prevents us seeing the injustice and avoidability of mass impoverishment.

We have explored seven myths about the economy. Seven commonly cited notions – especially by politicians – which they often talk about as though they were unarguably true. In fact, as the data show, they are unarguably false. The fact that these myths persist has a hugely damaging impact on policy formulation, and on the lives of millions of people.

Metaphors are often taken literally

There are also phrases that we use as though we are describing reality, when to take these phrases literally would make little sense. Familiarity with these metaphors can mean, however, that we fail to see that they are metaphors. Subconsciously, we feel as if they are describing reality – or at least a desirable future reality.

Three widely used metaphors, with particular power to shape our thinking, are: the concept of the invisible hand of market forces; the notion of free markets; and the idea of economic laws.

METAPHOR #1: THE INVISIBLE HAND OF MARKET FORCES

We owe the concept of the invisible hand of market forces to Adam Smith and his book, *An Enquiry into the Nature and Causes of the Wealth of Nations*.[18] In a much-cited passage, Smith says:

> As every individual, therefore, endeavours as much as he can, both to employ his capital in support of domestic industry, and so to direct that industry that its produce may be of greatest value; every individual necessarily labours to render the annual revenue of the society as great as he can. He generally, indeed, neither intends to promote public interest, nor knows how much he is promoting it. By preferring the support of domestic to that of foreign industry, he intends only his own security; and by directing that industry in such a manner as its produce may be of greatest value he intends only his own gain; and he is in this, as in many other cases, led by an invisible hand to promote an end which was no part of his intention. Nor is it always the worse for the society that it was no part of it. By pursuing his own interest, he frequently promotes that of the society more effectually than when he really intends to promote it.

The invisible hand of market forces is self-evidently a metaphor – nobody, not even the members of the Adam Smith

Society, believes that there is a literal 'invisible hand' guiding our economy. Nevertheless, there is a problem: the phrase is so widely used, and so much taken for granted, that it is tempting to assume that the economy does indeed behave as though there were an invisible hand guiding every transaction in such a way as to produce the best possible outcome.

Specifically, the final sentence suggests that more good is done for society by pursuing self-interest than could be done by actually attempting to do good. This is an extremely convenient line of thought for anybody who is concerned more with self-interest than the interests of society. Not only does it absolve them from guilt, it enables them to claim enormous merit from their actions.

Often the pursuit of self-interest *is* of great benefit to society – when automotive manufacturers seek to profit from the possibilities of electric vehicles, for example, they simultaneously contribute to the possibility of a significant reduction in damaging atmospheric pollution. But when they programme their engine management software to cheat on emissions testing, they do not.

As the discussion on free markets, below, makes clear, pursuit of self-interest can often be to the enormous detriment of society. The notion of an all-powerful invisible hand working for the greater good is hugely attractive. The reality of the world is that it requires a very visible hand to promote the interests of society.

METAPHOR #2: FREE MARKETS

The idea of free markets is not self-evidently a metaphor. Often when we use the phrase, we think that we are describing a possible, and indeed desirable, reality. But as the Cambridge economist Ha-Joon Chang has pointed out, there is no such thing as a free market: 'Every market has some rules and boundaries that restrict freedom of choice.'[19]

The notion of a free market becomes extremely problematic if we attempt to take it literally. In a market where companies free from government interference were literally free to do anything short of physical violence to increase their profits, the results would be disastrous. Banks would be free to mis-sell products and services to their clients, to carry out insider dealing, to rig indices, to reduce their capital buffers, to put the world economy at the risk of another global financial crisis – and all the evidence from recent years is that they would make full use of these freedoms. Large industrial companies would be free to pollute without limit – as indeed they did before legislation attempted to prevent pollution. Pharmaceutical companies would be free to advertise their products however they liked and to launch new products without the costly and time-consuming process of clinical trials – all of which they have done in the past. Tobacco companies would be free to advertise and to sell their products even to children – and of course they would do so.

Most people talk about the benefits of 'free markets' without intending such a literal interpretation of the word 'free'. Very few people would like to see tobacco companies free to deploy their sophisticated marketing techniques in infant schools, while the need for banking regulation is almost universally accepted, et cetera. What they really mean is that they are in favour of clean, competitive markets. To achieve clean, competitive markets, however, requires effective regulation. This confusion of terms – and in particular, the use of the word 'free' when the intent is for effective regulation – can easily lead to confusion of thought, and from there to poor policy and misguided legislation.

In the UK, this confusion has manifested at the highest levels of policy-making. For example, then Prime Minister Theresa May has spoken about 'A free-market economy, operating under the right rules and regulations'.[20] This is an oxymoron. What she presumably meant was 'a strong and properly regulated mixed economy' or 'clean competitive markets'. But these are very different things from a free-market economy.

METAPHOR #3: ECONOMIC LAWS

Economics sometimes describes itself as the science of allocating scarce resources. As befits a science, economics has armed itself with a number of laws.

Laws abound in other scientific disciplines. In mathematics, the Law of Quadratic Reciprocity has no exceptions – and no exception will ever be found because the law has a rigorous proof. In physics, there were no known exceptions to Newton's laws until the late-nineteenth century when it became clear that, at speeds approaching the speed of light, reality deviated significantly from Newton's assumptions. A more accurate description of reality was developed by Albert Einstein with his special and general theories of relativity. Nevertheless, for most normal purposes, Newton's laws are accurate enough even today. Crucially, scientists are clear about the circumstances when this is not the case.

In the case of many economic 'laws', however, exceptions are commonplace. In some cases, the exceptions are more common than the instances where the 'law' holds true. In other sciences, these economic 'laws' would not be called laws. They might be termed disproven theories or rejected hypotheses. Yet in economics, they retain their status as laws.

This is detrimental to clear thinking about economic policy. If my proposed policy follows an economic 'law', I might expect that policy to be sound. Conversely, if my proposed policy conflicts with an economic 'law', I might conclude that the policy is wrongheaded. If, however, the 'laws' are no more than metaphors and bear no relationship to reality, then these policy conclusions will be incorrect. The fallibility of economic laws is evident from a brief examination of three such laws: Say's Law, the Law of Marginal Productivity and Okun's Law.

Say's Law, named after the French economist Jean-Baptiste Say, states that production creates its own demand.[21] Say's Law was derived from theoretical reasoning about the economy. According to Say, producers only create a product in order to sell it – the only motivation for production is the desire to consume (and not, for example, to pay down debt). Workers and suppliers, similarly, work in order to get money so that they can consume. In other words, workers' wages, suppliers' profits and producers' profits all exist only to be spent on consumption. While any entrepreneur might occasionally make a mistake and any individual product might fail to find a buyer, the total value of all goods manufactured is nevertheless affordable. Say deduced from this that it is impossible to have a general glut – a surplus of supply over demand – or, equivalently, a deficiency of demand relative to productive capacity.

A general glut – more production than people want to buy – manifests in a recession with significant and sustained periods in which the resources used to produce goods in many sectors are underutilized. Sustained involuntary unemployment and factories lying idle (or operating below capacity) are symptoms of a general glut. Most obviously, in a general glut total production reduces from levels that had previously been attainable. In other words, GDP falls. Of course, we know that in practice GDP does sometimes fall – indeed, we are still suffering from the aftermath of the Global Financial Crisis, which caused a fall in GDP in countries around the world. According to Say's Law, since it is impossible that the problem lies on the demand side – that it stems from deficient demand – it must lie on the supply side: there must have been a shock to productive capacity.

However, in the case of the Global Financial Crisis, there were powerful forces that reduced demand (the 'credit crunch' followed by the private sector paying down its debt, rather than consuming) but there are no clear candidates for a supply shock of sufficient magnitude to have produced the global recession. In other words, Say's Law is incompatible with the kind of economy that can, in practice, produce a Global Financial Crisis. It is not a law in the real world.

Another economic 'law' is the Law of Marginal Productivity, which can be applied to the distribution of income. According to the theory, in the words of economist J. B. Clark:

> The distribution of income of society is controlled by a natural law, [which] if it worked without friction, would give to every agent of production the amount of wealth [added value] which that agent creates.[22]

If true, this would be enormously reassuring. Each member of society would be rewarded according to their contribution to society. The problem with the theory lies in the definition of 'added value', which sounds like a description of contribution to society but in reality is much closer to a description of bargaining power. We saw earlier in this chapter how firefighters, teachers, doctors and nurses can

seem to have a lower value to society than reckless financiers, tobacco marketers and pornographers. In fact, they
simply have less bargaining power.

In a fascinating book on the real-world applications of game
theory, Barry J. Nalebuff and Adam M. Brandenburger illustrate how the concept of 'added value' in economics is different
from our normal understanding of the phrase.[23] They describe
a game played at Harvard Business School between Adam and
twenty-six of his MBA students. Adam has twenty-six black
cards and the students have one red card each. The head of
the Business School has offered to pay US$100 to anyone who
can hand in a pair of cards, one black one red. The game is for
Adam and the students to negotiate, on an individual basis, to
create the matching pairs.

The bargaining is essentially symmetrical: each student needs
Adam and Adam needs each student – and the most likely result
is that they agree to split the US$100 equally. If Barry repeats
the game at the Yale School of Management but *deliberately
destroys* three of his black cards, the symmetry is broken: all
the students need Barry but Barry does not need all the students.
In fact, the last three students will get nothing at all, so there
is a real penalty for not settling with Barry. Since any student
who refuses Barry's offer runs the risk of being one of the last
students, *all* the students are in a very weak bargaining position
and essentially must take whatever Barry offers them.

Having played this game many times, Nalebuff and
Brandenburger found that in the first game the students can
expect US$50 each, whereas in the second they are lucky to
get US$20. This is because, in the technical sense in which
economists use the phrase 'added value', the students' added
value in the second game is reduced to zero.

As we would normally look at it, Barry – having reduced the
size of the pie – makes a *negative* contribution to society. We

might expect that his reward would be reduced, or even zero. From the point of view of economic 'added value', however, Barry now has *100 per cent of the added value* and his reward is dramatically *increased*.

In other words, if it is true at all, the Law of Marginal Productivity is true only in a highly technical sense that bears no relationship to the way in which it is normally understood – as meaning that market forces reward most highly those who contribute most to society. Once this becomes clear, the justification of huge differentials in income and wealth on the grounds of 'meritocracy' are exposed as a sham.

Lastly, there is Okun's Law. This states that change in the unemployment rate in an economy has a straight-line relationship to real GDP growth. Although Okun's Law was derived from statistical observation, and therefore has some grounding in reality, it has not stood up well to long-term scrutiny. When Edward S. Knotek II of the Federal Reserve Bank of Kansas City examined the data, he found that:

> Okun's Law has not been useful as a stable relationship, since its parameters have varied considerably over time and over the course of the business cycle. In addition, it has not always been a reliably strong relationship, especially in quarterly data.[24]

But despite this lack of stability, Okun's Law has not been renamed Okun's conjecture or Okun's heuristic, which might more accurately describe its status. Instead it retains its status as an economic law.

In striving to be a science, economics has adopted a number of 'laws' that, if true, would have deep impacts on our society and profound implications for policymakers. Unfortunately, many of these so-called laws are either not grounded in reality or do not mean what they purport to say. They are not laws in the sense that physical or mathematical laws are laws – they are better regarded as metaphors.

CHAPTER 10

Economic Models

All models are wrong, but some are useful.

George Edward Pelham Box[1]

This chapter is about economic models – in particular macroeconomic models that seek to explain and predict the behaviour of the economy as a whole – and why these models so often get it wrong. It begins with a quick discussion of models in general and what makes a good model, before considering the specific types of flawed models most widely used to predict the economy and looking at alternative approaches that may offer more hope of realism – although pinpoint accuracy of prediction will always remain out of reach.

Models and maps must be fit for purpose

As children, we play with models, with dolls, with action figures, with toy battleships and spaceships. If the game is good enough, we can even forget that we are only playing with models. As adults, the same thing happens but principally with conceptual models – ways we look at the world to help us manage its complexity. If a model has proven to be useful, we can easily forget that it is wrong or even that it is a model rather than reality itself.

Conceptual models come in a variety of shapes and sizes. They can be very sophisticated and highly mathematical, like the models physicists use to understand the universe: general relativity or quantum mechanics. Or they can be very simple, like the model some politicians use to understand the economy ('It's like running a corner shop'). Being complex, sophisticated and highly mathematical does not in itself make a model a good one, but neither does being simple and straightforward.

In thinking about what does make a good model, it can be helpful to reflect on one specific type of model: maps. Maps are useful not just because of what they contain but because of what they leave out – a map that left nothing out would have to be at least 1:1 scale and would be too unwieldy to be of any practical use. On the other hand, trying to plan an afternoon's walk across the fields to a country pub using a motorway route-planning map would be impossible, as it contains none of the relevant details.

One of the most useful maps in the world is not even to scale: the London Underground map. This topological map of the city's underground network was first created by a technical draughtsman, Harry Beck, in 1931.[2] Producing the map was Beck's own idea and the first draft was produced in his spare time. London Underground was initially cautious about publishing it because it was so different from other maps that had been produced up to that time. But the map proved hugely popular with the public because it was highly functional, and was quickly widely adopted. Beck's topological map is shown below.

With the exception of the River Thames, whose course is shown as being made up of a series of straight-line segments (and

Figure 34: London Underground map

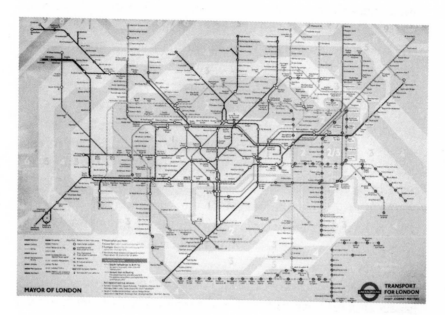

Source: Alamy

rounded corners), the map ignores all of London except for the tube network. The tube lines themselves are also represented as being made up of straight-line segments. The distances between adjacent stations on the map are not proportional to the distances on the ground.

Nevertheless, the map is extremely useful for navigating the London tube network because it accurately represents two things: first, the sequence of stations on each line; and second, the points of intersection between lines. Since these are the two key things that a traveller needs to know to plan a journey, the map is enormously helpful.

For comparison, opposite is a (much more) geographically accurate map of the network.

Although there may be purposes (such as ordering rails for replacement tracks) for which this second map is a better model of the network, for everyday challenges such as working out how to get from Pimlico to Piccadilly, the first map is much easier to use.

Comparing these two maps can help us to think about what makes good – and bad – models. We can see that a model can be good without being detailed or accurate as long as it clearly achieves its objectives. To be sure that a model is good, we need to be clear as to a) what its objectives are and b) whether we can be confident that it meets those objectives.

To be sure that the output of a model meets its aims, we also need to be sure that the structure of the model is correct. In particular, are the key assumptions on which it is founded valid? Furthermore, are we sure that any specific problem given to the model is accurately described, that the model processes that problem correctly and that it gives an output that is accurate and clear?

Figure 35: Geographically accurate tube map

In the case of the topological map, its objectives are to help passengers plan a journey between any two points on the network. In relation to this objective (though not necessarily to all objectives), the topological map is a better model than the geographically accurate map.

An important reason why the tube map works so well as a model is that its underlying assumptions are a very good match to the real-world problems that passengers face. In this case, the underlying assumptions are that the difficulty and time of navigating a route are reasonably approximated by the number of stops in total and the number of intersections. Implicitly, the precise distances between stops are not critical.

The whole structure of any model depends on its underlying assumptions and, therefore, the value of its output is also critically dependent on the soundness of those underlying assumptions. Since these underlying assumptions are often not made explicit, they can be a source of serious weakness that is quite difficult to detect.

What happens when underlying assumptions are not well chosen? In particular, what happens when simplifying assumptions are *too* simple? Imagine a tube map based on the simplifying assumption that all tube lines are straight. The very centre of the map might almost work, as shown overleaf.*

But there are fundamental flaws in this map. Most obviously, the Circle line does not exist – a circle cannot be represented as a straight line. Other tube lines which branch and loop (such as the District line, the Northern line and the Central line) can only be partly represented. Straight lines (on a flat surface) can intersect at most once. In the real world, many tube lines intersect at several stations. Assuming that all

---

* Even within this very limited area, it doesn't quite work. Charing Cross lies on both the Northern and Bakerloo lines, but since straight lines can intersect at no more than one point this map cannot show that.

Figure 36: Tube map assuming all tube lines are straight

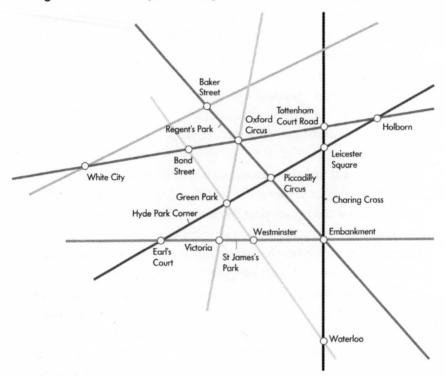

lines are straight is a simplifying assumption too far. If you want to navigate around London, you had better not use this map.

This analogy gives us a basis for assessing the main models used to analyze national economies.

Conventional macro-economic models are not fit for purpose

There are many types of macro-economic model in use, ranging in sophistication from complex mathematical models that can be run only by experts through to simple models that ordinary people can carry around in their minds. Probably the three most widely used types of model are General Equilibrium models, econometric models and simple mental models. Like all models, all three are wrong – the question is: which are useful?

GENERAL EQUILIBRIUM MODELS

Many central banks run models known as Dynamic Stochastic General Equilibrium (DSGE) models. The name alone is off-putting. Let's take each part in turn. 'Dynamic' simply means not static (i.e. that the model operates over an interval of time rather than simply at one specific point in time). 'Stochastic' means that the model allows for some factors to have probabilities associated with them rather than specific values (for example, the oil price can have a probability distribution linked with it rather than an assumption that the price will remain fixed during the forecast period). 'General' means that the model covers all markets in the economy simultaneously: the labour market, the market for goods and services, the market for capital et cetera. 'Equilibrium' means that each of these markets is simultaneously in equilibrium with the others (workers, for example, are paid precisely enough to motivate them to work the required number of hours, while firms produce precisely enough goods and services at precisely the right price to enable them to satisfy the demands of households, pay their workers and provide an acceptable return on investment).

The assumptions underlying these models are of particular interest. First, there are fundamental assumptions that determine the very nature of the model; and secondly, there are a series of simplifying assumptions introduced in order to guarantee that the model will be able to produce an answer.

The most fundamental assumption is that the economy is constantly, and fairly quickly, moving towards a stable equilibrium from which it is disturbed only by external shocks. In order to make the mathematics work, so that there will always be a stable equilibrium, a series of further simplifying assumptions were introduced:

- all participants in the economy (households, workers, firms et cetera) have perfect information and behave perfectly rationally, and all do so in the same way (so that in effect there is a single representative firm and a single representative household);
- external shocks will be small and the model will therefore operate at all times close to equilibrium – and can therefore be reasonably approximated by the assumption that all relationships are linear (i.e. all lines are straight lines);
- the financial sector merely acts as an intermediary between other participants in the economy, and because it has perfect information and behaves perfectly rationally, financial market prices will always be right – there will never be bubbles or crashes.

This last assumption means that many DSGE models omit the financial sector altogether. Finally, most DSGE models look principally at flows in the economy, and take little or no account of stocks.

Although it is known that all of these simplifying assumptions are untrue in the real world, proponents of DSGE models refer to them as having micro-foundations. In other words, they are supposedly founded in an understanding of microeconomics. This is their great virtue. As the distinguished (and

Nobel Prize-winning) economist Robert Solow put it in his testimony to the US House of Representatives Committee on Science and Technology in 2010:

> Here we are, still near the bottom of a deep and pro-longed recession, with the immediate future uncertain, desperately short of jobs, and the approach to macroeconomics that dominates serious thinking, certainly in our elite universities and in many central banks and other influential policy circles, seems to have absolutely nothing to say about the problem... I do not think that the currently popular DSGE models pass the smell test. They take it for granted that the whole economy can be thought about as if it were a single, consistent person or a dynasty carrying out a rationally designed, long-term plan, occasionally disturbed by unexpected shocks, but adapting to them in a rational, consistent way. I do not think that this picture passes the smell test. The protagonists of this idea make a claim to respectability by asserting that it is founded on what we know about microeconomic behaviour, but I think that this claim is generally phony.[4]

It is well-known that the predictive power of DSGE models is very poor, but what is even more concerning is that because of the structure of the models and their underlying assumptions, certain important features of the real world *simply could not happen* in such models. One noteworthy example is the Global Financial Crisis, which could never have been predicted in a model missing the financial sector. In the words of another Nobel Prize-winning economist, Joseph Stiglitz, 'not only did the model fail to predict the Crisis; it effectively said that it couldn't happen. Under the core hypotheses (rational expectations, exogenous shocks), a crisis of that form and magnitude simply couldn't occur.'[5]

In the same way, long-term unemployment is impossible in a model in which all markets clear quickly. And of particular interest to this book, mass impoverishment can never be an issue in an economy where there is a single representative household. If these features of the real-world are important problems – which they clearly are – policymakers have *no hope of deriving any relevant insight* from DSGE models as they are currently constructed.

ECONOMETRIC MODELS

Econometric models come at the problem from the other end. Instead of developing a comprehensive model based on theories or assumptions about how each type of agent will behave, the econometric approach starts with a relatively small number of economic variables, some of which are believed to depend on the others. The econometric approach is to then look at the data that illustrate past relationships and, where these can be found to be statistically significant, use these relationships to predict the impact of future policy choices.

Proponents of DSGE models criticise the econometric approach because they claim it does not have micro-foundations (see above). In one sense, the econometric models are very well-founded: they are based on real-world data, which is not true for DSGE models. What the critics mean is that econometric models reflect past relationships between economic variables, and any policy choice might affect those relationships so predictions about the future cannot be relied upon. Furthermore, since econometric models consider only part of the system, it is hard to be sure that there is a self-consistent future being predicted.

It is true that econometric models also have a poor record

of predictive accuracy. In fact, all known forms of macroeconomic model demonstrate a poor predictive record. As Simon Wren-Lewis of Oxford University has said:

> Macroeconomic forecasts produced with macroeconomic models tend to be little better than intelligent guesswork. That is not an opinion – it is a fact. It is a fact because for decades many reputable and long-standing model-based forecasters have looked at their past errors, and that is what they find.[6]

SIMPLE MENTAL MODELS

Under these circumstances, it is perhaps not surprising that many people, policymakers among them, prefer to rely on their own mental models. One model in particular has become very prevalent. This model says simply that 'markets are the best way to allocate resources'. According to this model, since public sector spending is non-market-based, it is likely to lead to misallocation of resources. The *best* thing government can do, therefore, is to get out of the way, to reduce its spending as far as possible, to reduce taxation as far as possible and to allow the magic of market forces to solve any economic problems. The *worst* thing government can do is to interfere to solve problems itself, because however well-intentioned its actions, it will only make matters worse.

This model has the great virtue of clarity and simplicity: it gives immediate guidance to policymakers on a whole range of economic issues. What should happen to taxes? They should be resolutely driven downwards. What should happen to government spending? It should also be constantly reduced. How should we tackle unemployment? Reduce interference with businesses, either in the form of regulation or from institutions such as trade unions.

Two highly influential politicians who adopted this philosophy were Margaret Thatcher in the United Kingdom and Ronald Reagan in the United States.

An obvious theoretical weakness of this model is that its prescriptions are the same in all circumstances. Regardless of the economic problem, the answer is to limit government, lower taxes and reduce government spending. Taken to its extreme, this would result in an end state with zero taxes and zero government spending, and therefore zero government and zero law enforcement – in a word, anarchy.

Proponents of this model do not usually support it by means of theory, however – partly because to do so requires a series of assumptions that are known to bear little relationship to the real world – but on grounds of pragmatism and choice. Government, they say, is slow, bureaucratic, inefficient and prone to picking losers. The private sector is dynamic and innovative, constantly evolving in response to consumer demand (i.e. it provides consumer choice). Given a choice between having activities carried out by government, or allowing the private sector to carry them out and allowing markets to make decisions, there is really no contest.

The best test of the model, therefore, is also pragmatic. How has it worked in practice? How effective have the market-based reforms instituted by Reagan and Thatcher been in driving economic growth? How well have they helped us to reduce unemployment? How well have they contributed to the prosperity and level of choice available to the average consumer? As we saw in Chapter 2, the post-war era can be split into two periods of about thirty-five-years each: the first from the end of the Second World War up to around 1980, (known as the Golden Age of Capitalism) and the second from the beginning of the 1980s to the present day (the Age of Market Capitalism).

During the first of these periods, there was a broad con-sensus in the UK and the United States that government had an important role to play. This period saw the UK create the National Health Service and the Welfare State. During the second of these periods, the consensus – under parties of both left and right – has been much more market-focused. There has been an emphasis on reducing tax rates, controlling public spending, privatizing government-run activities and deregulat-ing the private sector wherever possible. This second period has, in effect, been a practical test of market-based reforms. Looking at the results during these two eras gives us an idea of how well the market-based mental model has worked in practice.

And as we saw in Chapter 2, the Golden Age of Capitalism vastly out-performed the Age of Market Capitalism. The data lend no support to the idea that market-based reforms have been of benefit to the mass of the population of either the US or the UK. The 'twenty years of economic growth and pros-perity' that Republican politician Jeff Duncan referred to are not recorded in the data compiled by the Bureau of Economic Analysis, the Census Bureau or the Bureau of Labor Statistics. In fact, what the data show is that from 1945 up until about 1980 there was indeed a Golden Age of Capitalism, which has been followed by thirty-five years of poor results on almost every measure. In summary, the evidence does not support the idea that the simple mental model that says 'markets are the best way to allocate resources' is a reliable guide to policy-making.

These data seem so much in contradiction with what we repeatedly hear today that it poses the question, 'If the results during the period since 1980 were really so much worse than those before, why do so many intelligent, successful, well-informed people feel that the market-based reforms were a success?' It may be that following the money can lead us to at least part of the answer.

The top 0.1 per cent of the US population numbers around 320,000 people. This group includes senior politicians, financiers, top journalists and newspaper proprietors, senior lawyers and top civil servants. In short, it includes almost all of those who have their hands on the levers of power. Many members of this group, as research by the eminent economists Emmanuel Saez and Gabriel Zucman shows,[7] *have* found the last thirty-five years to be a time of great progress – their own wealth has soared – and most of their friends will agree with them. In a way, it is not surprising that what we hear is the narrative of economic triumph, even though the data show no evidence of any such success for the rest of the population.

We have considered three types of economic model: the highly sophisticated Dynamic Stochastic General Equilibrium models, the slightly simpler econometric models, and a very simple – and very widely adopted – mental model that says simply that markets are the best way to allocate resources. In the case of the first two, which are capable of making explicit predictions, we have seen that there are theoretical reasons to be sceptical about their predictions that in practice display poor accuracy. For the third kind of model, which does not produce explicit forecasts, we have looked at the performance of the economy since policy shifted in the direction that the model recommends and we see that, in the most important respects, economic performance has worsened. In other words, the three principal types of model that have been used to formulate economic policy are all fatally flawed. Even more fundamentally, the assumptions on which they are based mean that they have nothing to say about vital questions like financial stability and mass impoverishment.

This is a serious problem. We *have* to formulate economic

policy. When unemployment is high, we need to know which policies are likely to bring it down. When the banking system causes a financial crisis, we need to understand what sorts of reforms can reduce the chances of a recurrence. When growth stagnates, we need to know how to reignite it.

The economics profession has responded to this challenge in three main ways. One group has sought to explain that in practice there is very little wrong with conventional macro-economics – and, indeed, that conventional macroeconomics predicts that certain things will be unpredictable, and therefore the occurrence of an unpredicted Global Financial Crisis is a mark of the success of the theory.

A second group takes the problems with existing models seriously and has attempted to address some of the specific criticisms – e.g. the lack of a financial sector – but still largely within the overall construct of equilibrium modelling.

A third group is attempting a more fundamental rethink of economics. It has been prepared to reject some of the fundamental assumptions on which most models have historically been built. These include the assumption that individuals act rationally with perfect information, that banks act as intermediaries (lending out deposits they receive from customers) and, most fundamentally, that the economy is constantly moving towards a stable equilibrium.

The problem with rejecting these assumptions is that without them the mathematics becomes much more complex. In fact, explicitly solving the equations, in the way that we were taught to do at school, is not possible. Even proving that these equations have a reasonable solution may not be possible. A new approach is needed to underpin the modelling of these more realistic assumptions and the equations that represent them.

An alternative approach may be possible

One candidate for such an approach is System Dynamics, the brainchild of Jay W. Forrester, who also developed core memory for computers. Beginning his career as an electronic engineer, Forrester became interested in cybernetics (self-governing systems) and, in particular, the challenges in understanding the interactions between self-reinforcing and self-balancing feedback loops in electronic control systems (known respectively as positive and negative feedback). A key insight he developed was that the same sort of self-reinforcing and self-balancing feedback occurs in business and in the economy as a whole. The diagram below illustrates a simple set of dynamics relating to the introduction of a new and superior technology into a market where word-of-mouth drives rate of adoption.

Figure 37: Simple example of system dynamics in business

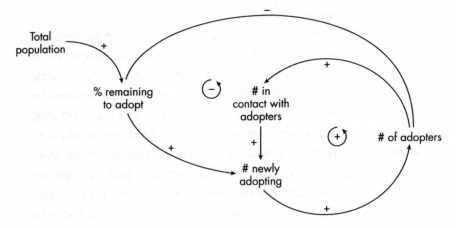

In this example, there are two main feedback loops. The first is a positive feedback loop at the right of the diagram. Here, the more people who adopt the new technology, the more people who come into contact with adopters and who, in effect, are converted by the adopters, adding to the total number of adopters. If this were the only dynamic at play, the number of adopters would grow exponentially and without limit. In the real world, there is a finite population and this introduces the second dynamic. This dynamic is a negative feedback loop towards the centre of the diagram, where the more adopters, the lower the percentage of the population remaining to adopt, and therefore the lower the percentage of those in contact with adopters actually available to be converted. In this very simple system with only two loops, it *is* possible to solve the equations explicitly and derive a formula for the penetration of the new product – the so-called S-curve, or logistic curve. In any real business system, and even more so in the economy as a whole, there are dozens of feedback loops, some positive and some negative, all interacting with each other constantly. In these cases, solving the equations explicitly would usually be impossible, but it *is* possible to run a computer simulation of even quite complex systems.

Using this approach – which economists such as Stephen Keen,[8] Wynne Godley and Marc Lavoie[9] have adopted – it is possible to model an economy with much more realistic underlying assumptions. For example, these models can be designed to deal with both flows and stocks in the economy, to include the financial sector and a realistic description of how money is created and destroyed, to include more than one firm and more than one household, and to operate without the assumption of perfect rationality and perfect information. Perhaps most importantly, these models can be truly dynamic in the sense that everything that happens in one period of time can have an explicitly modelled effect on what happens in the next.

We will never achieve great predictive accuracy

When the Queen visited the London School of Economics in November 2008, she famously asked, in reference to the Global Financial Crisis, 'Why did nobody see it coming?' It was a good question. Most economists, both in academia and in central banks were taken by surprise by the crisis. But there were a few exceptions – and some of these are working on new approaches with great potential. Even if they are successful, however, it seems unlikely that economics will ever be able to achieve great precision in forecasting.

WHY 'NOBODY SAW IT COMING'

The economics profession responded to the Queen's question in a letter from Professors Tim Besley and Peter Hennessy.[10] It explained that the problem was 'principally a failure of the collective imagination of many bright people, both in this country and internationally, to understand the risks to the system as a whole'. They also commented:

> So where was the problem? Everyone seemed to be doing their own job properly on its own merit. And according to standard measures of success, they were often doing it well. The failure was to see how collectively this added up to a series of interconnected imbalances over which no single authority had jurisdiction. This, combined with the psychology of herding and the mantra of financial and policy gurus, led to a dangerous recipe. Individual risks may rightly have been viewed as small, but the risk to the system as a whole was vast.

This is, of course, a perfect description of the fallacy of composition in action – and a good summary of how high the stakes are when this kind of thinking becomes widespread. It is not quite true, however, that nobody saw the crisis coming. Dean Baker clearly identified the risks as early as 2002[11] and the Dutch researcher Dirk Bezemer managed to find a dozen respected commentators who explicitly predicted the global financial crisis.[12] Interestingly, what many of them had in common was that they did not rely on general equilibrium models of the form described above but on models that included stocks as well as flows (and where stocks and flows were consistent) and explicitly modelled the financial sector and money creation. Bezemer's list included Stephen Keen, Wynne Godley and Marc Lavoie, whose alternative approaches are summarized above.

The new approaches seem so far to be more comprehensive (in that they include monetary stocks and flows in a consistent way), more realistic (in that the assumptions that they use about economic agents' decision-making processes are not known to be false in the real world) and hold out the prospect of greater predictive power.

STABILITY OF SYSTEMS

But there is one fundamental problem that may prove to be intractable even in these alternative models – not because there is anything intrinsically wrong with a model, but because of a feature of the real world: instability. Any system that contains self-reinforcing loops – positive feedback – runs the risk of being unstable in the sense that a minute change in the input may produce a very large change in the output. In the field of meteorology, for example, it is known that the weather system is unstable. The meteorologist Edward Lorenz famously asked, 'Does the flap of a butterfly's wings in Brazil set off a tornado in Texas?' His conclusion was that it could.[13]

If the same thing is true in economics, and I am unaware of any cogent arguments to the contrary, then the predictive power of economic models will always remain limited. They may be able to identify unsustainable trends such as bubbles, but they are unlikely ever to be good at predicting the timing of the bursting of the bubble.

WHAT WE SHOULD EXPECT

Even if economics does turn out to be unstable in this sense, so that making accurate long-range predictions will never be possible, there can still be an enormous contribution from the type of alternative model we have discussed. First, to a much greater extent than any of the other models listed, these alternatives enable us to identify trends that are unsustainable (such as the build-up of private-sector debt in the run-up to the Global Financial Crisis). Secondly, even in the absence of a precise forecast, they allow for far better analysis of policy options and economic scenarios than conventional approaches.

We should therefore expect not forecasts with pinpoint precision but models founded on realistic assumptions about the real world that are complete and stock–flow consistent. And we should expect policymakers to explore alternative policies and alternative scenarios using these more realistic models rather than simplistic mental models.

CHAPTER 11

Rhetoric Over Reason

Histories make men wise;… the mathematics, subtle; natural philosophy, deep;… and rhetoric, able to contend.

Francis Bacon[1]

R hetoric, as Francis Bacon noted in 1625, makes men able to contend – that is, to argue persuasively and to shape the opinions of others. Rhetoric unsupported by knowledge of history, mathematics and science risks being empty. Rhetoric without reason is one of the enablers of a post-fact world.

The rhetoric that justifies the economic status quo and supports the continuation of the process of mass impoverishment is very powerful. It appeals both to the aspirational side of our natures and to the more cautious, anxious side. Many of the most resonant phrases have been repeated so many times that we come to think of them as not merely true, but as axiomatic. When this happens, it becomes difficult to think clearly about the issues – solutions become literally unthinkable because to think about them would fly in the face of what we 'know' to be true. In this chapter, we explore the power and resonance of some of these key phrases and look at whether the facts support the rhetoric.

Most importantly, we consider the emotional power of rhetoric over hard fact – why the Devil seems to have all the best tunes.

The confident repetition of falsehoods

Many of those in positions of power and influence, whom we would expect both to know the facts and to be honest in describing them, do no such thing. There are numerous high-profile examples of utterly misleading comments by respected leaders. We can distinguish these cases of falsehoods – where perpetrators know the facts but say the opposite – from the myths of the previous chapter, which are often believed by those who propound them. When these falsehoods are repeated and echoed throughout the media, we can be forgiven for coming to think that we 'know' these things and for supporting policies based on these falsehoods.

We 'know', for example, that the root of our economic problems going back to the Global Financial Crisis has been profligate spending by governments. For example, by governments in the peripheral Eurozone countries of Portugal, Ireland, Italy, Greece and Spain – the so-called PIIGS. We 'know' that had those countries run their economies in the same way as Germany, the Eurozone would be in a far stronger position now. We 'know' that because of the mess that these countries created, there is a need to take hard decisions now – but it is important not to be afraid of austerity, which in fact leads to improved growth. We 'know' that there is a huge problem of government debt, which is at unprecedented levels, and if not tackled now will leave enormous problems for our children and their children.

If all of these things that we think we know are indeed true, then the policies that many Western governments are following today are probably correct – and those who responded to the surveys by saying that they expected their children to be worse off than they were are probably right. The world of Cowen's hypermeritocracy[2] may well come to pass. If, on the other hand, some of these things are half-truths or even outright wrong, then we may be staring solutions in the face without seeing them, or at least without giving them serious consideration. It is not an exaggeration to say that the future – or at least the shape – of Western civilization is at stake, so it is worth digging into each of these points in a little more detail.

FALSEHOOD #1: PROFLIGATE GOVERNMENTS WERE THE CAUSE OF THE EUROZONE CRISIS

One of the reasons we think we know that the crisis was caused by profligate governments is that we have been told so many times by those who ought to be in a position to know.

> *Indeed, it is expansionary policies and weak fiscal positions that created the current problems of high debt and low competitiveness in the crisis countries in the first place.*
>
> Ludger Schuknecht[3]

The sentence above comes from a letter from Ludger Schuknecht of the German Finance Ministry to Martin Wolf of the *Financial Times*. Mr Schuknecht is a senior member of that ministry and an outspoken and confident commentator on economic issues. It is interesting, therefore, to compare his very clear pronouncement with the equally clear data in the IMF database.

The obvious yardstick to measure whether a government is behaving prudently or in a profligate way is compliance with criteria 2 and 3 of the Maastricht Treaty, to which EU governments signed up in February 1992. Criterion 2 specifies that governments must run a deficit of no more than 3 per cent of GDP, while criterion 3 specifies that the ratio of government debt to GDP should be not more than 60 per cent.

According to the data,[4] the most prudent governments in 2007 included those of Spain, Ireland and Latvia – three countries hit particularly badly by the crisis but which were widely praised for their sound economic management at the time. All of these countries were significantly more prudent in 2007 than Germany was. Portugal was also very close to, though just outside, the zone of compliance. And while Italy had a very significant government debt to GDP ratio, its deficit was under control at the time the crisis struck. The UK also lay within the prudent zone before the crisis – and, although it is rarely mentioned today, in 2007 the Conservative Party (then in opposition) pledged to follow the Labour government's spending plans.[5] Conversely, the United States, the country that recovered most strongly from the Global Financial Crisis, was just outside the zone of compliance.

With the single exception of Greece, there is *no factual basis* for Ludger Schuknecht's comments about the crisis countries. The countries that were hardest hit were principally those that had *not* had weak fiscal positions before the crisis. Yet this disconnection from the facts has in no way reduced the influence of the narrative of previous government profligacy on EU economic management.

If it wasn't profligate governments that caused the crisis, then what was it? The answer is surprisingly obvious. It is called the 'Global Financial Crisis' for a reason: it was a crisis caused by, originating in and transmitted globally by the Financial sector.[6]

In the United States, for example, losses relating to subprime mortgage lending were estimated at around US$1 trillion.[7] Even if we assume that the average loss per loan was US$100,000, this would require 10 million bad loans to have been made – this is not a few bad decisions, this is bad lending on an industrial scale. The problem in Spain and Ireland was the same: bad lending to an overheated property sector. Profligate governments have essentially nothing to do with the Global Financial Crisis. Governments can, on the other hand, be held responsible for the ineffectiveness of their regulation of the financial sector, which was a major contributory factor to the crisis.

FALSEHOOD #2: AUSTERITY LEADS TO GROWTH

Perhaps the most impressive example of rhetoric triumphing over reason is the case of austerity. No less an authority than Jean-Claude Trichet, who was then the president of the European Central Bank, commented:

> As regards the economy, the idea that austerity measures could trigger stagnation is incorrect... I firmly believe that in the current circumstances, confidence-inspiring policies will foster and not hamper economic recovery, because confidence is the key factor today.[8]

This message was echoed by the UK Chancellor of the Exchequer, George Osborne, who talked about 'expansionary fiscal consolidation'.[9] The idea behind both quotes was that as soon as business realized that government spending was due to fall, and therefore that future taxation could afford to be lower, their confidence would rise and they would invest aggressively and drive growth in the economy.

This idea that business investments are driven not by businesses wishing to capitalize on an unmet demand in the market but by possible future tax rates seems bizarre to me. Every investment case I have ever seen starts with customer demand and the ability of the company to meet it. (Of course, decisions such as where to locate the corporate headquarters and in which jurisdiction to take profits are often driven by tax considerations, but these are merely ways that companies seek to minimize their tax liabilities on the returns on those investments.)

There is, however, no need to *theorize* about the impact of austerity: different governments adopted significantly different policies from 2008 onwards and we can compare the impact of these policies – in particular the degree to which they adopted a policy of austerity – with the growth or contraction in their economies. In other words, the facts will show what worked in practice.

Figure 39: Growth vs Degree of Austerity

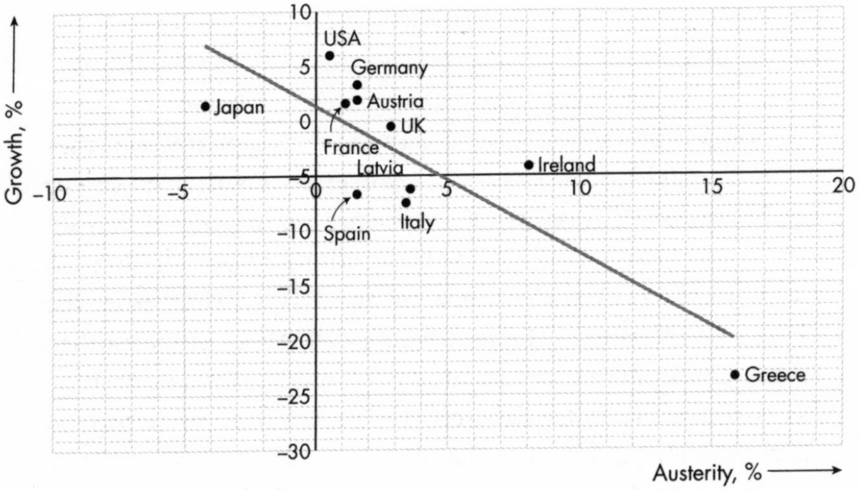

Source: WEO database[10]

For each country, the chart shows on the x-axis the degree of austerity imposed over the period 2008 to 2013 (as measured by the change in its structural balance) and on the y-axis the extent to which the economy has grown over the same period. There is a clear downward trend illustrated by the line that represents the statistical line of best fit. The obvious conclusion – confirmed by further, more detailed, research by Olivier Blanchard and Daniel Leigh of the IMF[11] – is that austerity is contractionary, not expansionary. The country that has imposed most austerity and therefore shows the clearest picture of its impact is Greece, which reduced its structural balance by over 15 per cent and saw its economy collapse by around 23 per cent as a result.

The doctrine of expansionary fiscal consolidation, which was never very plausible, has been shown to bear *no relationship to the facts*. This is not merely a theoretical issue – millions of jobs have been lost as a result of these policies, and the damage done to the lives of their victims is incalculable.

FALSEHOOD #3: THERE IS AN UNPRECEDENTED LEVEL OF GOVERNMENT DEBT

It is widely quoted that government debt has in many countries reached such high levels that these governments have no choice but to tackle deficit reduction as a matter of urgency. If they do not, the story runs, we will be bequeathing to our children an unendurable level of debt. For example, David Cameron, the UK Prime Minister at the time, said in 2015: 'To every mother, father, grandparent, uncle, aunt – I would ask this question. When you look at the children you love, do you want to land them with a legacy of huge debts?'[12]

Yet again, the data show a different story. The chart below shows a long-term picture of the UK's government debt levels.

Figure 39: Long-term history of UK government debt

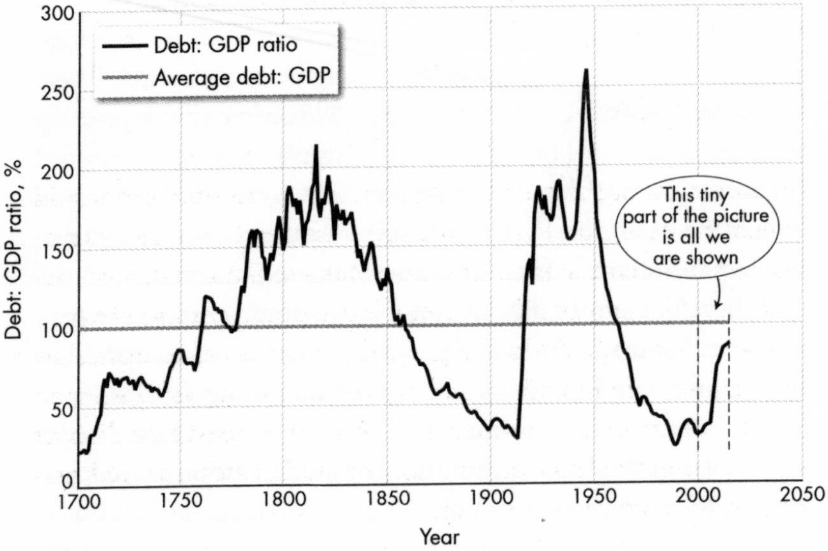

Source: *Bank of England*[13]

The data, compiled by the Bank of England, show three centuries worth of information relating to government debt. It is clear that since the financial crisis, UK government debt has indeed risen sharply from well below 50 per cent to around 80 per cent today.

What is most striking, however, is that this number is still some way *below the average* of the last 300 years and is nowhere near the peaks of the early 1800s and 1940s, both periods after which Britain enjoyed extremely healthy economic growth.

It is impossible, looking at these data, to believe that there is such urgency about debt reduction that we should sacrifice key elements of our civilization to achieve it. If we dismantle the NHS and the Welfare State to reduce government debt, leaving our children and grandchildren with no safety net and with healthcare unaffordable to most people, our descendants will ask us what on earth we thought we were doing.

Misdirection

Misdirection in the performing arts is 'a form of deception in which the attention of an audience is focused on one thing to distract its attention from another. Managing the audience's attention is the aim of all theatre; it is the foremost requirement of theatrical magic.'[14] In the theatre, we are the willing victims of misdirection; in politics, we are the unwitting victims – and the stakes are somewhat higher. There are at least two distinct kinds of misdirection in politics: the introduction of red herrings and the reversal of roles.

RED HERRINGS

In discussing the problem of mass impoverishment, for example, the introduction of red herrings – factual but not directly relevant and therefore misleading statements – is a favourite device. In this way, attention can be deflected from the root cause of the problem.

The first type of red herring is to identify, within the class of victims of current economic policy, one group that has done relatively better. This group can then be blamed for the ills suffered by the remainder and policy can be directed against this group in the interests of 'fairness'. It has become commonplace to blame baby-boomers for the problems experienced by the young. In the UK, for example, the Conservative politician Lord Willetts has written a book titled, *The Pinch: How the Baby Boomers Took Their Children's Future – And Why They Should Give It Back.*

Rather than exploring the root causes of mass impoverishment or what might be done to halt it, it is much more convenient to point out that since older people benefitted from a social contract that has been gradually whittled away to pay for tax cuts for the wealthiest in society, there is a significant wealth gap between young and old – and to pretend that the significance of this fact outweighs the enormously greater and far more damaging gap between rich and poor. (In fact, there are *some* respects in which policy *has* benefitted significant segments of the older generation at the expense of the young – for example, housing policy, which has benefitted all home-owners at the expense of those not yet on the housing ladder – but most of the problems relate to policies whose effects benefit the rich, not the mass of the older generation.)

A simple thought experiment exposes how this red herring works in practice. Imagine two neighbouring countries, Democracia and Plutocracia. At the beginning of our experiment, both countries are in the same situation: the average income is US$32,000: for members of the bottom 80 per cent of the population, income is US$20,000; and for members of the top 20 per cent, income is US$80,000. Both rich and poor save 5 per cent of their income and earn 5 per cent per annum on their savings. After thirty-five years, the savings of the bottom 80 per cent average just over US$90,000 while those of the top 20 per cent average just over US$360,000.

In the second thirty-five-year period, policies in the two countries diverge. Although in both countries average income rises by 50 per cent to US$48,000, the gains are distributed very differently. In Democracia, they are shared equally – the bottom 80 per cent now earn US$30,000 while the top 20 per cent now earn US$120,000; in Plutocracia, slightly more than 100 per cent of the gains go to the top 20 per cent, who now earn US$168,000, while the bottom 80 per cent now earn only US$18,000.

At the end of the second thirty-five-year period in Democracia, the average savings of the bottom 80 per cent amount to over US$135,000 – 50 per cent more than the previous generation. At the end of the second thirty-five-year period in Plutocracia, however, the savings of the young amount to only US$81,000 – they are poorer than the previous generation. Although to an outsider, it is clear that the problem was caused by rising inequality, the politicians of Plutocracia – in the interests of 'intergenerational fairness' – decide that it is time to reduce the benefits paid to the older generation. In other words, the answer is to level down within the bottom 80 per cent, not to seek to level up towards the rewards received by the top 20 per cent.

Another example of this approach is to point out that civil servants now have better pensions than most private sector workers (as a result of the widespread closure of defined benefit schemes by private sector companies) and to conclude that the problem is that civil servants' pensions are too good, rather than drawing the more reasonable conclusion that pensions in the private sector have now become inadequate. Again, the proposed solution – tackling the 'gold-plated pensions' in the public sector[15] – means levelling down within the 99 per cent. This type of red herring – levelling down – is extremely powerful in preserving the processes of mass impoverishment. By pitting one part of the 99 per cent against another, it can justify further impoverishment in the name of fairness.

Other groups that can be blamed with rhetorical success and then targeted for levelling down include immigrants, the unemployed, single mothers, Northerners, Southerners, Millennials (whose work ethic is apparently not what it should be) and even the disabled (the reality of whose disabilities can be called into question).

If the question is who to blame – and it is not self-evident that blame is productive – then the adage 'follow the money' is a useful guide. None of the groups listed above are notable for the great wealth of their members. There is only one such group, and it is, by definition, the very wealthy.

Another form of red herring is to treat the problems of a particular policy as being a minor price to pay for the benefits, even when this is not the case. For example, whenever the issue of mass impoverishment in the West is raised, proponents of free trade often note the important – and very real – benefit of global free trade in lifting hundreds of millions of people in China out of poverty. In the US, as we saw in Chapter 2, the economy as a whole is *far richer*; it is just that most *people* in it have become slightly poorer. The problem is *not* that wealth has flowed away from the US towards China, it is *the way that it has flowed within the US* which has caused mass impoverishment. In considering US mass impoverishment, what happens in China is a red herring.

REVERSAL OF ROLES

In recent years, an increasingly common rhetorical tactic appears to be inverting the roles of exploiter and exploited. In the United States, there has been talk of 'makers and takers', the makers being the wealth-creators and the job-creators (see below) whose hard work is exploited by the takers, who pay far less tax and may even receive tax credits.

In the United Kingdom, the same concept is denoted by the phrase 'workers and shirkers'. As we saw in Chapter 3, in the US, the 'makers' have taken more than 100 per cent of the benefit of the country's economic growth for the last thirty-five years, leaving the 'takers' poorer than their parents were a generation ago. Complaining that, having appropriated such a disproportionate share of the country's wealth, they are now paying a disproportionate share of the taxes is rather like killing one's parents and then pleading for mercy on the grounds of being an orphan.

In Mitt Romney's now infamous campaign speech – which he believed was behind closed doors – he said

> There are 47 per cent of the people who will vote for the president no matter what. All right, there are 47 per cent who are with him, who are dependent upon government, who believe that they are victims, who believe that government has a responsibility to care for them, who believe that they are entitled to health care, to food, to housing, to you name it. That that's an entitlement... 47 per cent of Americans pay no income tax. So, our message of low taxes doesn't connect... And so, my job is not to worry about those people – I'll never convince them that they should take personal responsibility and care for their lives.[16]

Romney may have regretted being quite so explicit in writing off almost half of his compatriots as takers but, overall, demonizing the victims of their economic policies while lauding the beneficiaries has proven to be an immensely successful rhetorical device for politicians around the world.

In their book *Breadline Britain*, Stewart Lansley and Joanna Mack give the example of Maria Miller, then a minister in the Department for Work and Pensions, who claimed that in the UK '... there isn't a shortage of jobs. What there can be is a lack of an appetite for some of the jobs that are available.'[17] In other words, there are no *genuinely* unemployed people – only the work-shy. As Lansley and Mack point out, while it is true that there were around 400,000 vacancies across the UK at that time, the number of people actively looking for work and available to start immediately was over 2.6 million. That is a shortage of 2.2 million jobs. The facts were clearly not on Maria Miller's side – but her rhetoric was effective.

Why the Devil has all the best tunes

I noticed a very strange thing when writing this book. I would research a topic, assemble the facts and reach a conclusion. And then I would hear a speech or read an article saying the opposite and, even though intellectually, I knew it was nonsense, *I found that part of me would believe it*. For some reason, the rhetoric would still resonate with me. Eventually, I came to the conclusion that this was because it fits with the national mood, the spirit of the times.

RHETORICAL RESONANCE

Nor is it just me who has this problem: after finishing a draft of this book, one of my brothers sent me an article entitled, 'Do we really want Britain to become Italy?' and asked me whether it was accurate. The key points of the article ran:

Let's face it, Britain has a debt problem... Over the past 10 years, the government has warded off... financial doom... borrowing £1.2 trillion... the amount it owes its creditors has risen from 36% of GDP in 2007 to a staggering 85%...

The Tories had vowed to address this as a matter of urgency, but public fury at their austerity policies has weakened Tory resolve... Britain's underlying debt level, in sum, will remain at about 75% of GDP for the foreseeable future.

Is that a problem?... We could go on for years like that. But when the next recession hits... the debt ratio is likely to soar way above 100% of GDP. At that point, 'Britain becomes Italy'... And that is a very bad place to be.[18]

On the post-fact spectrum, this article would sit at the 'deliberate misrepresentation' point. As Figure 31 says, 'comment may be based on real-world events, but reporting is not completely factual and is deliberately misleading'. The article begins by asserting that Britain has a debt problem because debt rose to 'a staggering' 85 per cent of GDP in 2017. The fact is that for the last 300 years, the UK's debt to GDP ratio has averaged over 100 per cent.[19] It was well over 100 per cent before the Industrial Revolution and over 200 per cent before the Golden Age of Capitalism – two of the most successful periods of economic growth in UK history. Therefore 85 per cent is not 'staggering'. It is below average. Let's face it, Britain does *not* have a debt problem.

The article goes on to observe that the public dislikes austerity and implies that the Tories should not have weakened their resolve but should have continued to slash public spending. The article mentions *none* of the costs of austerity set out in Chapter 2 – lower growth, stagnant productivity, failing public services and mass impoverishment. Let's face it, Britain *does* have an austerity problem.

The article admits that we could go on for years with a debt to GDP ratio of 75 per cent but then implies that this would no longer be true when the next recession hits – the last

300 years of history apparently counting for nothing. Finally, the article claims that if debt to GDP were to exceed 100 per cent, Britain would become Italy. Italy is part of the Eurozone and no longer has a central bank of its own. It has no control over its currency or its interest rates. None of this is true for Britain, and none of it would become true if debt to GDP tipped over 100 per cent. Britain has an independent central bank, the Bank of England, which can control our interest rates even when the debt to GDP ratio rises.[20] And that's a very good place to be.

This article, had it been deliberately constructed to do so, could hardly have had less substance. Yet despite that, it remains rhetorically effective. I knew that it was nonsense but for some reason, I half-believed it. Part of the reason, I suspect, is that it resonates with the *Zeitgeist* – the spirit of the times.

THE ZEITGEIST

Consider the immediate aftermath of the Second World War. The UK faced a major problem of reconstruction. More than half of national income had been diverted to the war effort and over 5 million people mobilized into the Armed Forces. Some 5 per cent of national wealth had been destroyed and 1 per cent of the population lost[21] (and the equivalent figures were even worse in some other countries). Government debt to GDP stood at over 200 per cent. This was, of course, a far greater challenge than we face today.

But the national mood was different then. As Margaret MacMillan, Professor of International History at Oxford University, explained: 'The shared suffering and sacrifice of the war years strengthened the belief in most democracies that governments had an obligation to provide basic care for all citizens.'[22] That shared suffering and sacrifice may have been necessary to win the war. As evolutionary biologists David Sloan Wilson and E. O. Wilson put it: 'Selfishness beats altruism within groups. Altruistic groups beat selfish groups. Everything else is commentary.'[23]

Along with a mood of altruism and solidarity, there was also a sense of hope. After six hard years, during the early part of which defeat seemed inevitable, the UK and its allies had emerged victorious. Even more than is usual after a war, the victors felt that good had triumphed over evil. Yes, there was a challenging task of reconstruction – but that was nothing compared with the challenges of the War itself. The national mood was one of hope and solidarity.

That all seems a long time ago. The Global Financial Crisis and the subsequent Great Recession has affected the current national mood. Many people now expect the next generation to be worse off than the last[24] and, as we have seen, although this outcome is not inevitable, their fears are not without reason.

The official response to the Global Financial Crisis has had two main planks: Quantitative Easing (QE) and austerity. The benefits of QE went disproportionately to the top 5 per cent,[25] while the costs of austerity were felt mainly at the bottom. There is no sense of shared sacrifice but an increasing tendency to blame. We blame the baby-boomers. We blame Generation X. We blame the unemployed. We blame the elite. We blame immigrants. We blame the native British. This has weakened the sense of solidarity within society. The national mood today is one of fear and isolation.

The *Zeitgeist* today is the opposite of the post-war national mood. And that affects our priorities. If I feel isolated and fearful, my main concern is to protect myself and my family. If I feel hopeful and part of a cohesive group, I want to work to create an attractive future for the whole group. Post-war Britons would have found the article my brother sent me negative, defeatist and divisive. We find it resonant.

Unless you are hyper-rational, you will probably find that you too have this problem.

The Devil's Dictionary

Inspired by the (satirical) work of Ambrose Bierce,[26] there follows a guide to rhetorical phrases that can be used to disguise the speaker's intent. Of course, these words still often have their true meanings but they are increasingly used to gloss over regressive policies, to make them sound responsible and attractive.

Phrase	Comment	Translation
Competitive-ness	This is often used to refer to the unit costs of labour, which remain uncompetitive until those in the West are comparable with those in India and China.	Mass impover-ishment
Creative destruction	This powerful concept absolves us from any concern about negative effects of our decisions – they only *seem* to be destructive.	Destruction
Expansionary fiscal consolidation	The belief that slashing public spending can only be a good thing and will cause rapid growth in the economy.	Impeding economic growth
Hard-working families	This useful phrase lumps together those in well-paying jobs or with private incomes with normal people, struggling to get by.	The rich (and the rest)

Phrase	Comment	Translation
Job creators	This phrase is used to refer to those possessed of great wealth, whether this wealth resulted from setting up and growing a business and thereby creating jobs, was inherited, or even resulted from mismanagement of a business that actually destroyed jobs.	The very rich
Pro-business	This seldom means anything to do with what is good for the economy, or even what is good for businesses in general. It most often means listening to political donors who want less regulation of their businesses.	Anti-regulation
Reform	Dismantling the welfare state.	Taking from the most vulnerable
Responsibility	This often refers to reducing public spending, even – perhaps especially – when to do so would damage the economy.	Irresponsibility
Scroungers, shirkers or takers	This refers to people of modest or no income who are in receipt of state-funded benefits or who are dissatisfied with their lot. They are contrasted with 'workers' and 'makers' and of course 'hard-working families'.	Normal people
Tough decisions	Decisions which are tough for the majority of the population – though very seldom for the decision-maker.	Bad decisions

Phrase	Comment	Translation
There is no alternative	Popular among politicians who are pursuing an unpopular course on the grounds that to do anything else would not be responsible (see 'responsibility').	I don't want an alternative
Wealth creators	See 'job creators'.	The rich

Armed with this phrasebook, we can see that when a politician says:

> Given the profligate way our predecessors ran the country and the enormous levels of debt we are consequently saddled with, it is vital that we manage responsibly to restore growth and stability to our economy. We will not shrink from tough decisions. We are resolutely pro-business, pro-families and pro-hard work. For too long hard-working families have been paying for scroungers and shirkers – from now on the rewards will go to the wealth creators.

Even if they are well-intentioned and believe every word of what they say, the practical impact of their plans is much closer to the paragraph below:

> Given that there was a Global Financial Crisis caused by ineffective regulation of the banking and shadow banking sectors, we have decided to respond irresponsibly even though this will damage the growth and stability of our economy. We will not shrink from taking bad decisions, and our policies will be unpopular. We are

resolutely anti-regulation and care passionately about our own families. For too long the rich (and the rest) have been paying taxes that benefit ordinary people – from now on the rewards will go to the rich.

CHAPTER 12

Catch-23 – The Narrative of Unaffordability

*There was only one catch and that was Catch-22,
which specified that a concern for one's safety in the
face of dangers that were real and immediate was the
process of a rational mind. Orr was crazy and could
be grounded. All he had to do was ask; and as soon as
he did, he would no longer be crazy and would have
to fly more missions. Orr would be crazy to fly more
missions and sane if he didn't, but if he were sane he
had to fly them. If he flew them he was crazy and didn't
have to, but if he didn't want to he was sane and had
to. Yossarian was moved very deeply by the absolute
simplicity of this clause of Catch-22 and let out a
respectful whistle.*

Joseph Heller[1]

We saw in Part One how over the last thirty-five years
(the Age of Market Capitalism), the economy has
performed poorly relative to the 1950s, 1960s and
1970s (the Golden Age of Capitalism). Specifically, we saw that
a process of mass impoverishment has begun in both the United
States and the United Kingdom (as well as other countries), so
that even as the economy continues to grow in real terms – in

other words society as a whole gets richer – the gains are being shared in such a way that the majority of the population actually become poorer.

We also saw that there is a real danger of these issues compounding in future: even lower growth, an even lower share going to the mass of the population, even faster mass impoverishment, the dismantling of the social safety net, worse health care, poorer education, lower social mobility – an end, in short, to the social contract that we thought defined a Western democracy.

Few people, though there are some, want to see this outcome but we have been led to understand that there is unfortunately no alternative. There simply isn't a bottomless pit of money that can be used to fund an ever-rising healthcare and benefits bill. For example, the UK's former Prime Minister, David Cameron, used this argument to defend his policy of austerity, claiming that he had no choice: 'If there was another way, I would take it. But there is no alternative.'[2]

Fixing the problems that we can all see is, apparently, unaffordable. If this is right, then, however unpleasant it is, we must resign ourselves to the end of this current phase of Western civilization and prepare ourselves for a return to something more like Victorian Britain. This was a world in which all the benefits of society went to a tiny proportion of people at the top – those who quite explicitly wielded all the power while the lives of the remainder were poor, nasty, brutish and short. This will, of course, be unfortunate for anybody who happens to lie outside the top 1 per cent of society. But if there is no alternative, there is no alternative.

However, if it is *not* right, then we need quite urgently to rethink how we run society. The stakes are high. This chapter explores that narrative of unaffordability and concludes that it is highly plausible but fundamentally unsound, and therefore extremely dangerous. It is a form of circular reasoning like that of Catch-22. It is, perhaps, Catch-23.

Why the narrative is so plausible

The narrative of unaffordability is plausible because it both *sounds* right and *feels* right. It *sounds* right because we have been systematically exposed to so many flawed economic models (see Chapter 10), so many myths and metaphors (see Chapter 9), and so much persuasive rhetoric (see Chapter 11) that it becomes very difficult for us even to question whether the narrative might be unsound.

In those chapters we saw evidence that, for example, thinking about running a national economy in the same way that one thinks about running a household is extremely misleading. So is believing that government debt in the US and the UK is at dangerous levels, a view that shows no understanding of historical reality. So is believing that profligate government spending was the cause of our current economic problems, which ignores both the fact that the Global Financial Crisis was what its name suggests – a financial crisis caused by a massive failure of the financial services industry – and that many of the governments hardest hit by the crisis were widely praised for their economic management in the period before.

Astonishingly, we saw that both the US and the UK are richer today than they have ever been. Nevertheless, we are so used to hearing these myths – and believing them – that it sounds right to say that we cannot afford to tackle our problems. Perhaps even more importantly, it *feels* right because it reflects our own experience: most people feel that they *don't* have enough money, and that they should be careful with it and ration their spending. Of course, each person's income is somebody else's expenditure and *vice versa*, so a society full of people rationing their spending is a society of people cutting each other's income.

Even to consider the question of whether unaffordability at the level of our society as a whole is a real phenomenon, when at the personal level it so clearly *is* real, is very difficult and requires considerable intellectual courage and honesty.

Paradoxically, the worse the results that follow from policies based on this narrative, the more people personally suffer from scarcity and the more plausible the idea of unaffordability at the level of society becomes. If Brexit – justified on the basis that it would free up £350 million per week for the NHS – weakens the UK economy, or if Donald Trump's tax reforms increase the US deficit, there is a risk that the idea of unaffordability will become *more*, not less, believable because of these failures. A sense of unaffordability therefore becomes self-reinforcing.

The state of government finances will then be used to demonstrate that the costs of Medicare, Medicaid and the NHS have become unaffordable, and that welfare payments need to be slashed. In the end, if these policies do so much damage that the pie begins to shrink, the narrative of unaffordability will become a self-fulfilling prophecy. That is the Catch-23.

An unsound narrative

It is easy to forget that society as a whole is getting richer. The pie is growing. In real terms, as we saw in Chapter 11, both the US and the UK are richer than they have ever been (and this despite the Global Financial Crisis and the Great Recession that followed it). As societies, *anything we could afford ten years ago, we can afford now* – and more. Of course, it does not follow that everyone in society is richer, and we saw that a dangerous process of mass impoverishment means that, in fact, they are not. But the wealth has not disappeared, it merely resides elsewhere.

Emmanuel Saez and Gabriel Zucman have painstakingly worked to understand where the wealth *does* reside in America. Because wealth is so very highly concentrated that missing a few of the very richest people can distort the entire picture, survey-based approaches run the risk of missing a small number of hugely important data points. Saez and Zucman therefore used tax returns to make a comprehensive set of estimates of wealth distribution in the United States since 1913. Their results are striking.[3]

The post-war period, and in particular the 1970s, was not a good time for the top 0.01 per cent of the population. Their share of national wealth fell to around 2 per cent. In the thirty-five years since then, however, it has grown enormously and now stands at around 11 per cent. The last thirty-five years have also been good – though not nearly to the same extent – for the rest of the top 0.1 per cent. The big losers are the bottom 90 per cent, whose share peaked at around 36 per cent and has now fallen to around 22 per cent. Over the last ten years, in real terms, the average wealth of a member of the bottom 90 per cent of the population has declined from US$66,466 to US$58,745. Over the same period, the average wealth of a member of the top 0.01 per cent has risen from US$121 million to US$260 million.

The total wealth of a society is related to the value of the goods and services that it can produce – i.e. to its GDP. As we have seen many times, real GDP per capita has continued to rise and societies in total have continued to become richer in most leading countries. The question, then, is not whether as a society we can *afford* to sustain our social contract, but whether we *choose* to do so and, if so, how we will pay for it.

If the immediate source of funding to maintain the social contract is to be government (and it is hard to see how it could be maintained otherwise), then there are three kinds of policy that could be explored:

1. additional revenue through taxation;
2. additional borrowing;
3. money creation.

We are consistently assured in the strongest possible terms that to exercise any of these options would lead to certain and imminent ruin for the nation. As always, it is therefore worth looking at the facts.

First, taxation. The facts on US taxation are summarized below. Clearly, higher tax rates are not an impossibility in the United States. A top rate of 70 per cent or more was the norm up until about 1980.[4] Since then, the rate has steadily declined and now stands below 40 per cent. A powerful chorus of persuasive voices tells us that these lower taxes are the route to economic growth. Peter Ferrara, former Senior Policy Advisor to the National Tax Limitation Committee and now one of President Trump's key economic advisers, believes that there is a clear link between higher taxes and lower growth:

> Put most simply, penalizing investors, successful entrepreneurs and job creators with higher taxes, to reward the less productive with government handouts, to make everyone more equal, is a sure-fire way to get less productivity, fewer jobs, lower wages and reduced economic growth.[5]

If there were such a clear and simple link, it would show up in the facts. For the first thirty-five years of the post-war period, during the Golden Age of Capitalism, the top marginal tax rate was at least 70 per cent. As we saw in Chapter One, the average growth rate during this period was 1 per cent higher than the average growth rate since taxes have been reduced. If we look in more detail at the long-run correlation between growth and level of taxation, what we find is the following (and you may want to see the detail in the Appendix on the *99-percent.org* website).

The two periods of highest growth were from 1936–40 and 1941–45, the wartime period during which the economy was actively managed by government. The 1960s and 1970s look particularly good in terms of per capita GDP growth, and the only period since then which has come close to matching it was 2001–05. In other words, the data show no evidence whatsoever of any trade-off between the top rate of tax and medium-term growth. In fact, quite the opposite. There is a tendency for higher growth in years where the top tax rate is higher. This is probably because higher taxes (and spending) tend to redistribute money from the very wealthy, who like to save a significant proportion of their income, to normal families (or as Peter Ferrara calls them, 'the less productive') who need to spend a higher proportion of it – in other words, more economic activity is driven per dollar when those dollars go to the middle class than when they go to the very wealthy.[6]

It is clear that the first option, taxation, is both possible and likely to be economically beneficial. If we, as a society, continue to choose not to take this option, we should at least be aware that we have made a choice based on personal preferences rather than economic necessity or good practice.

The second option is borrowing. Again, we are constantly told that following this path would be disastrous and lead to economic collapse. Many commentators take the line that government debt is already so high that we are in imminent danger of collapse. They claim that no business could survive if it ran its finances in the same way as the government. For example, UK Debt Bombshell, which claims to provide 'no-nonsense economics', says:

> We've been maxing out a new credit card almost every year, even in the good times. If a company were run like this, it would have long been declared bankrupt. So how much longer can we defy financial gravity? Well, we're about to find out.[7]

As we saw in Chapter Eleven, however, claims that government debt is at dangerous levels are nothing more than highly effective rhetoric. The fact is that *on average* the UK, for example, has sustained a higher ratio of debt to GDP for the last 300 years than it has today. An imminent disaster that takes more than 300 years to manifest is perhaps not so imminent.

The claim that businesses cannot run with an ever-expanding debt is equally nonsensical. As businesses grow, they typically *do* take on more debt, often over many decades. BP plc, for example – originally founded in 1909 as the Anglo-Persian Oil Company – has seen its debt grow dramatically over the years. Its liabilities were forty-four times higher in 2015 than they were in 1975.[8] In the 'no-nonsense' language of UK Debt Bombshell, they have been maxing out a new credit card almost every year. And BP is not unusual in this respect. It is usual for large companies to grow their debt year after year – and, of course, they are not declared bankrupt.

Even if the UK government were a household, its debt would not be worrying. Imagine, for example, a successful young couple looking to buy their first house with a joint income of £100,000. Imagine also that this couple has a prudent, old-fashioned bank manager who will only advance mortgages when he is very clear that the debt will be manageable. He refuses to lend them more than three times their joint income. In other words, no more than £300,000. The ratio of UK government debt to GDP is approximately 82 per cent. Tax revenue is approximately 36 per cent of GDP.[9] The national debt is therefore approximately 2.3 times income – well within the limits of what the old-fashioned, prudent bank manager would lend, and far less than many households do in fact borrow.

The cost of the interest on all this debt, we are told, will constitute an unbearable burden on our children and grand-children. We owe it to them to take tough measures now. But again, the facts do not support this narrative. Because interest rates are so low, borrowing is currently extremely affordable. In 1920, the costs of interest on government debt were around 9 per cent of GDP. Today, they are under 3 per cent.[10]

A business that has opportunities to invest in projects with a rate of return above its cost of capital would take those opportunities – indeed its directors have a fiduciary duty to manage the business in the long-term interests of its members, and that means making value-creating investments. At the time of writing, the cost of a long-term (ten-year) UK government bond is 1.85 per cent. If the UK government were the board of a company, it would therefore have a fiduciary duty to make any investment with a return above 1.85 per cent. But the UK government, unfortunately, has no such duty and has decided that the UK cannot afford to invest in, for example, flood defences, cutting the budget by almost £100 million and asking to see an average of £8 worth of damage avoided for every £1 spent.[11] This is equivalent to asking for a 700 per cent return.

No business with a cost of capital below 2 per cent would refuse to make investments unless they had a 700 per cent expected return. They know that making a sound investment makes them richer, not poorer – and the same is true for the country as a whole. No Swabian housewife would think to save money by not fixing a leaking roof in the house. Yet we are assured that this is prudence on the part of the government.

History suggests we could borrow more. The experience of long-lived businesses suggests that we could borrow more. Analogy with a normal household suggests that we could borrow more. Moreover, interest rates are near all-time lows. There is simply no factual basis for suggesting that government borrowing is not an option.

Politicians in particular do not like to talk about money creation. As we saw in Chapter 9, the Prime Minister of the United Kingdom went so far as to pour scorn on the idea, deriding it as being like a 'magic money tree'. He claimed that there was no such thing, and implied that money creation was impossible despite the fact that the Bank of England has clearly spelled out how it created £375 billion of new money since the Global Financial Crisis in order to stabilize the economy.[12] The former Prime Minister's claim is literally true – there isn't a tree – but figuratively it is a lie and a very important one.

The fact is very simple: money creation is possible, and we have done it recently and on a large scale. When there is risk of inflation, money creation may not be a good policy. When the economy is chronically weak, money creation may be necessary. As Lord Turner, former chairman of the UK's Financial Services Authority, says in his book, *Between Debt and The Devil*:

... inadequate nominal demand is one of very few prob-lems to which there is always an answer. Central banks and governments together can create nominal demand in whatever quantity they choose by creating and spending fiat money. Doing so is considered taboo – a dangerous path toward inflationary perdition. But there is no technical reason money finance should produce excessive inflation, and by excluding this option, we have caused unnecessary economic harm... money finance of fiscal deficits is technically feasible and desirable, [and] it may be the only way out of our current problems.[13]

Lord Turner points out that there is no technical reason why money finance should produce excessive inflation. Others have gone further. In the US, several economists, including the Nobel Prize-winning Paul Krugman, have supported the idea of a US$1 trillion coin:

Treasury [is allowed] to mint platinum coins in any denomination the Secretary chooses... And by minting a US$1 trillion coin, then depositing it at the Fed, the Treasury could acquire enough cash to sidestep the debt ceiling – while doing no economic harm at all.[14]

Similarly, in the UK, if the government minted three £500 billion coins and deposited them in a non-interest-bearing account of the Bank of England – not for spending, just to look at – they would have zero economic effect. But they would have a powerful psychological effect. UK government debt is around £1.8 trillion.[15] With three coins, net debt would be reduced to around £300 billion, or about 15 per cent of GDP. This is lower than it has been at any time since 1700. The idea that 'the state of government finances' makes action unaffordable would be blown out of the water.

We have examined the idea of unaffordability but failed to find any factual basis whatsoever for the idea that we cannot afford the social contract that defines Western civilization. In fact, there are three distinct ways in which we can afford to maintain our civilization and all of those ways have been proven to work in practice – and quite recently too. But this has not stopped politicians from making extraordinary claims, such as that made by the UK's former Chancellor of the Exchequer, George Osborne, as quoted in the *Independent*:

> Mr Osborne said earlier this month that people on low incomes would suffer if their tax credit cuts did not go ahead. 'Working people of this country want economic security. The worst possible thing you can do for those families is bust the public finances, have some welfare system this country can't afford,' he told BBC Radio 4's *Today* programme.[16]

In Mr Osborne's world, apparently, taking money from the poorest and most vulnerable is in their own interests because the problem of unaffordability is so severe. This position is so extreme that even some of those who originally supported deficit-reduction, find it hard to credit that he really believes it. Lord Turnbull, who was one of those and formerly Permanent Secretary to the Treasury, commented to Osborne:

> When you talk about debt, you talk about debt as though it were impoverishing the future... The majority of UK debt is owned by UK citizens, who have an asset. They own the gilts. They pay taxes to you obviously, but then they get interest in return. So the idea that this debt is impoverishing people is, I think, an economic fallacy.

I think what you're doing actually, your real argument, is you want a smaller state... But you don't tell people that's what you're doing. What you tell them is a story about impoverishment and debt, which I think is a smokescreen. The whole idea of the urgency and extent of reducing debt? I just can't see a justification for it.[17]

The history of the United Kingdom's National Health Service, the NHS, is interesting in this context. The NHS was founded in 1948 at a time when the ratio of government debt to GDP was over 200 per cent, and the cost of servicing that debt was over 5 per cent of GDP. Also in 1948, the National Assistance Act was passed which abolished the Poor Law system and established a social safety net to protect the poorest and most vulnerable, completing the work of the National Insurance Act of 1946.

If we had adopted our current patterns of thinking in 1948, we would have concluded that it might be a highly desirable idea in principle but completely unaffordable and totally unrealistic in practice. If the mind-set so prevalent in politics today had been the dominant mind-set in 1948, it is doubtful whether anyone would even have put forward the ideas of creating the NHS or the Welfare State. They would have seemed ludicrous.

Society as a whole is richer than it was and is likely to become richer still. Anything we could afford to do in the past, we will be able to afford to do in the future, if we choose to do so. Remember what Warren Buffett said about the vast increase in output coexisting with mass poverty:

I was born in 1930. There's now six times as much real output per capita in the United States than there was, in real terms – six times. If you'd told my parents that under these circumstances, there would be millions and millions of people living in poverty, they would have said it was impossible.[18]

The existence of previously unimaginable levels of wealth, in other words, has not stopped the narrative of unaffordability from taking root – with devastating consequences. The social contract is maintained by government, and as we have seen government has three distinct ways – all of which are demonstrably possible and have worked in the recent past, and indeed still work in other countries – of funding the social contract. Whether we do so or not is a political choice not an economic necessity.

The dangers of accepting the narrative of unaffordability

A narrative that is wrong but plausible is dangerous. To the extent to which it is believed – and it appears to be widely believed by policymakers of both left and right – it constrains policy choices.

If we believe in the narrative, investing in healthcare provision to make sure that all sectors of society are as healthy (and as productive) as possible is unaffordable. Investing in flood defences to prevent enormously expensive inundations of towns and cities is unaffordable. Investing in new technologies for renewable energy to prevent destructive (and colossally expensive) climate change is unaffordable. Maintaining roads so as to limit damage to the vehicles using them is unaffordable. Investing in education to improve the skills and prospects of the next generation is unaffordable. Protecting the young, the elderly and vulnerable is unaffordable. In fact, the type of civilization that we thought we had created is now unaffordable.

The narrative of unaffordability is a masterpiece of misdirection: it has convinced us that the *political* question of how to share the increasing wealth of society is a purely *economic* question, constrained by iron laws of economics. According to this narrative, we have no choice. There is no alternative. The post-war social contract is unaffordable. Even though society as a whole is far richer than it has ever been, in some mysterious (and never explained) way we can afford far less than we could afford before.

If we believe in unaffordability, then addressing the major problems of society becomes a luxury that we cannot afford. Taken to an extreme, the continued existence of most of the human race could become a luxury that we 'cannot afford'. Some economists, such as Bradford DeLong, Professor of Economics at UC Berkeley, are already beginning to warn about 'peak human' by analogy with the peak in the horse population that occurred just before the invention of the motorcar.[19] DeLong makes the point that historically – e.g. during the Irish potato famine – those in power have been prepared to see millions die because it was 'unaffordable' to keep them alive.

Tackling the narrative of unaffordability is therefore – quite literally – a matter of life and death.

PART 3

BUILDING THE FUTURE

All civilization has from time to time become a thin crust over a volcano of revolution.

Havelock Ellis

mmortality is elusive. People die and civilizations collapse – even those that believe that they will last forever. Among the longest-lasting civilizations, the Ottoman Empire and the Khmer Empire, both lasted for more than 600 years. The kingdom of France endured for over 800 years and the Republic of Venice survived for 1,100 years.[1] Most civilizations have had a much shorter life than these. Adolf Hitler's so-called 'Thousand Year Reich' lasted a mere twelve years.

Part One of this book set out the case that in some countries – including both the US and the UK – the social contract that defines Western civilization is under serious threat and that a continuation of current trends would lead to a dismantling of this contract and to the gradual disappearance of the kind of Western democratic civilization we have known since the end of the Second World War.

Part Two demonstrated that the notion – based on the narrative of unaffordability – that *There Is No Alternative* to our current approach to running society is not consistent with the facts – it is a mental construct buttressed by myths and metaphors, flawed models and misleading rhetoric. But it is not true.

Part Three shows that if we discard the narrative of unaffordability and take steps now to accelerate economic growth and to ensure that the benefits of that growth are shared more fairly, we can create an attractive future for coming generations.

Seeing the solutions doesn't need any complex theory. It just needs us to open our eyes to the facts. We can see what works and what doesn't work, both in our own history and by looking around the world. Then we just need to make sure we do what works.

Far from there being no alternative to our current plight, there is a wide spectrum of different forms of capitalism available to us – and some of them work much better than others. The choices we make as societies have consequences in terms of median income, percentage of the population living in poverty, life expectancy and social mobility, and all of these things have an impact on the happiness of the population. Looking at the top ten countries in the World Happiness Rankings shows that the US and the UK can both afford to be much better countries than they are. Unaffordability is not the problem. The problem is the choices that we make or, more accurately, the choices that are made for us by our elected representatives.

The flip-side to the myth of unaffordability is the opportunity that is open to us, if we reject that myth, to create a future of abundance for all. Achieving such a future will require a revolution – but it need not be a revolution in the streets. It can be just a revolution of the mind. A fact-based revolution. And it can be victimless.

If we consciously strive for a future of solidarity and abundance, we can achieve it. There are simple, practical steps that will preserve our democracies, regenerate growth and share it fairly – to create a second Golden Age of Capitalism. These steps are set out in 'The Abundance Manifesto'. The US has done it before – Roosevelt's New Deal – as has the UK in the aftermath of the Second World War. We just need to do it again.

We all have a role to play in making sure that our society chooses to head towards that Golden Age rather than continuing towards a scorched-earth future of mass impoverishment and plutocracy.

CHAPTER 13

Fifty Shades of Capitalism

When I say 'capitalism', I mean a full, pure, uncontrolled,
unregulated laissez-faire capitalism – with a separation
of state and economics, in the same way and for the same
reasons as the separation of state and church.

Ayn Rand[1]

We are told that we have to love free markets: the USSR tried socialism and that failed – and there is no alternative. This chapter shows that in reality we have a huge variety of choices open to us in thinking about how to run our society, and we'll explore some of the criteria that might help us make those choices.

The spectrum of possibilities

There are over 200 countries in the world.[2] Each one runs its affairs slightly differently from the others, and almost all of them allow capitalism to play a large role in their economies. This means that there are, in fact, far *more than fifty different shades of capitalism* for us to explore. We do not have to accept as the only alternative to communism the fundamentalist definition of capitalism suggested by Ayn Rand.

Indeed, Rand's point of view represents an extreme point on the spectrum of possibilities – just one possible meaning of the word 'capitalism'. Unlike Rand, most people who say that they are in favour of 'free' markets really mean that they are against excessive regulation. Very few are in favour of allowing tobacco companies to distribute free samples in infant schools or letting major companies combine to form monopolies or permitting drug companies to sell drugs without first conducting proper clinical trials. Et cetera.

The diagram below represents a selection of points along the spectrum between the two extremes of Randian capitalism and Soviet-style communism. It is worth noting that even Rand envisaged a small role for the state: to protect the rights of individuals, in particular property rights. At the other end of the spectrum, even in a state-controlled dystopia like North Korea, there is some private sector activity.[3]

This observation may be enough to suggest to you that neither end point on the spectrum is likely to sustain civilized society. The question that we might wish to ask ourselves is about choosing an acceptable balance: defining the form of capitalism that works best – or at least well enough – for society as a whole.

Figure 40: Spectrum of possible roles of the public and private sectors

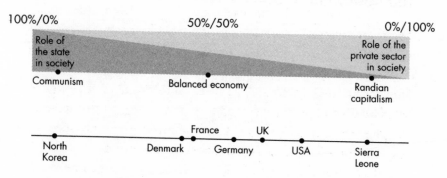

Source: WEO Database[4]

How should we choose?

If there are, as stated above, more than fifty different shades of capitalism potentially available to us, how should we start to think about which shade would suit us best? An obvious idea is to choose a system that is good for people to live under. One, admittedly subjective, way of assessing the system in any given country is to look at the degree to which the citizens of that country are happy with their lives. Surveys to assess perceived happiness are carried out across the world. The diagrams below are based on the rankings contained in the 2015 World Happiness Report, which ranked 158 of the world's countries according to their citizens' perception of their own happiness. The top ten countries, according to the 2015 report, are shown below.

Figure 41: World Happiness Report 2015 results

Rank	Country	Score
1.	Switzerland	(7.587)
2.	Iceland	(7.561)
3.	Denmark	(7.527)
4.	Norway	(7.522)
5.	Canada	(7.427)
6.	Finland	(7.406)
7.	Netherlands	(7.378)
8.	Sweden	(7.364)
9.	New Zealand	(7.286)
10.	Australia	(7.284)

Source: World Happiness Report, 2015[5]

It is interesting to look at whether these top countries have anything in common. In particular, is there anything similar about how they are run? The top ten countries all have governments that are quite active in the economy. No member of the top ten has a government representing less than 34 per cent of the country's GDP, and several have governments representing around 50 per cent.

At the other end of the spectrum, those countries whose governments play a minimal role – such as Sierra Leone, Madagascar and the Yemen – score far worse on the ranking. The position of Angola at 137, however, illustrates that having an active government is no guarantee of domestic happiness, and it would be easy to find other examples of this. While we should be careful not to read too much into these data, the facts are that the most successful countries have governments that play an active role.

Although the happiness of a country's citizens is arguably the most important indicator of how well it is governed, it is interesting also to look at a selection of objective measures such as median income, life expectancy, percentage of the population living in poverty and social mobility.

MEDIAN INCOME

It is clear that where there is a large difference, the higher the income the better the happiness score. Within the high-income countries, however, the picture is less clear. The United States has the highest median income but ranks only at number fifteen in the happiness rankings. Denmark, by contrast, ranks at number three but has a median income of only US$22,000.

PERCENTAGE OF THE POPULATION LIVING IN POVERTY

A different way of looking at the income of the population is to examine the percentage of people in the country who are living in poverty. This picture bears some similarities to the previous one but the pattern is stronger. At the large scale, those countries where poverty is commonplace score far worse on the happiness rankings. But at the small scale as well, within the group of most prosperous countries, the correlation appears to hold – by and large, the higher the percentage of the population in poverty, the worse the happiness ranking.

The conclusion is that poverty eradication ought to be a very high priority for all governments – even those in prosperous countries, especially Germany, the United Kingdom and the United States.

LIFE EXPECTANCY

Perhaps unsurprisingly, a country's happiness ranking seems to be quite strongly related to the life expectancy of its people. Among the developed countries, all except Denmark and the United States have a life expectancy of over 80 years.

SOCIAL MOBILITY

Social mobility, the ability of children to succeed financially even if their parents were not rich, is important to people. The data show that the higher the social *immobility* – i.e. the more that a father's income determines his son's income – the worse the happiness ranking.

The American dream, of course, is a paean to social mobility. Interestingly, the data show that of the leading countries, the US scores less well on social mobility than all except the United Kingdom. Conversely, all those countries in the top ten for which social mobility data are available score extremely well. Again, improving social mobility should be a key policy objective even in already prosperous societies, and in particular in the US and in the UK.

AFFORDABILITY

We have already seen the power of the narrative of unaffordability – even within very prosperous countries – when it comes to discussion of policy choices. These data show that there is no factual basis for such a narrative.

The United States is as rich, per person, as – or richer than – every country in the top ten, with the single exception of Norway. The fact that the US does not make the top ten is not down to lack of money. Switzerland has an almost identical per capita GDP to the US and it has managed its society in such a way that its citizens are among the happiest in the world.

To a lesser extent, the same point applies to the UK. New Zealand is a slightly poorer country in terms of GDP per capita but it runs its society in such a way that it is a member of the top ten when many richer countries, including the UK, are not.

CHAPTER 14

The Victimless Revolution

Those who make peaceful revolution impossible will make violent revolution inevitable.

John F. Kennedy[1]

If mass impoverishment is a trend that represents a real threat to Western democracy (as set out in Part 1) and if the barriers to tackling this trend lie only in our minds and in the collective decisions that society takes – not in the resources that are available to that society – (as explained in Part 2) and if, as well as the historical example of the Golden Age of Capitalism, there are countries that manage to avoid the problem today (as illustrated in Chapter 13), then it is clear that strenuous efforts should be made now to reverse the trend. These efforts will require the exercise of political power.

Unfortunately, power, like wealth, is highly concentrated. In fact, of course, the two things are highly correlated – being very wealthy confers a huge amount of influence, while influence can be deployed to boost one's wealth. As we have seen, in the United States the top 5 per cent have significantly greater wealth than the bottom 95 per cent of the population combined – and they probably have greater power as well.

Tackling mass impoverishment will require a reversal of direction and a change in many policies adopted over the last thirty-five years. This is a kind of revolution. The question is, *what* kind? Will the bottom 95 per cent have to take to the streets to reclaim control of their country – and if so, will they be successful? Or will there be a revolution in mind-set, as there was thirty-five years ago, but in a very different direction – leading to new policies and a shift towards the kind of economic thinking that produced the Golden Age and that shared the benefits so much more fairly?

The evidence suggests that society is rich enough to make this a painless revolution – there can be big winners without real losers. A revolution in mind-set will be sufficient:

- the flipside of the narrative of unaffordability is a sense of solidarity and abundance – and this sense has the great advantage that it is supported by the evidence and leads to a far better world;
- the obstacles to abandoning the narrative of unaffordability seem formidable but they may be less entrenched than they seem;
- the key is a change in mindset, and this change is supported by the facts. It requires no complicated theory and no leap of faith. Simply looking at the evidence of our own and other economies shows that we have the chance to build a future world of solidarity and abundance for our children to live in. A fact-based revolution is all that is required.

Solidarity and abundance

We saw, in Chapter 13, how powerful the narrative of unaffordability is. We have come to believe that even though society is far richer than it was thirty-five years ago, in some mysterious and never quite explained way, we can no longer afford what we used to afford. This belief is deeply rooted – we have heard the story so many times and from so many different quarters that even though the rational part of our minds accepts that real GDP per capita *has* grown and that society is therefore richer, it just doesn't *feel* true. The rational part of our minds tends to lose the argument.

It is therefore worth taking time again to consider whether abundance is really affordable. Since the wealth of society is related to the total value of the goods and services it produces, in order to ensure abundance for all we need only to make sure that two things are true:

- sufficient valuable goods and services will be produced;
- there will be an equitable distribution of the value of these goods and services.

For both of these, there are grounds for optimism.

ENSURING THAT SUFFICIENT VALUABLE GOODS AND SERVICES ARE PRODUCED

Sufficient valuable goods and services will be produced if there is capacity to produce them (supply) and enough demand for them – and if supply and demand are able to find each other. The world's working-age population continues to grow, so the supply of labour should not on its own be an obstacle. In any case, new technology, as we saw in Chapter 5, will enable the world to produce everything it produces today with half the workforce so that even in societies with ageing populations, shortage of workers is unlikely to produce supply constraints. New sources of energy and end-use efficiency measures are being developed,[2] as are new materials.[3] There are no readily apparent obstacles to continued growth in the wealth of society.

There is also no obvious shortage of demand. With an ageing population, the demand for healthcare and related services will be particularly high. The need to avoid damaging climate change creates enormous demand for new energy sources, for more energy-efficient forms of heating and transportation, for better ways to recycle, et cetera. Many Western countries have a civil infrastructure – roads, sewers, flood defences – that urgently needs investment. Improved education is also a priority in many of these countries.

There is, however, a growing problem in matching supply to demand. An important part of the mechanism that we use for this matching process is money – and if there is not enough money, or it is not in the hands of those who experience the demand, then the matching will not take place. The supply will not 'see' the demand. In this sense, 'poor people have no needs'.

Businesses will experience a demand shortfall, even as the real needs of society grow ever more severe. Civil engineers will sit idle even when there is an obvious need for flood defences; builders will lay off staff even when there are new houses, schools and hospitals that urgently need to be built. This is part of the problem we face today.

Even in recent decades, when growth rates have been lower than previously – partly as a result of this matching problem – we have seen very significant growth in the total value of products and services produced by all the world's leading economies. The OECD produces long-range forecasts for all major economies, which show most leading economies growing at 2 per cent *per annum* or more.[294] Even the slowest-growing are forecast to achieve a real increase in wealth of over 1 per cent *per annum*.

Figure 42: Long-term growth forecasts for selected leading economies (2015–50)

Country	Projected annual growth rate
China	3.6%
Australia	2.9%
UK	2.4%
US	2.1%
OECD average	2.1%
Denmark	2.0%
France	2.0%
Canada	2.0%
Japan	1.1%
Germany	1.0%

Source: OECD

Over the next thirty-five years, as over the last thirty-five – though maybe not to the same extent – most societies will become far richer. Even 1 per cent annual growth will accumulate over thirty-five years to a 42 per cent increase. Two per cent annual growth would correspond to a doubling in value over thirty-five years.

Most developed societies will be around twice as rich – according to the OECD forecasts – as they are today. Their populations will not have grown so fast,[5] so per capita GDP will be higher than it is today. The big question is whether their populations will share in this great increase in wealth. The pie will be bigger but will most people get a larger slice?

ENSURING AN EQUITABLE DISTRIBUTION OF THE VALUE OF THESE GOODS AND SERVICES

Part 1 demonstrated that, unfortunately, society as a whole becoming richer is *not* sufficient to ensure that most members of that society also become richer. Several countries have begun a process of mass impoverishment in which, despite real per capita growth, most people are becoming poorer over time. If we assume that real growth will continue – which is, of course, very good news – we are still left with the question of whether most people will benefit from that growth. Figure 43, below, shows three possibilities for sharing that growth, all based on the data we saw in Chapter 1.

Figure 43: Alternative scenarios for income growth in the US, by segment of the population

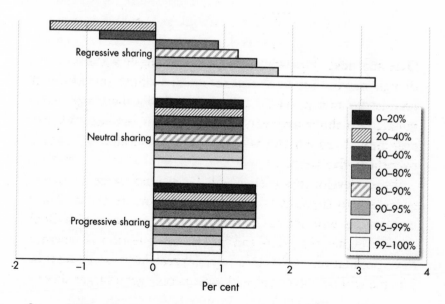

Per cent

Source: CBO[6]; author's projections

The three scenarios are:

1. **Regressive Sharing:** We attempt to preserve historical income growth rates by segment, protecting the lowest 20 per cent and giving priority to the richer segments, as in recent decades. The impact of this assumption is, as you saw in Chapter 1, to squeeze the middle-classes, who will experience a decline in their real incomes and will, by 2050 be living in or near poverty. In this scenario, in 2050 the bottom 20 per cent will still have a household income of under US$27,000, but now the next 20 per cent will also be living at that level.

2. **Neutral sharing:** Growth rates are equalized so that all segments experience the average growth rate in real income – 1.3 per cent per annum. All segments get richer year by year and inequality remains constant over time. In this scenario, the bottom 20 per cent of households will have an income in 2050 of US$41,000.

3. **Progressive sharing:** Policy is shifted in order gradually to reduce inequality over time, so that the poorest segments – in particular the bottom 90 per cent of the population – see their income rise faster than the richest. All segments are actually getting richer in real terms year after year; nobody is becoming impoverished. In this scenario, the bottom 20 per cent will have an income in 2050 of US$44,000.

The difference in outcomes between the first and the last of these scenarios highlights three key points:

1. The changes in income growth rate themselves are relatively minor – and there is no need to impoverish

the rich to prevent impoverishment of the rest of the population;

2. The impact on society of these changes is huge – it makes the difference between plunging the bulk of society into near poverty and seeing them enjoy a comfortable middle-class existence;

3. Recent trends and current policies tend in favour of the first scenario – the disaster scenario. It will take deliberate and sustained action to bring about something approaching scenario three.

There are, therefore, enormous grounds for optimism, but none for complacency. Changes to economic policy are required to bring about the more favourable scenarios, but in themselves they are relatively minor – the only thing revolutionary about them is the thought process needed to bring them about.

Why the obstacles may be less than they seem

At first glance, the obstacles to change can seem insurmountable. We have allowed the genie of extreme income and wealth inequality out of the bottle, and in effect handed control of society to a small minority of the population. It is not obvious that they will hand it back. Indeed, it is unlikely that they will rush to do so but their resistance may be less than expected:

- at first glance, it seems obvious that the top 1 per cent has benefitted enormously from the changes of the last thirty-five years;
- deeper examination suggests that this benefit may be less than it first appears;

- in the long-term, even the very rich may be better off under a more equal system than they would be by attempting to perpetuate current trends.

HOW THE TOP 1% HAS BENEFITTED

There is abundant evidence, in this book and elsewhere, that the top 1 per cent of society has benefitted in terms of income and wealth. With wealth comes status, power and influence. Wealth buys access to the best education and the best health care. Wealth even buys justice. There is no question that if anybody benefits from the status quo, it is the top 1 per cent – and within that top 1 per cent, even more particularly, the top 0.01 per cent.

There is no doubt that the ultra-rich, on average, are happier than the bottom 99 per cent of the population but they may not be as much happier as the difference in their wealth might suggest.

WHY THINGS MAY NOT BE AS GOOD FOR THE RICH AS THEY SEEM

There are three main reasons why extremes of inequality may negatively impact the happiness even of the very rich: first, because they are emotionally more exposed – paradoxically – to inequality than the bulk of the population; secondly, because their wealth buys less than they expect; and thirdly, because they are isolated by their wealth.

Someone in the middle, or even towards the upper end, of the wealth and income distributions is in a way shielded from inequality. They are unlikely to know their position in the national or global pecking order and, if they did, the difference between them and the person one place higher in that order is negligible. Neither of these things is true for the ultra-wealthy. League tables of the richest are widely publicized, and some of those listed in these tables define their sense of self-worth in terms of their financial net worth, which can make a change in the rankings extremely painful. It was widely reported, for example, that the Saudi Prince Alwaleed bin Talal Al Saud was deeply upset by Forbes' ranking of his wealth in the 2013 billionaires list.[7] He believed he should have been listed among the ten richest people in the world but Forbes disagreed.[8] A quick glance at that list for 2016 shows the following:

Figure 44: The ten richest people in the world in 2016

Rank	Name	Net Worth ($ billions)	Increase needed to move up one place
#1	Bill Gates	75	
#2	Amancio Ortega	67	12%
#3	Warren Buffett	60.8	10%
#4	Carlos Slim Helú	50	22%
#5	Jeff Bezos	45.2	11%
#6	Mark Zuckerberg	44.6	1%
#7	Larry Ellison	43.6	2%
#8	Michael Bloomberg	40	9%
#9=	Charles Koch	39.6	1%
#9=	David Koch	39.6	1%

Source: Forbes[9]

The average increase in wealth required to move up just one place is 8 per cent – a considerable undertaking against a moving target. Larry Ellison, for example, is extraordinarily wealthy but Bill Gates has almost twice as much wealth. Even though neither of them is constrained in their lifestyles, it is a reasonable assumption that Larry Ellison is painfully aware of the gap between himself and Bill Gates.

A second way in which the very rich suffer from inequality is that many of the goods they wish to own are so-called positional goods that are limited in supply: a house in Eaton Square, an original Picasso, a cellar filled with Château Lafite Rothschild. As the rich become richer, supply of these positional goods does not increase. The price rises instead. Remember hedge fund manager Paul Singer's complaint that the very rich are living on the leading edge of hyperinflation.[10]

While, of course, the suffering resulting from this high-end inflation pales into insignificance compared with the problems faced by people at the other end of the spectrum wondering how to meet next month's rent, it does mean that – frustratingly – all that effort expended in becoming very wealthy doesn't make it much easier to own a Picasso or a van Gogh and to live in the Hamptons or Mayfair. Inflation arises when too much money chases too few goods. In most of the world, that is not much of a problem – in fact, in recent years deflation has been the greater concern for the economy as a whole – but for the very rich, it feels like a big issue precisely because they have too much money.

The third, and perhaps most important, way in which the rich suffer from inequality is in a feeling of isolation. Another hedge fund billionaire, Thomas Perkins, clearly feels under enormous threat from the bottom 99 per cent of the population. In a letter to the *Wall Street Journal*, he warned:

Writing from the epicenter of progressive thought, San Francisco, I would call attention to the parallels of fascist Nazi Germany to its war on its 'one per cent,' namely its Jews, to the progressive war on the American one per cent, namely the 'rich.'... From the Occupy movement to the demonization of the rich embedded in virtually every word of our local newspaper, the *San Francisco Chronicle*, I perceive a rising tide of hatred of the successful one per cent... This is a very dangerous drift in our American thinking. *Kristallnacht* was unthinkable in 1930; is its descendent 'progressive' radicalism unthinkable now?[11]

While this may be an extreme case, Perkins is not alone in feeling isolated and anxious. In a study carried out for the Bill and Melinda Gates Foundation by Boston College,[12] over 160 extremely wealthy respondents reported on their feelings about a wide range of human issues including finances, family and friends. The level of insecurity is surprising – one respondent was quoted as saying that he 'wouldn't feel financially secure' until he had US$1 billion in the bank. Others struggle with the problem of working when they do not need to work – as one explained: 'Financial freedom can produce anxiety and hesitancy. In my own life, I have been intimidated about my abilities because I inherited money.'

Several people commented that extreme wealth does not make it easy to form deep, trusting relationships. 'Wealth can be a barrier to connecting with other people,' explained one. 'Not feeling you should share some of the stressors in your life ("Yeah, wouldn't I like to have your problems"), awkwardness re: who should pay at a restaurant.' Another worried, 'I start to wonder how many people we know would cut us off if they didn't think they could get something from us.' As a result, many find it easier to socialize only with others who are also rich.

In fact, extreme nervousness about the future of the world seems to be widespread among the rich. As Evan Osnos, writing in the *New Yorker* put it in an article describing doomsday preparation among the rich: 'Some of the wealthiest people in America – in Silicon Valley, New York, and beyond – are getting ready for the crack-up of civilization.'[13] He chronicled their preparations in case of disaster: buying houses in New Zealand; undertaking survival training; constructing bunkers; and securing space in post-apocalypse facilities.

Of course, despite all this, on average the very rich do have far happier lives than those living in poverty, but the benefits in terms of happiness are not proportional to their wealth.

HOW EVEN THE VERY RICH MIGHT BENEFIT FROM A MORE EQUAL SYSTEM

We saw in Chapter One how, if policy is set to try to preserve the rate of increase in income of the very wealthiest, there will be a failure of our civilization before the next thirty-five years have passed. Preventing this catastrophe does not (fortunately) require an overturning of the social order and a massive impoverishment of the very wealthy but simply that policy is formulated to ensure that the benefits of economic growth are shared by the whole population.

For the bottom segment, the difference between the three scenarios we looked at a few pages ago is life-changing. In the Progressive scenario, life can be comfortable – not luxurious but increasingly comfortable, especially for a family with two working partners. In the regressive scenario, life is hand-to-mouth, uncertain, difficult, stressful and insecure. By contrast, the difference in lifestyle available to the top segment is not dramatic: they would certainly have less money, but almost certainly the prices of the positional goods that are so important at that end of the wealth spectrum would be rising less quickly. It would be no harder to acquire a Picasso than it is today.

Furthermore, the rich save more than the poor.[14] A dollar given to a poor person is likely to be spent quickly and therefore to translate into immediate demand in the economy, whereas the dollar given to a rich person is likely to be saved or 'invested' – for example, by buying a house in the Hamptons or a Picasso. These dollars are more likely to lead to asset price appreciation than they are to create additional demand for products and services. As a result, the redistribution is in itself likely to boost economic growth, and if this happens, then the scenario would turn out even more favourably than presented above.

Since in the very long run the rich cannot see their incomes grow faster than the growth in the economy (or else more than 100 per cent of the economy would have to be the incomes of the rich), a policy that promotes higher economic growth would ultimately lead to the rich (as well as the poor) being better off than under alternative policies. The history of the last 200 years illustrates this well. Even the wealthy in 1815 did not have access to the same quality of healthcare, transport, information and entertainment that an average family can enjoy today.

In other words, the needed revolution, surprising though it may sound, could be victimless. The poor would be immeasurably richer but the rich would not be immeasurably poorer. In the long run, they might be slightly richer too. Not only would they be richer but they would be more secure. Their sense of isolation would lessen. Their sense of guilt would be replaced with a sense of satisfaction and they would know that they had helped to re-build a great country.

For the intermediate segments, too, the benefits would be enormous. Living in a society with a sense of solidarity and abundance is much less stressful than living in one whose dominant narratives are around scarcity and isolation. In a society of solidarity and abundance, nobody would feel that they needed US$1 billion in the bank to be secure.

That such relatively minor changes could have such enormously beneficial effects seems almost so good that it cannot be true. It feels as if there must be some barrier in the real world that stops this from happening – but all the evidence shows that this is not the case: there is no barrier.

How the truth can set us free

We saw in Part 1 how, in most developed countries, economic output has increased dramatically over the last thirty-five years and that there has been substantial real growth (i.e. after adjusting for inflation). Nevertheless, in several countries, this real growth has not been enough to prevent the phenomenon of mass impoverishment. The problem lies fundamentally not in a shortage of skilled labour or equipment or energy, natural resources or even land – which would have shown up as a shortfall of real growth – but in the way that growth is shared (which has manifested as mass impoverishment).

Our problem lies in the systems – laws, structures, bargaining processes et cetera – that determine how the fruits of economic growth are shared within society. All of these systems have been put in place by decisions taken on behalf of society as a whole by the elite within them: the politicians, functionaries, businessmen, judiciary et cetera.

These systems also determine who has access to the levers of power and who, therefore, can influence the decisions that shape tomorrow's world. This means that the root of our problem lies in the internal, mental world rather than the external, physical world. We are imprisoned not by a lack of ability to produce the goods and services that the world requires. Not by a shortage of skilled labour or an inadequate supply of technology. Not by a shortage of energy or other resources. Not by lack of land. We are imprisoned by our beliefs – in particular, our belief in the narrative of unaffordability. And this narrative, as we saw in Chapter 12, is not supported by the facts but by flawed mental models, widely accepted myths and metaphors, and by a triumph of rhetoric over reason.

If we want to end mass impoverishment, we must address the distribution of economic output. If we wish to address the distribution of economic output, we must consider the systems that we have put in place to govern this distribution. To change the systems requires society to take different decisions. And to take different decisions, we must tackle the widespread and deep-seated belief that there is no alternative. While we continue to believe that there is no alternative, continued mass impoverishment with all that that entails will remain the most likely future scenario.

Part 2 of this book examined some of the most prevalent underpinnings for this belief: the mental models that policymakers use to think about the economy; the myths and metaphors that politicians and the mass media routinely peddle; and the rhetoric – unsupported by reason – that supports the narrative of unaffordability. The facts, we saw, are readily available and they contradict these models, these myths, these metaphors and this rhetoric. The facts, in other words, will set us free.

The evidence that such change is possible comes both from our own history – notably the Golden Age of Capitalism that followed the Second World War and succeeded despite far more serious problems in the external physical world than any we face today – and from other countries, as described in Chapter 15, which have managed to create and sustain a sense of solidarity and abundance in today's world.

The surest way to end mass impoverishment is a fact-based revolution.

CHAPTER 15

The Abundance Manifesto

... we also need a government that will deliver serious social reform – and make ours a country that truly works for everyone.

Theresa May[1]

In the first part of this book, we explored the *process of mass impoverishment*; we saw that if current trends continue, today's civilization will not survive until 2050. It will have been replaced by a plutocracy in which a small proportion of the population own practically all the wealth and wield almost all the power, the middle class will have all but disappeared – and most people will be living in or near poverty.

The second part of the book explored the question of *why we are not resisting* these trends. In a nutshell, we are not resisting because we have been conditioned to think that there is nothing to be done. And almost everything we *think* we know about the economy turns out to be untrue.

We have been encouraged to believe that the post-war period marked a long slow decline, reversed only by the Reagan and Thatcher reforms. The truth is that the post-war period was the Golden Age of Capitalism, during which *the economy performed far better* than it has in the era of Market Capitalism. Even the 'dreadful' 1970s saw better economic growth overall, and higher pay rises for the typical family, than we have seen in the decade from 2007.

We have been trained to believe the story that the only route to economic success is through free markets and individual self-reliance. That the private sector is always far more efficient than government. That only the private sector can create jobs. And that even if we wanted government to help, which we shouldn't, there just isn't enough money – government debt is too high, taxation is too high, money doesn't just come from nowhere. Asking government to help tackle the problem is simply unaffordable.

Most of us *have* believed these stories – I used to believe them myself. But, as we saw, *none of this is true.*

If the stories *were* true, then we would have no choice but to accept that the future will be grim for most people. If they are *not* true, then there is everything to play for – *and there is.*

If we stand back and look at the facts, we see that we *should* be planning for a future of solidarity and abundance in which, by 2050, everyone is at least 50 per cent better off than they are today. And what is truly remarkable is that we do not need a revolution to achieve this.

In fact, the steps we need to take are neither particularly difficult nor particularly radical. The first step is to safeguard the functioning of our democracy. The second step is to build a New Deal on this foundation: base policy on facts rather than stories; explicitly manage towards a future of solidarity and abundance; invest wisely in the future; and ensure clean, competitive markets that work for the benefit of society.

We *can* make this kind of change successfully – we have done it before.

The key foundation is a well-functioning democracy

As we saw in Chapter 6, a well-functioning democracy requires more than simply the fact that each person can cast only one vote: it requires a society in which influence on public discourse and public policy is determined as far as possible by the quality of someone's ideas, not the depth of their pocket. Influence on policy should not, in other words, be dominated by a small proportion of the wealthiest people in society.

It is clear that in many countries, we have drifted away from this ideal and that, by very natural processes, we are likely to drift further. If we do not act, the rules will increasingly be written by and for the benefit of the already powerful and wealthy. Now is the time for us to perform a democratic reset.

Five proposals for a democratic reset

1. *An elected government should have an explicit duty to govern for the benefit of its entire population, not for that of a small and influential sub-segment:*

   - economic policy must explicitly target the problem of mass impoverishment and ensure that all sectors of society benefit fairly from economic growth – one of the tasks of the Office for Budget Responsibility (or equivalent organization) should be to assess the impact of each proposed budget in terms of this explicit duty over the short-, medium- and long-terms; where there is redistribution, it should be progressive, not regressive;
   - the Office for Budget Responsibility should publish its 'impoverishment ratio' each year – that percentage of the population which is poorer in real terms than it was the year before – and its 'leave-behind ratio' – i.e.

the percentage that has seen its income grow more slowly than the economy as a whole (in other words, more slowly than per capita GDP): this is the percentage who are being left behind by government policies;

- maintenance of full employment for those able to work should be an explicit goal of government policies and central bank decision-making;
- all proposed legislation should be assessed by the Office for Budget Responsibility to determine whether it tends to concentrate or to distribute income and wealth – regressive legislation that tends to concentrate income and wealth should require a two-thirds majority in both houses.

2. *There should be a written constitution in countries that do not already have one, or a constitutional amendment in those countries that do, to enshrine Point 1 above and to ensure that the distribution of political power does not become as concentrated as the distribution of wealth:*

- corporate political donations (from any type of organisation, commercial or not) should be banned, as should political advertising by corporate bodies;
- donations from individuals, their families and family trusts should be limited to an amount affordable by the median household;
- there should be strict controls over lobbying and full transparency of all meetings, and of all funding of lobbying activities whether in-house or external;
- suffrage should be universal – not dependent on property ownership or compliance with an onerous or costly process of registration.

3. *The constitution should safeguard separation of powers to prevent the risk that capture of one part of the elite*

facilitates capture of the remainder – the legislature should be separate from and have no control over appointments to the judiciary; regulators should have a high degree of independence, both from the legislature and from those whom they are tasked with regulating; and the independence of academic research should be protected: academics should be free to conduct fact-based research and publish the results whether or not they support government policy, and private funding of academia should be carefully controlled to ensure that wealthy donors cannot shape the teaching and research agenda to suit their own political ends.

4. *Media ownership should not be concentrated – no single family, family trust or other organization should be able to own or control media that reach an audience of more than 10 per cent of the population – and as part of the separation of powers, media owners should not also play a role as legislators, in the judiciary or in other key functions of society.*

5. *The constitution should also protect against an elected government seeking to circumvent democratic safeguards – e.g. by reducing the power of a second, or revising, chamber, or by reshaping electoral boundaries for political ends, or by seeking to limit the independence of the judiciary or otherwise weakening the separation of powers described in Point 3.*

Some of these reforms seem innocuous – indeed it is hard to imagine any government that would admit that it would even *think* of acting against Principle 1. But while they may not admit it, behind closed doors, they do just so. In the UK in 1982, for example, the then Cabinet Secretary, Sir Robert Armstrong, prepared a confidential paper for cabinet ministers exploring ways of dramatically reducing taxation to increase the wealth available for (upwards) redistribution. He justified this as follows:

> Some of the options would make some people worse off. But it is very difficult – in many cases impossible – to effect changes in the role of government without making some people worse off, particularly where public expenditure and hence taxation are involved. It is therefore necessary to accept that possibility whilst always recognising that it is the proper function and duty of government to ensure that no one is made so much worse off that he or she is subjected to undue hardship.
>
> If poverty is thought of as a relative condition, adverse redistributive effects become hard to accept. If, however, it is recognized that there is such a thing as an absolute level of poverty from which people should be protected, and poor people should share in the increasing wealth of the country, but perhaps not in full proportion, then some redistributive effects can be accepted – as they must be if the amount of wealth available for redistribution is to increase.[2]

It is notable that the paper was not putting forward the trickle-down argument – that the magic of market forces would enrich the poor, along with the rich. Armstrong, and the ministers for whom he prepared his report, were in no doubt that some people (the poor) would be worse off but they felt that this must be accepted if the amount of wealth available for upwards redistribution was to increase.

Governments with an explicit duty to avoid regressive measures, and who were measured on and held accountable for their impoverishment and leave-behind ratios, would not feel free to explore policy options such as those set out in Armstrong's paper. Parties whose funding came from the mass of the population rather than from rich individuals and big businesses would be more concerned about the well-being of the population as a whole. They would feel compelled to end mass impoverishment.

The fourth proposal seems more contentious but even if enacted, it would still mean that ten firms or individuals between them could maintain absolute dominance over the principal media – and, to a large extent, over public discourse. Nevertheless, in many countries this would be a much better situation than currently exists.

As Chapter Five pointed out, there are many ways of rent-seeking for those with their hands on the levers of power. Without the kind of democratic reform set out above, even if one government manages to pass effective legislation that reduces or even halts mass impoverishment, it will only be a matter of time until another government comes to power and undoes the good work. For this reason, constitutional reform is *more important than any single policy*, however carefully designed that policy may be. It is an essential foundation for a future of solidarity and abundance.

This reset would create a system of government *for* the people – indeed that would be the constitutional duty of government – and *by* the people in the sense that anyone's influence on policymaking would be (at least to a much greater extent than today) determined by the quality of their ideas rather than by the amount of wealth that they can use to push them.

We can build a new deal on this foundation

A democratic reset is a firm foundation on which fact-based policy can be formulated. As Part Two showed, there is no fundamental obstacle to creating a new Golden Age of Capitalism, just persuasive stories. A powerful narrative underpinned by well-established but flawed mental models, pervasive myths and metaphors, and rhetoric unsupported by reason.

Fact-based policy will allow us to create a society based on abundance and solidarity rather than scarcity and isolation, to invest in the future, and to enjoy the benefits of clean, competitive markets – capitalism as it is meant to be.

Fact-based policy

Particularly since the Global Financial Crisis, political discourse in many countries has been dominated by the narrative of unaffordability. As we have seen, even though it is not based on fact, this story is extremely persuasive – however desirable something is, if it really is unaffordable, we simply can't do it – and extremely destructive as a result.

Of the three factors identified in Part 2, it is the rhetoric unsupported by reason that does most to keep this story alive. Myths and metaphors play an important supporting role, and all of these – rhetoric, myths and metaphors – are lent a spurious respectability by the mental models most widely used to think about the economy. Moving to a world in which policy is based on fact will require reform in all of these areas.

Creating a society capable of taking fact-based decisions and formulating and implementing fact-based policy will not be straightforward. Fact-based decision-making requires both access to the facts and the ability to interpret them. In turn, access to the facts requires well-funded research and a thriving segment of the media providing high-quality journalism, while ability to interpret the data requires decision-making skills and the ability to distinguish facts from falsehoods and feelings. The existence of reputable fact-checkers is therefore important and valuable.

Fundamentally, all of these things depend on a widespread appreciation of the value of facts and on a large class of people – ideally, of course, the entire population – whose education includes critical thinking, attitudes and skills. This is, of course, not a trivial undertaking. But then, the enormous costs of going post-fact have become clear to most people. Now is the time to undertake such a programme – though the benefits would materialize only slowly.

One approach that might help in the short term is to set up an independent, well-funded and high-profile Office for Factual Accuracy, whose sole responsibility would be to assess for factual accuracy the public pronouncements of high-profile individuals and organizations – politicians, public officials, major media outlets and large corporations. Each statement could be assessed on a sliding scale ranging from 'known-to-be-false' to 'known-to-be-true' and with intermediate levels of 'probably-false-based-on-the-evidence', 'evidence inconclusive' and 'probably-true-based-on-the-evidence'.

Had such an office been established and recognized in the UK, the tenor of the discussion around the EU referendum would have been quite different. And had such an office been established and recognized in the US, the most recent presidential election would have been transformed. Scrutiny by the Office for Factual Accuracy might have a salutary effect on politicians and their policy advisers – no one would want to make a speech that would be publicly marked as full of 'known-to-be-falsehoods'. Political parties would therefore need to run their own fact-checking on their policy proposals.

Finally, a reform of the discipline of economics is needed to equip policymakers with models that are fit for purpose – e.g. for the purpose of ending mass impoverishment. Fortunately, this reform is to some extent underway and new schools of economic thought are already in development.

Behavioural economics seeks to address the fact – known for decades in other disciplines and more recently discovered by economists – that humans are not rational, consistent beings (*Homo Economicus*) with perfect information about the economy, who seek to maximize the discounted value of their own cash flows.

Modern Monetary Theory seeks to ensure that the realities of a *fiat* currency (which can be created at will by government) and of sectoral balances which sum to zero are taken into account in policy-making.

Most fundamentally, the work of economists such as Steve Keen and Marc Lavoie challenges the use of linear equilibrium-seeking models as the basis for understanding how the economy works.

It may take many years before thinking is no longer dominated by the idea of modelling an economy as if it were driven by a single, representative *Homo Economicus,* operating in a monetary system that resembles the gold standard and rapidly settling into an optimal equilibrium from which it deviates only as a result of external supply shocks – but the time will surely come.

A shift to fact-based policy will weaken the grip of the narrative of unaffordability and open the way to creating a society based on abundance and solidarity.

Design policy for abundance and solidarity

The major benefit of a society whose dominant narrative is abundance and solidarity, rather than scarcity and isolation, is the possibility of ending mass impoverishment. The total wealth of a society is related to the value of the goods and services that it can produce – when we talk about 'living within our means' as a society, anything we can produce is affordable. And as long as we can keep producing more, we can afford to consume more.

As long as the pie keeps growing, there is no fundamental obstacle to each person enjoying a larger slice. And at a time when a significant number of people are unemployed (even if technically they do not all feature in the unemployment statistics) or underemployed, we can afford a great deal more than we are currently enjoying.

Knowing we can do better is reassuring but questions remain about how to ensure valuable additional products and services are created, and that money to buy them reaches the pockets of the wider population.

The narrative of unaffordability means that there are many important areas in which society has been spending too little and where enormous benefit can be delivered. The pie should be growing far faster. It should also be sliced more fairly. The constitutional reforms described above will naturally lead to a profound shift in the policy mix. An explicit focus on avoiding mass impoverishment will require governments to assess every policy on two dimensions:

- Will this policy increase the size of the pie? (Abundance)
- Will this policy help share the pie fairly? (Solidarity)

As Figure 45 below illustrates, this assessment shows that there are four types of policy:

- **Type I: Captured growth policies** – policies that will increase the size of the pie but lead to less fairness in how the slices are allocated;
- **Type II: Shared growth policies** – policies that will both increase the size of the pie and distribute the slices fairly;

- **Type III: Vulture policies** – policies that will shrink the pie at the expense of the poor;
- **Type IV: Balancing policies** – policies that will improve distribution of the slices but will not grow the pie.[*]

Figure 45: Policy mix to create a society of solidarity and abundance

		Ensuring Solidarity	
		Sharing the pie unfairly	Sharing the pie fairly
Creating Abundance	Growing the pie	**Type I: Captured Growth Policies** *Balance with types II & IV* Widespread automation Large scale immigration Free trade with low-cost countries Unfunded tax cuts	**Type II: Shared Growth Policies** *Focus policy here* Investment in: • R&D • Infrastructure • Education • Healthcare Direct job-creation Supporting Private Sector Investment
	Not growing the pie	**Type III: Vulture Policies** *Avoid* Funding tax cuts by reducing benefits and public services Regressive tax changes	**Type IV: Balancing Policies** *Use to balance Type 1 policies* Raising the minimum wage Paying benefits to those in need Progressive tax changes

---

[*] Note that not all Type IV policies will shrink the pie even though Economics 101 might suggest that they would. Evidence from minimum wage rises, for example, shows no evidence of negative employment effects (Belman & Wolfson, 2014).

During the era of Market Capitalism, the policy mix has been heavy on captured growth and vulture policies and light on shared growth and balancing policies. The result has been lower growth and less fairness. As Professor Philip Alston has reported:

> The costs of austerity have fallen disproportionately upon the poor, women, racial and ethnic minorities, children, single parents and people with disabilities. The changes to taxes and benefits since 2010 have been highly regressive, and the policies have taken the highest toll on those least able to bear it. The government says everyone's hard work has paid off, but according to the Equalities and Human Rights Commission, while the bottom 20 per cent of earners will have lost on average 10 per cent of their income by 2021/22 as a result of these changes, top earners have actually come out ahead.[3]

A policy reset would see a strong focus on Type II policies and a judicious blend of Type I and Type IV policies to ensure robust economic growth, fairly shared. And no more vulture policies.

As widespread automation replaces many jobs in their entirety and drives down the wages available in others, an increased focus on shared growth and balancing policies may be the only way of avoiding the dystopian outcomes presented in Part One of this book. Appendix V illustrates how such a system could be made to work – how widespread automation could indeed lead to abundance for all rather than an acceleration of mass impoverishment.

More immediately, the final report of the Commission on Economic Justice contains no fewer than seventy-three specific policy recommendations under ten headings.[4] All of these recommendations aim to promote prosperity and justice – or, in other words, abundance and solidarity.

Interestingly, a quick look at the Conservative Party's 2017 manifesto showed that it was full of good ideas for Type II policies – but unfortunately, distracted by Brexit and in the continuing grip of the narrative of unaffordability, none of them have been implemented.

There is no shortage of good ideas. We just need to have the courage to carry them out.

Invest in the future

As a society, we are systematically under-investing in the future. This under-investment impoverishes future generations. Investment can come from two sources: the private sector – which *will* invest when it can 'see' demand to invest for, but will not invest otherwise; and the public sector, which is currently in the grip of the narrative of unaffordability.

Once this narrative is weakened, the public sector will be free to invest in those areas in which the private sector – even in good times – will not invest enough, such as fundamental research and development, education, preventive healthcare, environmental protection and civic infrastructure. These are Type II policies.

We have become accustomed to thinking of the private sector as risk-taking, dynamic and innovative, and the public sector as slow, inefficient and bureaucratic. As Mariana Mazzucato explains in her book, *The Entrepreneurial State,*[5] however, an astonishing amount of private sector innovation is possible only because of fundamental advances driven by public sector investments.

Taking the iPhone as an example, she shows how many of the key elements so brilliantly assembled by Apple were originally funded (as was Apple itself as a fledgling business) by government. The iPhone took the world by storm because it combines so many innovative new technologies: it was the first truly smart phone, with Siri as an intelligent assistant; it had comprehensive Internet access; it had an easy-to-use touch screen interface; and it made innovative use of location services based on GPS.

All of these elements exist only because the early, high-risk stages of their development were funded by the public sector. The touchscreen, for example, was developed by CERN and perfected by Westerman and Elias originally at Delaware University; the Internet was developed at DARPA and the World Wide Web at CERN by Tim Berners-Lee; global positioning satellites (GPS) were another military technology; and SIRI was originally developed by the Stanford Research Institute on behalf of DARPA. *Without government-backed R&D, we would not have the iPhone.*

The world is struggling to meet its commitments to reduce greenhouse gas emissions. The development of new and more cost-effective technologies for energy generation (such as fusion, solar, wind and tidal power) and storage are vital to the long-term well-being of humanity. The same goes for technologies promoting greater efficiency in the use of that energy. At such a time, driving fundamental research and development – especially during early and high-risk phases when a commercial return cannot be guaranteed – is a vital role for government.

Nor is it just at the early stages of technological development that government has a key role to play. The UK, for example, has under-invested in civic infrastructure for several decades. The Conservative MP, Stephen Hammond (while he was Parliamentary Under Secretary of State for Transport) described the state of Britain's roads thus:

... we've underinvested in roads for decades. The World Economic Forum ranks the UK twenty-fourth in the world for the quality of its road network at the moment. By contrast, France and Germany are in the top ten. It is a simple fact that since 1990, France has built 2,700 miles of new motorway – more than the entire UK motorway network. We have built just forty-six, between 2001 and 2009. And between 1990 and 2001, annual spending on trunk road schemes in England fell by more than 80% in real terms.

The continual stop-go has had a huge impact. This is something that we, as a government, are working hard to address. Because we know that if we don't act now to improve our roads, the repercussions will be felt for generations to come.[6]

The situation in housebuilding is even worse. As the Chief Secretary to the Treasury put it:

The UK housing market, however, faces longstanding issues. Housing supply has failed to keep up with household formation levels for decades, leading to rising house prices and making good-quality housing unaffordable for many. Between 1999 and 2010, the UK built fewer new homes per 1,000 inhabitants than Germany, almost 30 per cent fewer than the Netherlands and over 40 per cent fewer than France.[7]

Britain needs to build over 240,000 new homes each year to meet demand[8] and falls far short of this target every year. While there are many factors on the supply side holding back housebuilding – such as shortage of land, inability to grant planning permission, incentives for housebuilders to hoard land until prices rise, et cetera – it is notable that in the early years of the Golden Age of Capitalism, the public sector built more houses than the private sector whereas today, in the grip of the narrative of unaffordability, it builds very few. The implications of this shortage are well known: house prices are becoming increasingly unaffordable to the young, and rates of home ownership are beginning to decline. Even those who can afford to buy risk being overstretched, while those trapped in rented accommodation pay a significant proportion of their income on housing costs.

Arguably even worse is the situation in relation to flood defences. In 2007, the UK suffered from serious floods as a result of what were at the time unprecedented levels of rainfall. Sir Michael Pitt was commissioned to lead a review into the floods and to recommend policy for future flood protection. In his letter to the Secretaries of State, he commented:

> The floods of last year caused the country's largest peacetime emergency since World War II. The impact of climate change means that the probability of events on a similar scale happening in future is increasing. So the Review calls for urgent and fundamental changes in the way the country is adapting to the likelihood of more frequent and intense periods of heavy rainfall. We have searched for practical solutions to highly complex problems and thought carefully about the public interest. Our recommendations are challenging and strong national leadership will be needed to make them a reality.[9]

Indeed from 2008 to 2010 there was significant investment in flood defences but after 2010, the impact of austerity led to these expenditures being considered unaffordable and the budget was sharply reduced.[10] As Sir Michael's report predicted, flooding on a similar scale *did* happen again: there were serious floods in 2015. Estimates of the cost of the damage caused to the UK run into many billions of pounds.[11] Spending on flood defences would have been a sound investment for the UK economy, while 'saving' taxpayers a few hundred million pounds has cost them over £5 billion.

Providing this kind of critical national infrastructure is clearly an area where if government does not spend the money, it will not be spent. And as every Swabian housewife knows, it is not prudent to leave a leaky roof or pipe unrepaired.

The situation is similar in the US. A recent assessment by the American Society of Civil Engineers suggests that to prevent serious damage to the economy, investment in civil infrastructure totalling US$3.3 trillion is required before 2025 – but they expect only US$1.9 trillion of that to be spent: *a funding gap of US$1.4 trillion.*[12] 'Saving' the US economy US$1.4 trillion in this way is estimated to cost over US$4 trillion by 2025 in terms of lost GDP.

The examples above show that, in the UK and the US at least, there is no shortage of high-return projects – projects, in other words, that will pay for themselves many times over. It is a false economy not to invest in these projects and it is the narrative of unaffordability itself that will impoverish future generations.

Create clean, competitive markets

The story of capitalism is compelling: where there is a need in society, there is a business opportunity. An entrepreneur can seize this opportunity by providing a product or service to meet the need. In producing this product or service, he will consume other products and services, raw materials and labour, and their costs to him, being set at market prices, will reflect their values for alternative uses. If, after meeting these costs, the entrepreneur makes a profit, this means that he has found a higher-value use for the products and services consumed and simultaneously created value for himself and for society as a whole.

In this way, enlightened self-interest automatically increases the benefit for society as a whole. In this ideal story of capitalism, making profit is synonymous with working for the greater good. And *any* interference, for example by government, with profit-making will necessarily reduce the public good. It is on the basis of this story that many people say they believe in free markets.

Unfortunately, as a matter of real-world observation, making profit is *not* always synonymous with working for the greater good. When a tobacco company grows its profits by selling more cigarettes, it is not clear that this is for the greater good. When a company boosts profits by paying below a living wage – and gets the taxpayer to top up the difference – it is not clear that this is for the greater good. When a company is loaded up with debt, pays huge dividends and then goes bankrupt leaving employees, suppliers and the taxpayer out of pocket, it is not clear that this is for the greater good.

The failure of British Home Stores in 2016 is a case in point. The Conservative MP David Davis described it as:

> ... the dark side of capitalism: increased borrowing and payment of ever bigger dividends; risk transferred from the private to the public when the business fails; [with] the low-paid and the taxpayer left to pick up the bill.[13]

In brief, the story is as follows. In the year 2000, Philip Green, who was subsequently knighted for his services to retail, bought BHS for £200 million on behalf of his wife, Tina,[14] who was resident in Monaco – a jurisdiction well-known for its low tax rates. Philip Green then argued that the business was worth more than he paid for it and wrote-back around £100 million of negative goodwill through the profit and loss account, thus making BHS appear surprisingly profitable. On the basis of this profitability, he was able to load the business with debt and to extract large dividends, rental payments and interest on loans estimated by the *Financial Times* at around £1.2 billion,[15] before he sold BHS for just £1 in 2015, when the business ran into trouble.

Around a year later, BHS filed for administration, putting the jobs of its 11,000 employees at risk. At the time of Philip Green's purchase, the BHS pension plan was in surplus (£17 million surplus in 2002); at the time of BHS's failure, the plan had a deficit of £571 million. As Davis commented: 'The BHS story is a case study in many unpopular aspects of modern capitalism: exploitation of limited liability, loophole-ridden tax law and intricate accountancy.'

Sadly, this is not an isolated example of capitalism failing to follow the ideal. The Global Financial Crisis was precipitated by subprime mortgage-lending in the United States that caused losses to the US banking system estimated at almost US$1 trillion[16] – very roughly equivalent to one year's profits from all US quoted companies – and additional losses to the banking system around the world.

To achieve US$1 trillion of losses is a remarkable achievement: if we assume that the loss on each bad loan averaged US$100,000, then it would require 10 million bad loans to generate US$1 trillion of losses. This is industrial-scale bad lending – a system gone wrong; and its global impact has been devastating and is still being felt. Andrew Haldane, Chief Economist of the Bank of England, estimated the impact of the

Global Financial Crisis at between US$60 trillion and US$200 trillion for the world economy.[17]

The financial system is still not fixed: banks have continued to behave unethically as shown by the more recent LIBOR scandal, for which many have received significant fines. Indeed, fixing the system has proven problematic: in the UK, for example, the Independent Commission on Banking recommended a package of measures to keep the world safe from a recurrence of the Global Financial Crisis[18] but its chairman, Sir John Vickers, subsequently became concerned that in the face of persistent and persuasive lobbying by banks, the Bank of England is in danger of watering down the Commission's recommendations to the point of ineffectiveness.

Mervyn King, the former governor of the Bank of England, agrees. In his book, *The End of Alchemy*, he concludes that banks should hold at least 10 per cent of equity (the foundation of their risk buffer), as against 3–5 per cent, which is common today, and that the risk of a second Global Financial Crisis remains high until the system is fixed.[19] Nor is the problem limited to retailers and banks. The automotive industry is reeling from a series of disclosures relating to emissions, and many other sectors have their own scandals.

Why does this happen? Are businesses run by psychopaths? Possibly some are, but there is a more systematic reason why such things tend to happen. Put very simply, the nature of market capitalism puts enormous pressure on those who run businesses. Corporate executives feel constantly under pressure to improve performance, and in particular to drive up reported profit. In practice, one of the easiest ways to do this is to externalize costs. Pollute without paying to clean up the pollution, pay below a living wage but still have living employees, avoid paying taxes, carry out transactions that look good in the short term (such as making unviable long-term loans). All these are ways of ensuring that reported profit is higher.

Because of the possibility of externalizing costs, many of the levers available to corporate executives to improve profit are *not* synonymous with working for the greater public good. They are not even necessarily synonymous with working for the long-term benefit of their own shareholders.

Even worse, if there is a straight competition between two otherwise similar companies in the same sector and one of them aggressively externalizes its costs, it will be more profitable than its competitor. If the situation is allowed to continue, it will be able to take market share from its competitor and ultimately drive its competitor out of business. If externalization is widespread, the forces of competition will act to allow the bad to drive out the good – the precise opposite of the capitalist ideal. Appendix IX provides a worked example of how this happens, and how companies that externalize their costs become an engine for mass impoverishment and for the destruction of the environment.

There are, in fact, many CEOs with high ideals who do seek to make their businesses a force for good. In the UK, for example, The Royal Society for the Encouragement of Arts, Manufactures and Commerce (RSA) has for many years promoted *Tomorrow's Company*, with the aim of encouraging businesses to manage in the interests of all their stakeholders and society, and for the long-term. They have found it an uphill struggle:

> There are emerging trends in British business that we cannot ignore. Despite considerable success in many areas, companies in the UK suffer from under-investment, low productivity, low real wage growth, employees that are demotivated and disconnected from management and

diminishing public support. The irony is that the returns to shareholders have also been poor.

The good news is that an alternative business approach already exists. Instead of the current focus on short-term incentives, targets and profit, it focuses on purpose, values, relationships and the long-term.

We recognize that this is easier said than done and short-term pressure is formidable. However, twenty years of convening companies, investors and policy-makers has proven to us that change can be achieved when the business and investor community work together to achieve a common goal.[20]

After twenty years' campaigning, they have found that CEOs are under such pressure to deliver short-term performance that other considerations too often become secondary.

Creating a market in which externalization is *not* widespread is a vital role for government. In free markets, the bad will drive out the good; in clean, competitive markets the good will drive out the bad. Regulation has a bad name and it is seen as interfering with businesses' ability to generate profits. This interference is, however, essential if we are to have clean, competitive markets; without it, we will continue to see massive externalization of costs, which will have to be borne by society as a whole, and we will see good businesses systematically driven out by bad businesses.

All competitive sports employ referees to ensure fair play and to make sure that the best, rather than the most unscrupulous, competitors win. In many sports, there are strict and onerous regulations to prevent drug-taking. When these regulations are insufficient, as they were in cycling for many years, the distortion of competition can be dramatic – the *Tour de France* winners list shows a gap with no winner from 1995 to

2005, and there are several other years in which the original 'winner' was subsequently stripped of his title as a result of drug-taking.[21] The regulations that were subsequently introduced are indeed onerous and intrusive – but the only losers from them are the cheats. Honest cyclists now have a chance to win.

It is the same in business: for capitalism to work for the benefit of society – to enable the RSA's vision of *Tomorrow's Company* to become a reality – there is a vital role for government to play as a referee.

Arguing that business regulations represent unjustified interference in the ability of businessmen and women to make profit is like arguing that sporting regulations constitute an unjustified restriction on the ability of athletes to compete. Asking bankers to design financial regulation is like asking Lance Armstrong in his prime to design the regulation of drug testing in cycling.

We have done more difficult things before

As the United Nations Trade and Development Report pointed out in 2017, a democratic reset of this kind has a clear precedent:

> The original New Deal proposed by President Franklin Roosevelt to the United States electorate in the 1930s represented a concerted effort to repair and rebalance the United States economy and society in the aftermath of the Great Depression. Famously, Roosevelt offered a positive alternative to a fearful society, making job creation and social security the pillars of a more hopeful strategy. He abandoned the austerity policies that had

promised a recovery through tax increases and cuts in government programmes, and offered instead recovery through enhanced government spending and targeted support for different regions and sectors (beginning with agriculture). This was to be made sustainable through strengthened regulation of markets, beginning with taming financial markets but more generally by managing competition.

In addition, it was expected to deliver more inclusive outcomes through redistributive measures beginning with labour market reforms to protect workers, followed by progressive fiscal measures and welfare programmes. Recovery, regulation and redistribution became the bases of the New Deal...

One important lesson from these efforts is that, to be effective, policy changes should be rapid and of sufficient scale and generosity; slow and small incremental increases are likely to be less inspiring or transformative.[22]

At the moment, while we remain in the grip of a narrative of unaffordability, some of these ideas may feel radical. For this reason, it is worth comparing the situation we find ourselves in today with the situation after the Second World War, when Great Britain took the bold decision to build a new world, and somehow found it affordable.

Not only was it affordable, it also coincided with the beginning of the Golden Age of Capitalism, an era of unprecedented growth and prosperity. As the chart below indicates, the cost of funding the war effort had pushed the ratio of debt to GDP to well over 200 per cent. It would have been easy, and plausible, to say that in such desperate times, government simply could not *afford* to do more for its population. It would have been straightforward to argue that ideas such as the creation of a Welfare State or of a national health care system were laudable but completely impractical, and would have to wait until the public finances had been restored to health, perhaps in a generation's time. Today's national mood would certainly have indicated such policies.

Figure 46: Comparison of the state of UK public finances today and in 1948

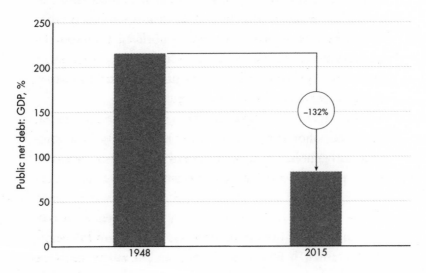

Source: Chantril[23]

Instead, based on the 1942 report by Sir William Beveridge,[24] the government conceived an ambitious plan to free Britons from five great evils, or 'giants' as Beveridge called them: *Want* [poverty], *Disease, Ignorance, Squalor* and *Idleness* [unemployment]. This was a radical plan for a comprehensive liberation of the British people from the fear, and the reality, of these evils.

Beveridge set out three key principles that were to guide the creation of the new welfare state, and it is clear from the third principle that he saw the solution to these evils as coming from a productive cooperation between the state and the individual – not from the state alone, nor from the individual alone – and that he was concerned to preserve incentives and opportunities for self-improvement:

> The first principle is that any proposals for the future, while they should use to the full the experience gathered in the past, should not be restricted by consideration of sectional interests established in the obtaining of that experience. Now, when the war is abolishing landmarks of every kind, is the opportunity for using experience in a clear field. A revolutionary moment in the world's history is a time for revolutions, not for patching.
>
> The second principle is that organization of social insurance should be treated as one part only of a comprehensive policy of social progress. Social insurance fully developed may provide income security; it is an attack upon Want. But want is one only of five giants on the road of reconstruction and in some ways the easiest to attack. The others are Disease, Ignorance, Squalor and Idleness.
>
> The third principle is that Social Security must be achieved by cooperation between the state and the individual. The state should offer security for service and contribution. The state in organizing security should not stifle incentive, opportunity, responsibility; in establishing a national minimum, it should leave room and encouragement for voluntary action by each individual to provide more than that minimum for himself and his family.[25]

The statistics in Chapter 2 demonstrate that Beveridge was right: investing to create the NHS and the Welfare State did not destroy enterprise; it ushered in the Golden Age of Capitalism.

Restoring the social contract is not an unaffordable pipe-dream – in fact, it is *the key to restoring economic dynamism.*

CHAPTER 16

Your Role in the Change

Activism is the rent I pay for living on the planet.

Alice Walker[1]

There are at least two ways of driving this kind of change: *top-down*, from a central authority such as government; and *bottom-up* from the population as a whole.

There is no doubt that bottom-up efforts have mitigated some of the worst impacts of mass impoverishment. The determined efforts of charities, churches and community organizations who provide food banks and hostels for the homeless prevent thousands of deaths each year and ease the misery for many more. Those who provide training for the young and reskilling for the not-so-young, and those who create new businesses in areas of high deprivation have all made the world immeasurably better.

But as we have seen, they have not been anything like enough to prevent mass impoverishment from blighting the lives of millions. The idea that as the public sector retreats, the private sector will fill the gap has been tested for over thirty-five years and found wanting. However stirring the stories, the idea that rugged self-reliance underpinned by voluntary support will be enough to reduce poverty is no longer plausible. Governments need to act.

We *do* need top-down action. But we need bottom-up action to drive it. And this is where *you* come in. Unless the population as a whole makes it clear to our elected representatives that mass impoverishment will not be tolerated, politicians will conclude that it *will* be – and they will continue to formulate policy accordingly. We know where that ends.

But you may feel that there is nothing you can do. You have no great power, and not even very much free time. How can you change the world? Fortunately, you are not alone. Most people are in the same situation as you. And this means that there are millions of you. If even one quarter of those millions spend just one hour a year making sure that politicians are aware of their demands, the effect will be dramatic.

You can also make certain that any newspapers you buy and other media you consume are taking a positive approach to the issues, rather than continuing to pay money to those whose editorial line perpetuates mass impoverishment. And as far as possible, you can avoid spending your money with businesses that systematically externalize their costs.

And there is one absolutely vital thing that you can do that really takes no extra time: make sure that you vote for the candidate or party doing most to address mass impoverishment. If there is no party with a credible plan, vote for the party whose plans are doing least to exacerbate mass impoverishment. Everyone can vote: at the ballot box, with their pocketbooks and with their feet – and if they do so, their combined impact will be enormous.

But perhaps you *do* have some time. Perhaps you are even a member of a political party or a non-governmental organization such as Oxfam or Greenpeace. If so, there is more you can do. You can make sure that as many as possible of your colleagues are aware of the issues – and the facts and figures – in this book. If you are politically active, you should make sure that your party has a positive plan to address mass impoverishment. And if you cannot get your party to listen, maybe you are in the wrong party.

It may be that in your working life, you can make an impact. If you are a teacher, perhaps you can help your pupils to realize the importance, and the difficulty, of sifting fact from fiction. (For example, is it fact or fiction that UK government debt is at dangerously high levels? Most politicians and almost all newspapers would lead you to believe that it is fact – but if you consult the sources of data, you see that it is fiction.[2]) If you are a journalist, you can start to highlight the facts presented in this book and to dismantle the myths. If you are a playwright, there are many powerful stories locked behind the statistics. If you are a businessman or woman, you can lend your weight to the creation of clean, competitive markets.

And perhaps you are a politician or policymaker yourself. If you are, you should strain every sinew to ensure that your party proposes and implements shared growth policies while steering clear of vulture policies. You are in a privileged position that enables you to make an enormous contribution to the change we desperately need.

Even if you can do none of these things, you can display the 99% sticker in your window, to show support. Whoever you are, there is *something* you can do, and you are not alone.

When you have finished reading this book, take a look at the website *99-percent.org* that will point you in the direction of resources, such as sample letters to elected representatives, and to groups and organizations in your area whose members are concerned about mass impoverishment and would welcome your help.

Whether your contribution is large or small does not matter. What matters is that you take action. As Philip Alston, United Nations Special Rapporteur on extreme poverty and human rights, said in his 2018 report on the UK,[3] 'the good news is that many of the problems could readily be solved if the government were to acknowledge [them]'. We need to make sure they do.

Conclusion

After more than 300 pages of facts and figures about the economy, you could be forgiven for thinking that the subject of this book is immensely complex. In fact, the data have been presented to deal with potential counterarguments; the argument itself is very simple. The pie is continuing to grow but more and more people find that their slice is shrinking. There are no real-world barriers to fairer slicing, though we have been misled into believing that there are. A few common-sense reforms will ensure fairer slicing and guarantee an attractive future for our children's generation. That's it. If your friends ask you what the book is about, that is all you need to say.

Summary of Part 1

Part 1 made the argument that, little by little, and in a way that is barely perceptible, some of the core features of our civilization are being whittled away. If we do nothing to change these trends, then before 2050 we will have reached a point of failure: life will be immeasurably worse (and measurably shorter) for the bulk of the population than it is today.

We saw data that showed that both in overall economic performance and the economic experience of a typical member of society, the *Golden Age of Capitalism* was far more successful than the era of *Market Capitalism*. During the era of

Market Capitalism, even though society as a whole has continued to get richer, in some mysterious way, many people have begun to get poorer.

In the US, the key driver has been rising inequality: both a fall in the share of national income that goes to wages, and the distribution of those wages becoming increasingly skewed towards the top-end. In the UK, the key drivers have been rising inequality (driven by a falling wage share) and almost stagnant GDP per capita. The experience of these two countries shows that it is vital to grow the pie and it is equally vital to slice it fairly.

Several ground-breaking technologies, ranging from materials science through medical advances to advanced information technology, mean that many important human problems will become solvable before 2050. Unfortunately, they also mean that employing humans for many purposes will become uneconomic. With the right set of policies, we could enter a technological utopia; with the wrong set, we will experience a nightmare. 2050 is not far away but no political party has any policy to deal with the challenge.

The practical impact of impoverishment goes way beyond the issue of unfairness: poverty brings reduced educational attainment and life chances, increased exposure to violence and ill-health, and reduced life expectancy. Ensuring that the increasing wealth of society is used to eradicate rather than exacerbate poverty is literally a matter of life and death.

Like any game, winning in the game of capitalism depends greatly on effort and skill. Unlike most other games, it also depends on one's wealth and social position at the start of the game. It is also a game in which the rules are constantly being rewritten, and the people doing the rewriting are almost all in the top 1 per cent. By a very natural process, therefore, unless the rest of society takes steps to prevent it, the rules will increasingly favour the rich at the expense of the rest. Without such steps, the trends of the last thirty-five years will continue or even accelerate.

If these trends do continue, we are unlikely to reach 2050 with our civilization intact. Either there will be a violent transition to a new state or mass impoverishment will have reduced the bulk of the population to a condition that we would now regard as intolerable.

Summary of Part 2

Part 2 argued that the barriers to action are illusory. They are mental constructs rather than features of the external economic world. If we allow these trends to continue, it is a choice – albeit an uninformed one – rather than a necessity.

We are becoming aware of the dangers of a post-fact society. We are not yet aware of how deeply rooted post-fact thinking is in the formulation of economic policy. Reinforcing this post-fact view of the world are myths and metaphors that are so often repeated that we take them for truth. Examples are that the private sector is always more efficient than government, that only the private sector can create jobs, that governments should manage their finances in the same way as individual households, that lower taxes automatically lead to higher growth, that markets can and should be free, and that the way in which markets distribute the wealth of society is a fair reward for the contribution made by each individual.

These myths and metaphors are further reinforced by the use of rhetoric – constant repetition of falsehoods like the idea that the Global Financial Crisis was caused by excessive government spending – and misdirection to ensure that the electorate focuses on the wrong issues.

And even economic models – both the sophisticated kind used by professional economists and the simple mental models used by many politicians – are unfit for purpose. If it is important (and of course it is) to avoid another Global Financial Crisis, to prevent sustained unemployment and to end mass impoverishment, we need models that can explain and address these issues. The underlying assumptions behind the models in widespread use today means that they have nothing to say about such problems. They are unfit for the purpose of solving these problems but are effective in reinforcing a post-fact view of the world.

In combination, these economic models, myths and metaphors, and powerful rhetoric create a narrative of unaffordability. According to this narrative, although it is deeply regrettable that one in six children is brought up in poverty, that the state of civil infrastructure worsens every year and that healthcare is in crisis, there is nothing we can do – we simply can't afford it. This narrative of unaffordability is the principal barrier to action. It obscures the simple fact that if society in total is getting richer, as it is, then anything we used to be able to afford, we can afford today – and more. We simply need to choose to do so.

Mass impoverishment is a political choice, not an economic necessity. The barrier lies in our minds.

Summary of Part 3

Part 3 showed that a reset is not only a practical possibility but one that needs only evolutionary – rather than revolutionary – change.

There are more than 200 countries in the world and almost all of them run some form of mixed economy in which capitalism coexists with a state sector. Some of these countries perform far better than others. In particular, some perform better than the US and the UK. There are, in other words, many shades of capitalism to choose from – and it *is* a choice – and some work better than those we have chosen.

Fundamentally, we face a choice between a world of solidarity and abundance in which all members of society benefit from economic growth or a world of isolation and insecurity in which a small number take all the gains while the bulk of the population drifts into poverty. Abundance requires a relatively modest but vital change to the order of things to ensure both that the pie continues to grow *and that the entire population benefits from that growth*. It is not necessary to impoverish the rich to share the gains but it is necessary to act. A fact-based revolution to create the necessary policy changes will avoid a revolution on the streets.

There are five key areas in which policy should change. First, there needs to be a democratic reset to make sure that it is the constitutional duty of an elected government to govern for the benefit of the entire population and to institutionalize certain measures to hold them to account. Secondly, there needs to be a conscious programme to enable fact-based policy-making. Thirdly, we need to invest wisely in the future, avoiding the kind of false economies that save one dollar today at the cost of US$10 in the near future. Fourthly, we need to ensure that the benefits of growth are shared. And lastly, we need to clean up capitalism to ensure that healthy competition means that good businesses drive out the bad ones, rather than the other way around. Just as cycling had to take a stand to prevent drug-users from beating clean cyclists, we need to take a stand to prevent companies that externalize their costs, pollute the environment and avoid their taxes from out-competing good businesses.

This change will happen if we all play our part. Some of us have time to spare and exert some influence on policy, but most of us do not. If we are in the former category, of course we can directly seek to drive this kind of change. But if we have neither time nor influence, we should remember that we are in the vast majority and that even without time and influence we can vote at the ballot box, with our wallets and with our feet – our combined impact is dramatic.

The stakes are high. If we take no action, the world of 2050 will be deeply unpleasant for most people. The good news is that barriers to action live only in our own minds: the trends we don't like are the results of political choices, not economic necessities. Both the experience of our own history and that of other countries today shows that there are many options for how we run our society, and some of them work much better than the one we have chosen today. The change we need is vital but not revolutionary. Five common-sense areas of policy change will suffice. If we all play our part, we can be sure that this change will come about.

If you remember only one thing from this book, it should be that while the pie is growing, it is *not* inevitable that most people's slices must shrink. So we should be planning for a world in 2050 where everyone is at least 50 per cent better off than today.

Appendices I–X

The appendices below are located on the *99-percent.org* website. For those with a healthily sceptical disposition, there is a wealth of further data and analysis as well as links to the original sources. Please take a look.

Appendix I – What Current Policies Would Mean for 2050 (Supporting analysis for Chapter 1)

Appendix II – Comparison of Golden Age and Market Capitalism (Supporting analysis for Chapter 2)

Appendix III – Mass Impoverishment (Supporting analysis for Chapter 3)

Appendix IV – The Impact of Poverty

Appendix V – Automation (Supporting analysis for Chapter 5)

Appendix VI – How Current Policy Sustains Mass Impoverishment (Supporting analysis for Chapter 7)

Appendix VII – Myth Busting (Supporting analysis for Chapters 9 to 12)

Appendix VIII – What Makes a Happy Society (Supporting analysis for Chapter 13)

Appendix IX – Two Stories of Value Creation

Appendix X – Bibliography (Full details and website links for data and citations)

Endnotes

How This Book Came About

1 McKinsey Global Institute, 2016
2 Tatlow, 2017
3 Wearden & Fletcher, 2017
4 Monaghan, 2017
5 Bulman, 2017

Chapter 0: Economics – The Five Things You Need to Know

1 Wren-Lewis, 2014
2 Ghizoni, 1971
3 McLeay, Radia, & Thomas, 2014
4 If you are curious, the paper by McLeay, Radia, & Thomas does an excellent job of explaining it
5 ONS, 2015
6 Credit Suisse, 2015
7 OECD, 2015
8 OECD, 2015

Part 1: The Burning Platform

1 Machiavelli, Niccolò, *The Prince*, 1532
2 Conner, 2012

Chapter 1: The Age of Anxiety

1 Benarde, 1973
2 Stanley, 2017
3 CNBC, 2014
4 Shelter, 2016
5 Centres for Disease Control and Prevention, 2017

6 Jivanda, 2014
7 Centre for Poverty Research, University of California, Davis, 2018
8 Centre for Poverty Research, University of California, Davis, 2018
9 US Census Bureau, 2018
10 Deaton, 2018
11 Again, Appendix I contains the basis for these estimates
12 US Census Bureau, 2018
13 O'Brien, 2014

Chapter 2: A Tale of Two Systems

1 Dickens, Charles, *A Tale of Two Cities*, London, 1859
2 Macrotrends, 2018
3 Spence, 2018
4 Lawson, 1992
5 Duncan, 2010
6 BBC, 2009
7 Pfanner, 2008
8 Financial Crisis Inquiry Commission, 2011
9 Evans, 2018
10 Campbell, Denis, 'Hidden toll of ambulance delays at A&E revealed', *The Guardian*, 2 April 2018
11 Campbell, Denis , Marsh, Sarah and Helm, Toby, 'NHS in crisis as cancer operations cancelled due to lack of beds', *The Guardian*, 14 January 2017
12 Bureau of Economic Analysis, 2015 / St Louis Federal Reserve Bank, 2015

Chapter 3: Mass Impoverishment – Coming to a Street Near You

1 Córdoba & Verdier , 2007
2 Robbins, 1935
3 Mankiw, 2009
4 Federal Reserve Bank of St Louis, 2018
5 St Louis Federal Reserve, 2016
6 Anderson & Pizzigati, 2018
7 Bureau of Labor Statistics, 2015
8 Food and Agriculture Organization of the United Nations, 2017
9 World Hunger, 2016

10 Sen, 2001
11 Federal Reserve Bank of St Louis, 2018
12 Statista, 2018
13 See the full analysis in Appendix III
14 May, We can make Britain a country that works for everyone, 2016
15 World Bank, 2018
16 OECD, 2018
17 Glasmeier, 2015
18 Centre for Research in Social Policy, 2015
19 Tiplady, 2017
20 Buffett, 2015
21 OECD, 2015

Chapter 4: An Alternative Morality

1 Wilde, Oscar, *Lady Windemere's Fan*; London, 1893
2 Oxford Dictionaries, 2018
3 Soros, George, *The Crisis of Global Capitalism: Open Society Endangered*, New York, 1998
4 Melin, 2017
5 Ziprecruiter.com, 2018
6 Morningstar.com, 2018
7 Davidson, James Dale and Rees-Mogg, William, *The Sovereign Individual* (London, 1997), p. 131
8 Sohn, 2014
9 Romney, Full Transcript Mitt Romney, 2012
10 Davidson, James Dale and Rees-Mogg, William, *The Sovereign Individual* (London, 1997), p. 310
11 Davidson, James Dale and Rees-Mogg, William, *The Sovereign Individual* (London, 1997), p. 393
12 Thiel, 2009
13 Davidson, James Dale and Rees-Mogg, William, *The Sovereign Individual* (London, 1997), p. 140
14 Cowen, 2013
15 Mason, Rowena, 'Benefit freeze to stay for working people costing typical family £300 a year', *The Guardian*, 27 November 2017.
16 Tighe & Rovnick, 2018
17 Morley N., 2017
18 Greenfield & Marsh, 2018

19 Fleming, 2018
20 Wikipedia, 2018 Wikipedia, 2018
21 Mayer, 2016
22 Freedland, 2017

Chapter 5: The Fork in the Road

1 Carney, Mark, 'Keeping the patient alive: Monetary policy in a time of great disruption', World Economic Forum, 6 December 2016
2 Miller, 2014
3 US Census Bureau, 2015
4 Rigby, 2016
5 Royal Academy of Engineering, 2013
6 University of Manchester, 2016
7 Walsh, 2016
8 Kirkpatrick & Light, 2015
9 Driverless car market watch, 2016
10 Yadron, 2016
11 Bostrom, Superintelligence: paths, dangers, strategies, 2014
12 United Nations, 2016
13 ITER, 2016
14 Culham Centre for Fusion Energy, 2016
15 Noakes, 2016
16 Hudson, 2013
17 Murgia, 2016
18 Rajesh, 2015
19 Smart Cities Council, 2016
20 The Ellen MacArthur Foundation, 2016
21 Andersen, 2006
22 Allen R. C., Capital Accumulation, Technological Change, and the Distribution of Income During the British Industrial Revolution, 2005
23 Allen R. C., Pessimism Preserved: Real wages in the British Industrial Revolution, 2007
24 Schwab, 2015
25 Bureau of Labor Statistics, 2015
26 Frey & Osborne, 2013
27 Faroohar, 2018

28 Manyika, et al., 2017
29 Heath, 2018
30 Cowen, 2013
31 Murphey, 1999

Chapter 6: Wealth, Power and Freedom

1 Chaggaris, 2012
2 Churchill, 1947
3 Piketty, *Capital in the 21st century*, 2014
4 Stein, 2006
5 Humanities Texas, 1963
6 Rucker, 2008
7 Lawler, 2015
8 Lewis S. , 2013
9 Jones, *The Establishment*, 2014
10 Swinford, 2014
11 Supreme Court of the United States, 2010
12 Greenhouse, 2012
13 NASA, 2016
14 Ipsos MORI, 2014
15 Brulle, 2013
16 Fischer, 2013
17 Mayer, 2016
18 Jones, *The Establishment*, 2014
19 Rosenberg, 2018
20 Supreme Court of the United States, 2010
21 Roosevelt, Franklin D., State Of The Union Address, 1941
22 Berlin, 2018
23 OECD, 2010
24 Office for National Statistics, 2015
25 Wolff, 2012
26 The *Economist*, 2014
27 Stein, 2006
28 Bigman, 2015
29 Tudor Jones, 2015
30 Soros, George, 'Billionaire George Soros: I Should Pay More In Taxes', ThinkProgress, 13 February 2012
31 Freeland, 2014

Chapter 7: Eight Scenarios

1 Bank of England, 2016
2 Allen, Monaghan, & Inman , 2017
3 Thomas N. , 2016
4 Corlett, Finch, Gardiner, & Whittaker, 2016
5 Institute on Taxation and Economic Policy, 2017

Part 2: Why We Don't Act

1 Alston, 2018

Chapter 8: Going Post-Fact

1 Moynihan, n.d.
2 Noble & Lockett, 2016
3 Goebbels, 1928
4 History.com , 2009
5 ONS, 2015
6 Political Science Resources, 2016
7 The Conservative Party Archive / Getty, 2009
8 Godley, Seven unsustainable processes, 1999
9 Baker, 2002
10 Rodrik, 1997
11 Greenspan, 2008
12 Alford, 2010
13 King, 2003
14 Brown, 1999
15 BBC, 2009
16 Bernanke, 2007
17 Greenspan, 2008
18 Cassidy, 2010
19 Wallace, 2015
20 Goff & Parker, 2011
21 Connolly, 2016
22 Pariser, 2011
23 Kuchler, 2016
24 BBC, 2016
25 Dilnot, 2016
26 OECD, 2014

27 Nickell & Saleheen, 2015

28 Lewis H. , 2016

29 Benton, 2016

30 Boczkowski, 2016

31 Carney, Mark, 'Keeping the patient alive: Monetary policy in a time of great disruption', World Economic Forum, 6 December 2016

32 Agerholm, 2016

33 BBC, 2016

34 Harris & Eddy, 2016

35 Spiegelhalter, 2016

36 Harris & Eddy, 2016

37 Phys.org, 2016

38 Yeats, 1920

39 Suskind, 2004

40 Nyhan & Reifler, 2006

Chapter 9: Myths and Metaphors

1 Popper, 1953

2 OECD, 2019

3 Library of Congress, 2015

4 OECD, 2010

5 Cowen, 2013

6 Blanchard & Leigh, Growth Forecast Errors and Fiscal Multipliers, 2013

7 Batini, Eyraud, & Weber, 2014

8 Cameron, Economy: There is no alternative TINA is back, 2013

9 Bank of England, 2015

10 Sky News, 2009

11 McLeay, Radia, & Thomas, 2014

12 Merkel, 2008

13 Federal Reserve Bank of St Louis, 2019

14 Office for National Statistics, 2016

15 Bennett, 2016

16 Rothwell, 2014

17 Payscale.com, 2018

18 Smith, 1776

19 Chang, 2010

20 Hughes, 2017
21 Say, 1821
22 Kumar, 2015
23 Nalebuff & Bradenburger, 1996
24 Edward S. Knotek, 2007

Chapter 10: Economic Models

1 Box, 1987
2 wikipedia, 2015
3 Balstone, 2015
4 Solow, 2010
5 Stiglitz, Where Modern Macroeconomics Went Wrong , 2017
6 Wren-Lewis, 2014
7 Saez & Zucman, 2014
8 Keen S. , 2001
9 Godley & Lavoie, Monetary Economics, 2012
10 Besley & Hennessy, British Academy reveals 'Dangerous Recipe' to the Queen, 2009
11 Baker, 2002
12 Bezemer, 2009
13 Lorenz, 1972

Chapter 11: Rhetoric over Reason

1 Bacon, 1625
2 Cowen, 2013
3 Schuknecht, 2012
4 IMF, 2015
5 BBC, 2007
6 Berg, 2011
7 IMF, 2008
8 Trichet, 2010
9 Skidelsky, Robert, 'George Osborne's cunning plan: how the chancellor's austerity narrative has harmed recovery', New Statesman, 29 April 2015
10 IMF, 2015
11 Blanchard & Leigh, Working paper WP/13/1, 2013
12 Cameron, David Cameron and the national debt monster, 2015
13 Bank of England, 2019

14 Wikipedia, 2015
15 Morley K. , 2015
16 Romney, Mitt Romney's '47 Per cent' Comments, 2012
17 Lansley & Mack, Breadline Britain, 2015
18 Aldrick, 2018
19 See Figure 40
20 See Appendix on website
21 Harrison, 1998
22 McMillan, 2008
23 Wilson & Wilson, 2007
24 McKinsey Global Institute, 2016
25 Islam, 2012
26 Bierce, 1911

Chapter 12: Catch-23 – The Narrative of Unaffordability

1 Heller, 1961
2 Cameron, Economy: There is no alternative TINA is back, 2013
3 Saez & Zucman, 2014
4 IRS, 2015
5 Ferrara, 2014
6 Dynan, Skinner, & Zeldes, 2004
7 UK Debt Bombshell, 2016.
8 Companies House, 2016
9 Office for Budget Responsibility, 2015
10 Chantril, 2015
11 Mason, Rowena, 'Government raised bar for funding of flood defence schemes', *The Guardian*, 11 February 2014
12 Bank of England, 2015
13 Turner, Between Debt and the Devil, 2016
14 Krugman, Be Ready To Mint That Coin, 2013
15 General government gross debt was £1,763.8 billion at the end of the financial year ending March 2018 according to the Office for National Statistics, 2018
16 Stone, 2015
17 Turnbull, 2015
18 Kaufmann, 2015
19 DeLong, 2015

Part 3: Building The Future

1 eupedia, 2016

Chapter 13: 50 Shades of Capitalism

1 Rand, 1946
2 CIA, 2015
3 Wee, 2013
4 IMF, 2015
5 World Happiness Report, 2015

Chapter 14: The Victimless Revolution

1 Kennedy, 1962
2 International Energy Agency, 2015
3 Ashley & Greenemeier, 2013
4 OECD, 2015
5 United Nations Population Division, 2017
6 Congressional Budget Office, 2014
7 Lopez, 2013
8 Dolan, 2013
9 Forbes, 2016
10 O'Brien, 2014
11 Haaretz, 2014
12 Wood, 2011
13 Osnos, Evan, 'Doomsday Prep for the Super-Rich', *The New Yorker*, 22 January 2017
14 Dynan, Skinner, & Zeldes, 2004

Chapter 15: The Abundance Manifesto

1 Statement from Prime Minister Theresa May, 2016
2 Armstrong, 1982
3 Alston, 2018
4 The IPPR Commission on Economic Justice, 2018
5 Mazzucato, 2013
6 Hammond, 2013
7 Treasury, 2013
8 Castella, 2015

9 Pitt, 2008

10 Department for Environment, Food and Rural Affairs, 2015

11 Burn-Callander, 2015

12 American Society of Civil Engineers, 2016

13 Davis, 2016

14 Murphy P. , 2016

15 Burgess, Ford, Guthrie, & Toplensky, 2016

16 IMF, 2008

17 Haldane, 2010

18 Independent Commission on Banking, 2011

19 King, 2016

20 RSA, 2017

21 topendsports.com, 2016

22 United Nations, 2017

23 Chantril, 2015

24 Beveridge, 1942

Chapter 16: Your Role in the Change

1 Walker, 2013

2 Bank of England, 2019

3 Alston, 2018

Acknowledgements

This book would not exist without data. And so my first debt is to the diligent but unsung statisticians who collate economic data. In the UK, statisticians at the Bank of England, Companies House, DEFRA and the Office for National Statistics have provided huge amounts of vital information. In the US, members of public bodies including the Bureau of Economic Analysis, the Bureau of Labor Statistics, the Census Bureau, the Congressional Budget Office, the Federal Reserve Bank of St Louis, the Inland Revenue Service and the Office of the Chief Actuary have all provided invaluable sources of data. And internationally, the OECD, the World Bank, the International Monetary Fund and the United Nations have done the same.

Of course, these standardized datasets cannot tell the full story – in particular about extremes of wealth and poverty – but researchers around the world have worked painstakingly to plug the gaps. I am particularly grateful to Facundo Alvaredo, Anthony Atkinson, Thomas Piketty and Emmanuel Saez for permission to cite their ground-breaking work on the World Top Incomes Database (now replaced by the World Inequality Database); Nick Balstone for his geographically accurate map of the London tube system; Jeanne Brooks-Gunn and Greg Duncan for their painstaking study into the practical impact of poverty on children; the Centre for Research in Social Policy for its calculations on the minimum income required for a normal life; Christopher Chantril for his data on UK public spending; Credit Suisse for their international survey of wealth; Forbes Magazine for their list of the world's richest;

Carl Benedikt Frey and Michael A. Osborne for their pioneering work on the future of work in the face of automation; Amy T. Glasmeier and her team for their minimum income calculator; Ipsos MORI for data on attitudes to climate change around the world; Payscale.com for data on pay by skill set; Thomas Piketty for data showing that returns on capital increase with the size of the initial endowment; Robert C. Allen for demonstrating the stagnation of wages during the Industrial Revolution; Emmanuel Saez and Gabriel Zucman for their work on wealth inequality in the US over time; The Resolution Foundation for its analysis of the impact of the 2016 budget on rich and poor households; Edward N. Wolff for his analysis of the shrinking wealth of the middle class; and the World Happiness Report team for their survey showing which countries have the happiest populations.

I would also like to express my thanks to The Ellen MacArthur Foundation for permission to reproduce the infographic explaining the circular economy.

And there are hundreds of others whose insights I have briefly quoted in this book. I am grateful to them all, though they are too numerous to thank individually here.

The Bibliography on the *99-percent.org* website gives full details of all of these contributions.

Equally important are those who have provided encouragement, guidance and advice throughout the writing of this book. I would like to thank Dr Jonathan Aldred, Nicholas Anderson, Steve Coomber, Louis Cox-Brusseau, Professor Fiona Devine, Andrew Harrop, Professor Steve Keen, Tom Kibasi, Ken Lever, Henry Maxey, Piers Messum, Andrew Prentis, David Pitt-Watson, Hugh Pym, Sten Scheibye, Simon Thomas, Anthony Werner, Raoul Wedge-Thomas, and Rich Wylor-Owen.

I am enormously indebted to the team at Head of Zeus.

Acknowledgements

To Anthony Cheetham and Neil Belton for believing in the project, to Florence Hare for her thoughtful editing, and to Matt Bray for his creative design.

My agent, Peter Cox, deserves particular thanks. Without his insights, encouragement, tenacity and determination, this book would never have seen the light.

And finally, I must thank my family. My wife Shirin and my children, Henry and Leila, have given me the time and space – at the cost of significant disruption to their own lives – that I needed to write this book. I love you all and I am forever in your debt.

About the author

Mark E. Thomas lives deep in the
Herefordshire countryside with his
wife, two children and a cat.